Hidden Agendas

HIDDEN AGENDAS

Politics, Law and Disorder

Derek Lewis

HAMISH HAMILTON · LONDON

HAMISH HAMILTON

Published by the Penguin Group
Penguin Books Ltd, 27 Wrights Lane, London w 8 5 t z, England
Penguin Books USA Inc., 375 Hudson Street, New York, New York 10014, USA
Penguin Books Australia Ltd, Ringwood, Victoria, Australia
Penguin Books Canada Ltd, 10 Alcorn Avenue, Toronto, Ontario, Canada m 4 v 3 b 2
Penguin Books (NZ) Ltd, 182 – 190 Wairau Road, Auckland 10, New Zealand

Penguin Books Ltd, Registered Offices: Harmondsworth, Middlesex, England

First published 1997
1 3 5 7 9 10 8 6 4 2

Copyright © Derek Lewis, 1997

Set in 12/14 pt Monotype Bembo
Typeset by Rowland Phototypesetting Ltd,
Bury St Edmunds, Suffolk
Printed in Great Britain by Clays Ltd, St Ives plc

A CIP catalogue record for this book is available from the British Library

ISBN 0–241–13730–6

To all who work in our prisons
and those on the outside who help them

Contents

Introduction

The 1,014 days for which I was Director General of the Prison Service in England and Wales were the longest, toughest, most traumatic and yet most satisfying of my life. A private sector outsider brought in to change the service, I came up against the widely differing and often hidden agendas of government ministers, party politicians, civil servants, prison governors, public sector unions, private sector contractors, prisoners and pressure groups. Although I and the Prison Service rarely seemed to be out of the headlines, usually as the butt of critical comment, a startling transformation was taking place just beneath the surface. The satisfaction of seeing that progress unfold was ample compensation for the pressures of the job and the acrimonious end to my term of office. And if that were not enough, I also had the privilege of getting to know many people within the service, in organizations outside and in the wider political world who showed dedication, talent and integrity. It was an experience that left me with an addiction to prisons and a deep concern for their future and for all those who work in them.

There are many lessons to be learned from my time as Director General. I hope this book will in some small way help to ensure that those lessons really are learned and not forgotten. For that to be possible, the truth needs to be told, even when it is uncomfortable for some of those involved. I hope they will read it in that spirit.

The book is dedicated to all those who work in our prisons and those on the outside who support and help them. They are too often criticized and too rarely appreciated for the difficult, dangerous and vital task they perform. It is for that reason that I am such an ardent supporter of the Butler Trust – an independent charity that makes awards to prison staff for excellence in their work. I also hope that what I have written will likewise do a little to raise the profile of the good work that is quietly done by so many.

A book of this type is never a solo effort and I am deeply grateful to many who have made it possible – to my agent, Caroline Dawnay, who urged me to write it; to Kate Jenkins and Clare Alexander of Hamish Hamilton, who encouraged and advised; to Jeremy Lewis who helped on the structure and performed an invaluable role as editor; and to many others who provided encouragement and ideas. I am particularly indebted to Julia Challinor, who provided vital inspiration, creative input and friendly criticism, to Louise, my wife, who word-processed the ever-changing manuscript with dedication and extraordinary patience, and to all of my family, including our Labrador, for accommodating the stresses and vagaries of authorship with such tolerance.

Much of this book was inspired and written at Achduart, our refuge in the Scottish Highlands. Meaning 'High dark place', it is perhaps a fitting association for a book that attempts to cast a little light on some aspects of our public and political life. Without the special support and assistance I received there, this endeavour would never have been started, let alone finished.

I

How It All Began

The old offices of Thames Television on the Euston Road had a mournful air about them in the summer of 1992. Thames, one of the longest serving ITV companies, had lost out in the race for a new franchise to an upstart newcomer, Michael Green's Carlton Television; Green had rubbed salt into the wounds by positioning an enormous poster advertising Carlton TV on the opposite side of the road. Most of the staff had about six months to go before the dole queue beckoned, and we felt as if we were working in a funeral parlour.

There was one bright spot, however. A new television channel, UK Gold, was due to go on air in three months, broadcasting all the best-loved programmes from the archives of Thames and the BBC, its founding shareholders, and I had been asked by the two companies to set it up. There was still one small unanswered question: where was the £35 million needed to launch the channel to come from? Neither the BBC nor Thames had any money, so new financial backers had to be found, and in double-quick time.

I was chewing over the options in quiet panic when a call came through from a headhunting firm, Saxton Bampfylde. Did I know anything about the Prison Service for which they had been asked to find a new chief executive? If I was at all interested, Anthony Saxton would very much like to talk to me. I knew virtually nothing about prisons, and couldn't imagine why they thought I might be interested in such a job, but I always enjoyed talking to Anthony and said I would be happy to do so.

When Saxton telephoned a few days later, he promised that it would be interesting and at worst I would have only wasted an hour.

We met on 27 August 1992. He had done his homework – visiting prisons, talking to governors and staff, and seeking views from those outside the service. He described a complex, unpredictable and difficult world, remote from my own experience and from that of most people. Prisons, he told me, had been the Cinderella of the public services for as long as anyone could remember. During the 1970s and 80s they had been neglected and conditions had become unacceptable. Management was weak and the trade unions had been allowed to become too powerful. Prisoners were slopping out and there was gross overcrowding. Violence and drugs were on the increase. Many prisoners spent most of the day locked up or idle. Little was being done to tackle criminality; in fact, the proportion of ex-prisoners who returned to crime – recidivists in the jargon – was horrendous. Not only was the Prison Service failing to perform, but it was inefficient and trapped in a tangle of bureaucracy. Some attempts had been made at improvement, including a programme of building new prisons and installing integral sanitation in older cells so as to eliminate slopping out. But it had been too little, too late.

The Strangeways riot in April 1990 represented the nadir in the fortunes of the Prison Service. Night after night the nation's television screens were filled with pictures of rioting prisoners on the roof of the prison, while prison officers and police stood by, apparently impotent. It took twenty-five days before the authorities regained control of a shattered prison; and the lives of many staff and prisoners were shattered as well. Strangeways, and the copycat riots that followed, had resulted in an inquiry by Lord Justice Woolf.

The worst and most dramatic prison riots in this country's history needed a thorough and far-reaching investigation, which is exactly what Woolf provided. His report runs to nearly 600 pages, and was based on evidence taken from over 300 individuals and organizations. An intelligent, deep-thinking and painstaking man who inspired people by his capacity to listen, Woolf recognized the limitations of prisons as a way of dealing with criminals. He also understood the powerful and conflicting demands placed on prisons, all of which had to be taken into account: the need to keep prisoners securely in custody, to maintain order and safety and to punish, while at the same time making every effort to rehabilitate them. And he emphasized the importance of maintaining certain standards of humanity so that prisoners were treated fairly, and prisons did not become seedbeds of violence and disorder. His report contained trenchant criticism of years of political and management neglect, as well as the bumbling failures of communication so evident during the Strangeways riot. Unlike some of its successors, Woolf's inquiry was a model of thorough objective investigation, reaching sound conclusions based on intelligent consideration of the evidence.

Woolf's report was greeted with cross-party enthusiasm, and within months the government had published a White Paper entitled 'Custody, Care and Justice'. A balanced document which contained the vast majority of Woolf's recommendations, it set out the goals of the Prison Service with great clarity.

The Woolf Report also gained widespread support within the Prison Service, from governors, trade unions and, most importantly, from individual prison officers. Here, for the first time, was a well-planned, long-term strategy for prisons, an agenda for change that would take the service through the 1990s and into the next century. The first comprehensive statement on prisons for decades, perhaps ever, it created new hope for prison governors as well as providing inspiration for those who had been brought up in the reformative tradition of borstals – among them some of the most gifted governors, who had been recruited with a mission to rehabilitate, but had found themselves thwarted by overcrowding, poor conditions and an increasing sense of hopelessness, made worse by an intransigent Prison Officers' Association determined to obstruct.

The Woolf agenda had even been accepted by those on the political right – though they had little choice as long as memories of Strangeways remained alive. After all, Strangeways occurred after the Conservative government had been in power for more than ten years, and there were no plausible excuses for the condition of our jails.

Some used Woolf to justify their particular hobby-horses. Pressure groups such as the Howard League for Penal Reform and the Prison Reform Trust focused on its caring aspects, conveniently forgetting how much there was about security and control. Their efforts gave Woolf a bad name in some quarters, where the report came to be associated with a soft, liberal, 'wet' view of punishment and imprisonment.

Kenneth Clarke – who had become Home Secretary after the spring 1992 election – appeared to sympathize with the caring aspect of Woolf. Among the background documents Saxton gave me was Clarke's speech to the November 1992 Prison Service conference. It was all about giving prisoners more time out of their cells, getting them into 'useful activities' and eliminating slopping out. He made no secret of the fact that he was also looking for significant efficiency improvements, and he was brutal about the management failings of the Prison Service – but nowhere in his speech did he refer to the fact that prisoners were escaping from the system at the rate of one a day, or the escape of two IRA prisoners from Brixton eighteen months earlier, assisted by a smuggled gun. Nor was mention made of the need for better discipline in prisons, or for curbing drug abuse.

As well as Woolf and the White Paper, Clarke had inherited the 1991 Criminal Justice Act, which had radically changed criminal policy in a number of ways. Sentencing had become 'softer' by limiting the ability of judges to take into account previous convictions. The use of remand became more sparing. The whole system enabling prisoners to earn early release was swept away at a stroke and replaced, for the most part, with automatic release at the half-way point in their sentences, except for those who had to earn parole. Such changes had driven the prison population down from its peak of 51,000 in 1987 to a record low of around 40,000 at the time of our discussions.

The one subject on which Woolf had made no recommendations was the constitutional structure of the Prison Service. For that

Admiral Sir Raymond Lygo, former chief executive of British Aerospace, had been called in. After declaring the Prison Service to be 'the most complex and difficult management task' he had ever encountered, his report recommended that 'If the Prison Service is to achieve the direction and unity for which successive reports have called, it must be allowed to operate much more independently of day-to-day ministerial control and more separately from the Home Office.' The service should be given the status of one of the new executive agencies, which had been designed to give the big public services, such as the Passport Office or Social Security, greater clarity of direction and the autonomy necessary to produce a better, more efficient service. The Director General of the service should be given the freedom to manage day-to-day operations without ministerial involvement; and the appointment of the new head should be determined by open competition, with candidates from the Civil Service being considered alongside candidates from the private sector – still a relatively new and controversial approach. His recommendations were now being implemented by Kenneth Clarke, who was in Saxton's terms, 'Mr Fixit', determined to 'get rid of the baggage' of unions and bureaucracy. Clarke had listened to the views of Sir Peter Levene, the Prime Minister's efficiency adviser, who believed that the whole service could be contracted out to the private sector.

As was the case with most top Civil Service posts, previous Director Generals had been appointed by a mysterious process, which took place almost entirely behind closed doors. The permanent secretary at the Home Office would consider possible candidates, and then consult with the Cabinet Secretary, Home Secretary and others; after which, an appointment would be announced, without the job having been advertised, with no opportunities to apply for it, and with no formal interview process. The result had been that a string of Home Office civil servants had served as Director General for an unspecified period before moving back to another job in the Civil Service or retiring.

One of the government's major reforms of the Civil Service had been to sweep away the closed-door cosiness of many such appointments, and expose them to open competition. The job of Director General was to be advertised, and headhunters had been appointed to seek candidates who might not read the job advertisements. The candidates would all be judged by the same criteria, before being subjected to psychological testing and an appearance before a Civil Service Selection Board. Hence our conversation.

I was beginning to realize that here was an institution that played a critical role in our society, about which I knew far too little. My curiosity had been aroused, and we agreed to resume in two weeks' time.

My second session with Saxton was given over to the structure and management of the service. He painted a frightening picture of an organization in disarray. There were some 130 prisons, just over 40,000 prisoners and just under 40,000 staff. The service cost the taxpayer over £1.5 billion a year to run. And yet there was confusion over who did what. There was a Director General and a Prisons Board, but no one seemed to know what they really did and their authority was unclear. The organization was highly resistant to change, and changes, when they did occur, seemed to take for ever. Governors were apparently unable to make basic decisions about such critical matters as how many people worked in their prisons, who they were, and what money was to be spent on. Open warfare appeared to exist between the field and the centre; the civil servants at the Home Office distrusted prison governors and thought them incompetent.

Saxton also outlined the part played by Sir Clive Whitmore, the Home Office permanent secretary, who would have a pivotal role in the appointment. He suggested that Whitmore was a reluctant participant in Clarke's venture: doubtful, perhaps, about the wisdom of the Prison Service acquiring agency status, a staunch supporter of the Civil Service, and certainly loyal to the existing Director General, Joe Pilling, he had been swept along by the drive and enthusiasm of his political master. Whitmore was dismissive of prison governors, who were allegedly so incompetent that 2,000 people in Prison Service headquarters, including 'sound' civil servants, were needed to keep them in order. In my experience, no normal organization could conceivably need such a bloated hierarchy.

But following Strangeways most governors were restless and anxious for change. They wanted to be given the authority and the tools to do the job, and to be allowed to get on with it. One prison, Brixton, had already seized the initiative under its new governor, Andrew Coyle, and had outlined its vision of the future in a plan called 'Brixton 2000'. Saxton gave me a copy. It set out what was wrong with Brixton – overcrowding, prisoners locked in their cells twenty-three hours a day, slopping out, mentally disordered inmates in awful conditions, too little for prisoners to do – and a plan for change that Brixton staff had developed themselves and clearly believed in. It provided convincing evidence that change was possible.

I wish the other briefing material had been as inspiring. For a large, complex organization it was pitifully scant – the Woolf Report, the White Paper, an unintelligible paper on computer plans, a recent Clarke speech, some vague material on operating performance. There were no forward plans, no budgets, no assessments of key people, no financial or operating reports. It gradually became apparent that such things simply did not exist: compelling evidence of what needed to be done.

Kenneth Clarke was determined to introduce the catalytic effects of competition into the Prison Service, just as he had into the National Health Service, and to convince opponents that their hostility to privatization was misplaced. Many Prison Service staff argued that making a profit out of imprisonment was immoral; it could only ever be a job for the state. In reality their views concealed a fear of change and the unknown and the possible threat to lifetime job security, traditionally the great selling-point of prison work. Ironically, public confirmation that the head of the new Prison Service executive agency would be recruited by open competition included an embarrassing Civil Service blunder. Part of the published job description stated that 'Tenders will also be invited later this year for the management of an existing establishment (Strangeways) and for some other establishments in later years.' In other words, private sector companies, as well as the existing management team, would be invited to bid for the privilege of running it. This was a dramatic departure – originally the private sector had been confined to running brand new prisons, so existing jobs were never threatened – and big news within the service and outside, because of Strangeways' notoriety. This sentence was to be removed if no announcement had been made at the time of publication: it had not but the sentence nevertheless remained, and the news simply escaped. Clarke, abroad on holiday at the time, was eventually contacted by telephone, and was said to be livid.

As the headhunters' quest for the right man continued, work on UK Gold progressed. I had found an American corporation willing to put up the entire £35 million, so funding was secure. The final touches were being put to our marketing plan, advertising campaign and initial programme schedule, and the satellite transponder was being tested. Long hours were spent with lawyers. In between I had my first formal encounter with Sir Clive Whitmore. It was an early meeting by Civil Service standards – 8.30 a.m. on 17 September. Sir Clive's reputation was impressive. A former private secretary to Margaret Thatcher, he had been highly regarded by her, and was considered one of the Civil Service's highest flyers. Although he occupied a large airy office with comfortable modern furnishings – not at all the traditional Civil Service stereotype – he appeared to be the archetypal mandarin. He was charming, and his welcome combined impeccable manners with a feeling of warmth. He sank into an easy chair and chatted about the Prison Service. Surprisingly perhaps, in view of the shocks and embarrassments it routinely served up for the Home Office – only the previous week a prison murder had hit the headlines – his affection for the service was apparent, albeit that of an uncle for a wayward nephew who needed to be taught how to do things properly, the Civil Service way.

It cannot have been an easy conversation for him. Clarke had made it clear he wanted someone from the private sector – even, it was rumoured, going so far as to tell Joe Pilling, the current Director General, that he did not want another civil servant. Whitmore had to be a consummate diplomat. He performed with rare professionalism, and it was easy for me to like him. His infectious enthusiasm for the challenge served to reinforce my growing interest, and he seemed relieved to have found someone who met Clarke's private sector brief.

I was then tested and interviewed by a psychologist, Barbara Cohen, to assess my suitability for the job – common practice in the private sector, but new to the Civil Service. We met one evening in a dingy conference room in the St Ermine's Hotel, just behind the Home Office. Compared with the rest of the selection process, this was serious stuff. With beguiling charm she probed my past, looking for areas of weakness, and then subjected me to a battery of computer tests designed to establish whether I had what it would take to do the job and how I would handle the pressures from ministers, MPs, select committees, the public and others. Her thoroughness was in marked contrast to the superficiality of the Civil Service Selection Board, which followed five days later.

A stilted letter from the government's Recruitment and Assessment Services made no concessions to warmth: 'Your interview will begin at 12.00 p.m. Will you please arrive ten minutes beforehand and report to the reception desk.' I had not been consulted on the timing and was already scheduled to address a gathering of advertising agencies, so Saxton Bampfylde negotiated a 2.00 p.m. slot a day earlier.

Were I successful, I would become a civil servant, albeit on a limited-term contract, and the letter also provided my introduction to Civil Service bureaucracy, in the form of detailed instructions about claiming my travel expenses, together with a complex two-page form for the purpose. Claims below £6 would not be paid, nor the first £5 of any claim, while 'Candidates who are unemployed may wish to consult their Jobcentre.' I could claim for travel to the interview, but not to the psychological tests. First-class rail fares would be refunded, but I could not claim mileage if I travelled in another candidate's car (difficult, as their identities were a closely guarded secret). Air fares from Orkney would be refunded, and I would be reimbursed at the rate of 5p a mile if I travelled by motor cycle or scooter. My chosen means of travel for the one-mile journey from Marylebone Road to Whitehall was by taxi, and as I read on I discovered that taxi fares were not refundable.

I was escorted from the waiting area to a drab room, sparsely furnished with a large round table. The board was chaired by John Holroyd, the first Civil Service commissioner, charged with maintaining propriety in Civil Service appointments. He was accompanied by Lord Woolf, Sir Clive Whitmore, Sir John Chilcot, permanent secretary at the Northern Ireland Office and (at that time) heir-apparent to Whitmore, and a senior business executive. They sat around one half of the table; opposite them were a single chair for me and a solitary glass of water. The chairman gave me a formal welcome and introduced his colleagues. Each had been assigned his two or three questions and was called upon to ask them in turn. They followed the pattern that Saxton had predicted – what was necessary to take the service forward, the relevance of my experience, my management style and my views on the private sector. None was very profound or difficult. All could be answered without too much detail and without creating hostages to fortune, and there were few follow-up questions. It was an unsatisfactory ritual from which I guessed they had learned little more than was in the psychologist's report. I was soon on my way out, passing in the waiting-room a lone figure hidden behind a copy of the *Financial Times*. I recognized him from the annual report. It was Joe Pilling – suffering the indignity of applying to retain his job.

Surprisingly soon after the selection board Saxton rang to say that Kenneth Clarke would like to meet me. I later learned that this was not the usual selection process: traditionally the board recommends a preferred candidate, whom the Secretary of State is asked to endorse – with one or two reserve candidates in case of strong objections to the first choice. On this occasion – never repeated – the Civil Service commissioner had agreed that the board should offer the Home Secretary a choice of candidates, from whom he would make the final selection.

At noon on 12 October, Whitmore escorted me down the corridor, past the photographs of previous Home Secretaries, to Clarke's office. It was not my first encounter with him. During my time at Granada, Clarke, then at the Department of Trade and Industry, had been our guest in the Royal Box at Covent Garden for a performance of *Tosca*. According to my briefing notes for the evening, 'He is amiable, sharp-witted and straightforward, and enjoys fairly vigorous discussions conducted with a touch of aggression. How he will make out at the opera I don't know: his hobby is listening to jazz.' He thanked us at the end of the evening, and left us with 'Wonderful performance, pity about the music.' At least he was honest!

We sat in comfortable chairs for a cosy fireside chat. In his shirtsleeves and smiling, Clarke sprawled in a chair with a large mug of coffee. I expected a formidable grilling. This was probably one of the most important appointments Clarke would make in his time at the Home Office and, if his tenure was long enough, it could affect his own reputation, but it proved no test of endurance. He was in expansive mood as we chatted cursorily about the Prison Service and its problems. He wanted to know how relevant I thought my experience was and what my views were of competition and the private sector. He seemed open-minded, but I knew of Sir Peter Levene's arguments for the almost complete privatization of the service. I told Clarke that I was positive about the private sector but had no preconceptions about the extent of its involvement. This was no time for making commitments that might prove unworkable. Clarke's progress up the political ladder had not changed him – he remained genial, outgoing, bluff, instinctive, a 'people person'. He described his relationship with the new Director General as that of a non-executive chairman in the private sector with a chief executive – very much like that he had enjoyed with Duncan Nichol, the chief executive of the NHS, when he had been Health Secretary. He was someone I felt I could work with in a relationship with which I was already familiar, and as we left the meeting, Whitmore confided quietly that he thought it had 'gone well'.

I returned to my office, with little time to reflect further on the Prison Service – we were now less than three weeks away from the launch date for UK Gold on 1 November.

★

Meanwhile, after six meetings on the Prison Service in as many weeks, the Home Office appeared to have ground to a virtual halt. How did government achieve anything when everything took so long? The Prison Service was scheduled to become an agency in four months' time, yet the recruitment of the person who was going to run it was leisurely to the point of negligence. I went on reading press reports about what was happening in the prisons, but it was another five weeks before an apologetic Saxton telephoned to say that Clarke would like me to do the job. Saxton and his associate Douglas Board needed to come round that very day to talk about salary and other benefits. I knew that the pay would be dramatically less than I was currently earning and might prove to be wholly unacceptable, so I was quite encouraged to find Saxton and Board talked in terms of around half, rather than a third, of my present salary. Although the private sector was beginning to conclude that bonuses did little to motivate and often distorted pay, bonuses and so-called performance-related pay were then very much in vogue in government circles and they were keen that part of my pay should be related to the performance of the service. I was perfectly happy with that. Another week or two were taken up with haggling over the financial details. Finally they came back with a proposal that was slightly higher than I had suggested. The Treasury had agreed and all appeared to be settled.

But life, I then discovered – and was to rediscover again and again – is never that simple in government. Norman Lamont, the Chancellor, had been asked to rubber stamp the salary package and was having none of it. I would be earning more than the Prime Minister, more than Sir Robin Butler, the Cabinet Secretary, and more than Lamont himself. Meetings followed between him and Kenneth Clarke. The Prime Minister was drawn in. Eventually an embarrassed Douglas Board asked me if I would meet Clarke again. The Prime Minister, Clarke said, had asked that the package be rejigged to avoid political embarrassment. It was my first glimpse of Clarke, the master of the offensive, in a difficult situation. He was passingly apologetic, but ebullient when explaining the need to readjust. Lamont wanted to reduce the basic salary and the bonus.

Clarke suggested a compromise. Whitmore, charged with making it all happen, set out to finesse the problem. Eventually he and I agreed to a drop in base salary made up by a more generous pension scheme, which would not attract much public attention. We had a deal, though no one had even discussed the targets or performance on which the bonus would be paid. Whitmore was quick to reassure me. I need not worry, he said: the Home Office believed that bonuses, although demanding, should be very much achievable. With a nod and a wink, he told me I could expect to earn most of it.

I now had to make my final decision. It was not easy. Most sensible people must have thought me crazy to take a 50 per cent cut in pay to endure the frustration, bruising and insecurity of the political and Civil Service world. But I gradually found myself being drawn inexorably towards it. It was entirely different from anything else that I had ever done, and the sheer fascination of this new world was magnetic. It was also a management challenge of Himalayan proportions – something I found difficult to resist. Clearly there were risks, but there was a good chance of achieving real change for the better. Something in me said that if asked by government to take on a job like this, one had a duty to respond. I wondered how I would feel in ten or fifteen years' time if I said no: almost certainly, I decided, I would regret having missed the opportunity and the experience. Some of those I spoke to warned me off, often in emotive terms, while others encouraged me to accept. An outsider at the start of a journey into an entirely new world, I had already glimpsed some of the hidden agendas that were to dominate the next three years: Clarke's political insistence on a private sector appointment, the Civil Service's determination to look after its own, and the pervasive obstruction of vested interests. But it was something I knew deep down that I had to do. I looked upon the future with enthusiasm, but no illusions about the odds I faced.

The days that followed were chaotic. I had hoped to visit some prisons as part of the final stages of my research, but when I discussed it with Sir Clive Whitmore he said we couldn't run the risk of a leak. What about talking to some of the key players, then? A bit difficult, he replied. Lord Woolf would be OK. Peter Lloyd, the Prisons Minister, was a problem: it wasn't clear whether there would be a job for him after the service became an agency. Judge Stephen Tumim, the Chief Inspector of Prisons, was far too indiscreet according to Sir Clive. And it was too soon to meet Joe Pilling: Whitmore would be getting him to clear his desk the following day, and a meeting would be better left until the New Year. Whitmore obviously felt badly about the way Pilling had been treated, and with good reason. Pilling had known for weeks that he would not remain in the job, but had been left in limbo. He had had to host the annual Prison Service conference and keep up the pretence of not knowing whether he would be staying. Whitmore assured me that he would be 'looked after' and found an equally senior job in another department.

Clarke decided only just before the weekend that he wanted to make a pre-Christmas announcement, which in practice meant Monday, 21 December. At that stage I had yet to receive a written offer of the job. A draft finally arrived late on Friday. Like so much else in the selection process – the job specification with its reference to Strangeways, the interview arrangements, the unplanned delays, the inadequate briefing, the U-turns on pay – it was another cock-up. The Treasury, apparently ignorant of its own legislation, had unknowingly suggested pension arrangements which would have earned me no pension at all. This was a potential job-stopper – no pension equalled no appointment, and a good deal of egg on Clarke's face, let alone Whitmore's. A series of anguished telephone calls followed over the weekend, trying to sort out the mess. One caller introduced himself irritably as 'Pain of the Treasury': he was obviously not used to working at weekends. No solution had been found by Monday morning, and there were anxious faces in Sir Clive's office. Pain was there, with a deputy secretary from the Treasury. Whitmore had lost a little of his normal calm. Clarke, returning by car from a weekend in his Nottingham constituency specially for the announcement, telephoned regularly from the M1 to find out whether there would be an announcement at all. We were still hopeful that the employment agreement could be signed before 3.00 p.m. and advised him to continue his journey. The morning's frenetic activity eventually paid off. We solved the pension problem, and at 2.30 p.m. I received the final signed offer of employment. At 2.35 p.m. I returned my acceptance, with twenty-five minutes to go before the public announcement.

Ten minutes later, as I waited in the Home Secretary's large but grubby conference room, one of the Home Office press team rushed in brandishing a copy of the previous day's *Sunday Express*. Agitated, he pointed to an advertisement for UK Gold which had a picture of Fletch and MacKay from the TV sitcom *Porridge* with the strap line 'Just what you would expect in one of HM Prisons: a riot'. It was an ad proposed by our agency two months earlier, which I had stopped on the grounds of political insensitivity. It had been deleted from our advertising programme but a copy had evidently been placed by mistake. There was nothing that could be done now.

The press conference itself was more like a photocall, with the odd sound-bite. A battery of cameramen had come to capture pictures, still and moving, of this strange new species – the so-called television executive who was about to try his hand at running our prisons. The questions were predictable. What did I expect to be able to contribute to our prison system? Considerable management experience and an open mind, I replied, but a recognition that I had an enormous amount to learn. What was Ken Clarke expecting to achieve? He said he wanted to see modern management methods introduced into the Prison Service. It was lucky that no one went on to ask what such methods might be. I suspect Clarke might have talked about competition, short-term contracts for managers (one of his hobby-horses) and perhaps performance indicators – but the rest of the answer might have been a little thin. He had, after all, had no personal management experience.

A curt and authoritative 'Right, that's it. Thank you' rang out from Audrey Nelson, chief press officer for the Prison Service. The press conference held to announce my appointment was closed.

2

On the Inside

There was little time to take stock after the press conference. I was now committed to the job in a very public way. I knew enough to be confident that it was the right decision, but I was well aware I had barely scratched the surface. Although I did not officially start for a couple of weeks, it was to be the beginning of a long love affair with prisons and those who work in them, and a learning marathon that had to be run at a sprint.

I expected an hour or two's briefing from my new boss, the Home Secretary, or some document setting out what was expected of me – the priorities for change and performance targets. But as far as Clarke was concerned, the job was finished with the public announcement, and Whitmore offered nothing. The Prison Service was awash with rumours about the brief I had been given. I was seen as a hatchet man brought in to cut staff numbers and privatize the service. The rumour-mongers might have been disappointed to learn that I had no brief at all.

In the absence of a formal induction, Whitmore introduced me to the Prisons Board. The five-minute car ride between Queen Anne's Gate and Prison Service headquarters behind the Tate Gallery was to become a frequent part of my routine. The service headquarters occupies a soulless 60s office block, typical of White-hall departments. In the 80s it enjoyed a modest facelift – air-conditioning that struggles to cope and a veneer of marble on the outside – but the interior remained as dark, dingy and claustro-phobic as ever. As I entered it felt vaguely familiar, and I realized

I had been there some twenty years earlier as a junior analyst at Ford, negotiating a price increase application with the Prices and Incomes Commission. Sir Clive whisked me straight up to the fifth floor home of the Prisons Board, where the five executive members had been ordered to assemble. We stepped out of the lift, crossed the hallway, and he opened the boardroom door. Barely pausing, he all but pushed me in. After a fleeting introduction, concluding with 'Here they are', he made an embarrassed exit. I was on my own, my induction programme over.

The reason for his haste was soon apparent. The atmosphere was tense and hostile. Joe Pilling had been a much-respected Director General during his sixteen months in the job and, more importantly, he was 'one of us' – a long-serving Home Office civil servant. There was not much enthusiasm for the brash intruder who had been so unceremoniously foisted upon them. I introduced myself and explained my background – fifteen years with Ford Motor Company in Europe and the US, a couple of years in Imperial Group, then seven with Granada before setting up the new satellite TV channel, UK Gold. It was a varied career that had given me management experience in many different settings. I hoped that experience would be useful to the Prison Service, but I recognized I had a vast amount to learn.

The ice broken, I asked them to introduce themselves. Brian Emes and Ian Dunbar were both former prison governors, now operational directors, each responsible for one-third of the country's prisons. Dunbar was well known for a document entitled 'A Sense of Direction', one of the early signposts for the future of the Prison Service. It had not yet featured in my reading, and I later discovered it was one of the many initiatives in the service that had fallen into disuse. Emes had played a key role in the Strangeways riot, when he and Brendan O'Friel, the governor, had disagreed over plans to bring the riot to an end. He was due to retire in a couple of months, when he would be replaced by another ex-governor, Tony Pearson. They represented the governor class, which had always encountered a glass ceiling at the now abolished deputy director general level, and had never made it to Director General. Rosemary Wool, a doctor of psychiatry, had served in a number of prisons but now had responsibility for prison healthcare. Finally, there were two career civil servants from the Home Office. Tony Butler, director of finance and personnel, was a genial and experienced Civil Service professional with hidden talent as a 60s rock guitarist. He was a Home Office high flyer and a former principal private secretary to Home Secretary Willie Whitelaw, for whom he had a deep regard and affection. He had a powerful intellect and, after the initial hostility had receded, was someone with whom I worked closely on the mould-breaking initiatives in industrial relations and the private sector. He was an immensely hard worker whose response to new challenges was to work even harder. His impish sense of humour could be relied on to relieve tense moments, while his skills in working the system and engineering compromises often produced results where a full-frontal attack would have failed. The other civil servant, Philippa Drew, made up the trio of operational directors. She was a very different proposition, and probably the most hostile of the group. As the daughter of a former permanent secretary, she gave the impression that she was driven by ambition to emulate her father. She was steeped in the Civil Service tradition and seemed to have no time for such new-fangled innovations of the present government as open competition, privatization and quantitative analysis. Her appointment as the third operational director had been a bold experiment by Joe Pilling – putting a policy civil servant without any relevant operational experience into one of the key jobs. She was tall, with a forbidding presence and a forensic intellectual style that could terrify colleagues or subordinates as she pounced on any flaw in their logic. Perhaps the contrast between the two characters was best summed up by her love of Wagner's *Ring* and Tony Butler's of 60s rock music. Her pre-emptive strike was made with cold formality. 'The new Director General ought to make it his business to be seen inside at least one prison on Christmas Day,' she said. I smiled and said I thought it would be an excellent idea, even though I would not have started the job by then. I would hope to visit several others over the Christmas period. I invited her to join me on Christmas Day, just in case her suggestion had been designed to discomfit me. She did.

With my introduction to the executive directors complete, I had to find out the views of other colleagues and start building relationships. I met the two non-executive directors first. One, Millie Banerjee, was a senior executive from BT; the other, Bill Bentley, a former executive with Shell. Although, like so much in the service, their role was not very precisely defined, they were there to provide an independent voice on the board. At first they seemed little improvement on the executives. They had argued strongly that Joe Pilling should retain the job, and were disappointed that their views had not been listened to. Given a succession of Prisons Ministers in recent years, and a change of Director General less than eighteen months before, they believed that the Prison Service needed stability in its leadership. But once the decision had been made, they said they would give me their support. It was a view I understood, and at least we were talking the same language – about how to get things done. Not an overwhelming welcome, it marked the beginning of a very constructive relationship.

My next task was to get to know the other senior people in the service. But first I had to work out who they were and find out how this labyrinthine organization worked. There was no guide book. The telephone directory was full of surnames with no first names, lots of grades and no sense of who worked for whom or what they did. The organization chart was not much better. Units in Prison Service HQ seemed to be called divisions (were there really *that* many staff?) and all carried impenetrable acronyms – DPF, DIP, DIA, DOC, DSP. I tried to sort out who had staff (support) functions and who had direct responsibility for running prisons – the line management – but it all seemed a glorious muddle. The field organization must be simpler, I assumed. But a glance at the map showed that the area manager for London South also covered the three prisons on the Isle of Wight, but none of the prisons in between, while the area manager for London North also had responsibility for the maximum-security Whitemoor prison, in the Cambridgeshire Fens. I learned that, like so much else in the Civil Service, it all came down to grades. Some governing governors were of the top 'governor 1' grade, others 'governor 2' or 'governor 3'. Some area managers were also 'governor 1', but some the more senior 'assistant director'. Protocol did not allow a 'governor 1' governor to report to a 'governor 1' area manager. Instead of changing the grade structure – something it took me another two and a half years to achieve – the whole organization structure had been distorted. The result made local co-operation between prisons more difficult, created a mismatch with other agencies such as the police, and forced area managers to waste time travelling which should have been spent on managing.

I arranged to see all fifteen area managers individually during my first two weeks, as well as a similar number of people holding senior staff appointments. It was a heavy commitment of time, but vital if I was to find out something about them, and what the issues in the Prison Service were.

My quest for knowledge was not easy. Despite their professed enthusiasm for helping me to learn about the Prison Service, civil servants were keen to select what information I should have – namely that which supported the status quo. I was handed long essays full of assertive statements, with very few facts to support them. I became used to the *Yes Minister* jargon of 'It doesn't work', 'We've tried it before', 'Too difficult', or 'Too risky'.

One week after starting work, I chaired my first meeting of the Prisons Board. I approached it with some trepidation, given the previous evidence of hostility – but also with some bemusement, since the role of the board remained a mystery. No one could tell me what it was supposed to do. No document required particular decisions or plans to be approved by the board. Some decisions were made by the Home Secretary or the Prisons Minister working in conjunction with individual members of the board or the heads of staff divisions: these decisions were then issued to the field as instructions, completely bypassing the board itself. Only the previous year, the searching of visitors to SSUs – special secure units within a prison for the exceptional-risk category A prisoners, such as IRA terrorists and gangland bosses – had been suspended by a junior civil servant from HQ, who had obtained the agreement of

Angela Rumbold, then Prisons Minister. The board had simply been excluded from a decision that was to contribute to the Whitemoor escape just two years later.

I had heard the board described as a talking shop, and the papers for the first meeting did nothing to allay those concerns. They were voluminous and verbose. It was unclear whether they were simply reporting the current state of affairs for the information of the board or requesting decisions. Civil servants in Prison Service HQ had prepared drafts of the new corporate and business plans required for agency status, but there was no identification of the issues the board needed to consider or decide on. And the boardroom itself was discouraging, with low, comfortable chairs down which members slowly slid before they started to snooze, and a complete absence of modern audio-visual equipment. I had already developed the sense of a disparate and inharmonious group, and my fears greatly outweighed my hopes.

I knew I had to stamp my mark on the board early. Here was the key set of people who had to work together as a team and become the core group of leaders and decision-makers in the service. I had to make sure that I was as well briefed for that meeting as anyone else, and many hours of preparation went into it. Nowhere in the papers, however, could I find that month's financial report. I asked for a copy, only to be told that there was no regular monthly financial report to the board. I was amazed. How could an organization responsible for spending £1.5 billion of taxpayers' money a year do without regular financial reports? I asked that one be instituted for the next board meeting.

But the problem was not simply confined to financial matters. There was very little information of any kind about how the various parts of the service were performing – and such as there was provided no basis for judging whether we were doing well or badly. The service had been worrying for months if not years about how to meet this need, but had become bogged down in disagreement about the solution. With such a complex service there was never going to be one neat set of information that would meet all our needs: but what we had to have were some broad indicators, however crude, which would tell us whether we were going in roughly the right direction. I asked for a simple report to be instituted, showing the latest results and whether they were better or worse than budget. Yes, our headquarters people said, that could be done – but there were lots of ifs and buts. Soon afterwards one of them told me that they understood that I wanted to find out whether results were better or worse than budget. They knew how to show that for escapes, but were puzzled about expenditure. Although it was clearly unacceptable to spend more than budget, they had also been taught not to spend less than budget, because it would be taken away from budgets in future years: in their different ways each was as bad as the other. Until then, the 'must spend it' philosophy of government departments had been a remote piece of folklore to me. Now I was staring it in the face, and I began to understand why it was rumoured that there was a warehouse full of personal computers purchased by the Home Office the preceding year to use up all the money. Wait a minute, I said: how would you feel if you were a taxpayer? Wouldn't you be grateful if the Prison Service did everything it was supposed to, but managed to spend less money? Wouldn't *that* be better than budget? Well yes, came the hesitant reply: we've never thought of it like that before.

Getting reports produced was only half the battle. The other half was getting the board to use them in a culture that had always regarded literary skills as a higher art form than quantitative analysis. Philippa Drew was the leader of the literary resistance, regularly protesting a lack of understanding of numbers and delaying meetings for lengthy explanations. The low regard in which numbers people were held was amply demonstrated by the briefing papers, which used pages of text when a simple table or graph of numbers would have told the same story more effectively. When numbers were used they often failed to add up, and changed inexplicably from one meeting to the next. Financial jobs in the Home Office were like household chores – something that had to be done, but a resented intrusion on the real work of policy-making. One senior member of the finance team confessed that he was 'not very good with numbers', and had never wanted the job anyway: he had taken it only because it would be 'good for his career'. As I gradually came to understand this, I was no longer surprised to find accounting systems so inadequate that individual prisons had no breakdown of where money was being spent, and were often provided with accounts that still included the costs of staff who had retired, died or been transferred long ago. The state of the accounting and control systems, and the almost complete absence of people with financial expertise, were scandalous, as was the resulting waste of taxpayers' money.

Within a few weeks I had seen ample evidence of how hostile, political, conspiratorial and divided the service could be. I was like the mouse observed by the circling hawk for the first wrong move. Though trivial, it came quickly. I had inadvertently dictated a short letter about UK Gold in the middle of a tape of Prison Service correspondence. The typist told her supervisor, the supervisor told her boss, who in turn told Tony Butler. He came to see me with the look of the hangman: 'It has been brought to my attention that you have been abusing public resources,' he said. I promised not to sin again, but it was obvious that it would be some time before I knew whom, if anyone, I could trust.

The staff in Prison Service headquarters represented only 5 per cent of those employed in the service. The rest were in prison establishments up and down the country, where the real business was done. The key group that I had to get to know was the prison governors. Each prison has several governor-grade staff – about ten on average – but there is only one governing governor (the 'number one governor', in the vernacular) in charge of each prison. Like the officer class in the army, they come from two sources: there are those who start at the bottom and work their way up through the ranks, and there are those who come in the Sandhurst way as assistant governors. Many of those who come up through the ranks have a battle-hardened, pragmatic and sometimes slightly cynical view of the work they do, particularly when it comes to rehabilitation. The direct-entry governors were recruited in the 1960s, 70s and 80s, often straight from university, lured by the attraction of what was billed as 'management with a social conscience'. Many went into the borstal system, as housemasters *in loco parentis* for a group of young delinquents – providing supervision, discipline and counselling, and taking them on outward bound activities. Their principal purpose in life was not security or punishment but care and rehabilitation. Now governing their own prisons, they had come face to face once again with many of the youngsters in whom they had invested so much effort and hope – recidivists like all the rest. For the most part, however, their idealism remained intact. It is hardly surprising that such governors viewed the caring aspects of the Woolf agenda with such enthusiasm, and its apparent later abandonment with such dismay.

Governors are a colourful, varied and humorous group. The service has more than its share of Scots who have migrated to the larger English service. There is the old Etonian who commands infinite respect from his staff, managing in a gentle, polite and low-key way that few would associate with prison. There are the mildly eccentric, like the one who sports a monocle and cane as he walks around his establishment. There are those who operate an authoritarian regime with staff, and others who allow a great deal of freedom. An increasing number of, and some of the best, governors of male prisons are women; and the right male governor can sometimes be the most effective with female prisoners. The only generalization is that the best take an enthusiastic, almost proprietorial, interest in their establishments, knowing their staff by name and many of the prisoners too.

Governors represent only one of the very different cultures at work in the Prison Service. Many older prison officers grew up with different traditions, in a form of cultural apartheid which flourished under the organization structure which existed until 1987. Prison officers were then the responsibility of higher ranking prison officers and ultimately of the chief officer – the Prison Service equivalent of the regimental sergeant major. Representing the gentleman officer-class, governors had little contact with ordinary prison officers. Prison officers learned to treat their governors with politeness and respect, but without expecting too much of them. Chief officers believed in discipline, attention to detail and proper procedures. For many of them, the very notion of rehabilitation was a foreign language. This tradition was reinforced by the recruitment of large numbers of new prison officers straight from the armed forces.

Running a unified and effective Prison Service with this great divide would have been difficult enough; superimposed on the stifling, woolly culture of the Home Office, it stood no chance. The Home Office was a late-comer to prisons, becoming involved only after the abolition of the old Prison Commission in 1963, when the autonomy of individual prisons was curbed and the Prison Service transformed into a department within the Home Office. Home Office civil servants carry a heavy burden of tradition and history, along with a highly developed awareness that they are dealing with very serious matters involving human rights and the liberty of the individual. Inevitably, the Home Office attracted people who shared its own liberal and humanitarian ethos. As the 1995 senior management review observed, this had led over time to the development of a distinct Home Office policy on law and order, largely independent of the government of the day. It was felt that such weighty matters were too important to be left to transitory ministers, who needed to be guided and restrained by their senior civil servants, rather like delinquent schoolboys.

Civil servants of this ilk occupied most of the senior staff positions in the Prison Service headquarters, which was created after the abolition of the Prison Commission. They retained their commitment to Home Office policy, continued to aspire to promotion in the main Home Office, and affected disdain for the 'dirty end of the business'. Theirs was a remote intellectual world, not one of practical results. The boundaries were pushed back still further when Joe Pilling appointed Home Office civil servants as operational director and area manager, normally the preserve of ex-governors. If his aim was to improve line management, it was destined to fail. One senior governor confessed that he had no need to worry when either of these two line bosses visited his prison, since he knew they were very unlikely to spot any weaknesses.

The fourth and newest culture at work in the Prison Service is that of the private sector, resulting from the government's desire to implement modern management methods, the involvement of private companies in the management of prisons and court escorting and the recruitment of staff from the private sector. With its enthusiasm for change, emphasis on results rather than procedure, and willingness to compete, it has found itself at odds with most of the existing traditions in the service. Prison governors who left the public sector to join private companies found that the demands made on them were heavy, and the penalties for failing to perform swift and unpleasant. The head of our new audit group returned open-mouthed from a security audit at Blakenhurst, one of the privately managed prisons. Whereas most public sector prisons barely produced a workplan to correct deficiencies by the time the audit team had left, virtually all the deficiencies at Blakenhurst had been corrected by the morning after they were identified. No wonder many in the Prison Service felt threatened by the arrival of this new force.

The interaction between different groups of Prison Service employees has a profound effect on it, but many from outside also contribute. Not all those who work in prisons are paid employees. Some are volunteers from outside organizations such as the Women's Royal Voluntary Service, while others belong to two unique Prison Service groups – prison visitors and members of Boards of Visitors.

Prison visitors are volunteers who visit prisons and befriend individual prisoners. Some inmates have no family on the outside, and for them a prison visitor is a lifeline to the real world, offering a respite from the company of their fellow-prisoners. Very often a prison visitor will provide advice and help as the prisoner comes close to his release date.

The role of Boards of Visitors is very different. Their principal job is to act as the eyes and ears of the Home Secretary within prisons, telling him directly when and where they think things are going wrong. Boards may concern themselves with the treatment of an individual prisoner – such as the mishandling of an application for parole – or with overall conditions in a prison, with overcrowding or cleanliness. Once again, their members are volunteers, doing the job because they think it worthwhile. Boards form part of the system of checks and balances, trying to ensure that there is no abuse or ill-treatment in a world where the basic right of freedom has been removed. Few other countries have anything similar to Boards of Visitors and they are, perhaps, one reason why we have very few instances of staff abusing prisoners. Boards may help individual prisoners who approach them with a problem, or provide assistance for those who work there, coming to the defence of prison governors who are under political attack – as was to happen at Whitemoor and Parkhurst.

I talked to representatives of all these groups, as well as to pressure groups such as the Howard League, the Prison Reform Trust, the National Association for the Care and Rehabilitation of Offenders, trade unions, the police and the probation services. All treated me politely but warily. Their questions were designed to winkle out any hint of a hidden agenda. They were convinced there must be one, and found it hard to believe that the only agenda I had was the very open one set out in the White Paper. I was beginning to realize how many people and organizations had to be got on side – including Princess Anne, the very active patron of the Butler Trust, a charity which makes awards to prison staff for exceptional work. I met her on a visit to my local prison at Chelmsford. Judging by her swift comment – 'Oh yes, I've heard about you' – she too feared the worst.

Prominent among the outsiders with whom I had to work were Her Majesty's Chief Inspector of Prisons and the prisons ombudsman. The Chief Inspector and his small team are independent of the Prison Service. Their task is to report to the Home Secretary and to Parliament on the condition of our prisons – a wide brief that has allowed inspectors to highlight whatever issues they think important. By contrast, the prisons ombudsman, created as a result of the Woolf Report, deals with individual prisoners' complaints of unfair treatment.

The Chief Inspector of Prisons when I joined was Judge Stephen Tumim. He was the second holder of the post, to which he had been promoted from relative obscurity as a circuit judge. When I first met him he was well established in the job after five years, and Kenneth Clarke had just extended his appointment by a further three – a move that was not universally applauded in the Home Office. In his early years he had had a reputation for working hard and often inconspicuously to improve the appalling conditions in the country's jails. His reports had become increasingly trenchant in their criticisms, and he had come to greater prominence through a report on suicides in prison in 1991 and his co-authorship of the second part of the Woolf Report. He had campaigned to reduce overcrowding and eliminate slopping out. An early reticence and dislike of the television cameras had evaporated. His reports increasingly contained verbal nuggets which were seized upon by the press – the Wolds was prone to 'corrupting lethargy', Wymott was 'close to anarchy' before the 1993 riot, Leeds suffered from 'a sub-culture of self-destructive behaviour', and the Prison Service needed to be 'left alone to get on with its job without too much digging and poking'. Although he had no formal powers to order changes, his criticisms were often enough to do the job.

Relations between the Prison Service and its official critic could never be completely smooth but, despite press reports to the contrary, my own personal relations with Tumim were fine. We met every couple of weeks for a session which invariably involved my listening as he held forth on various pet issues. In the early days these tended to be complaints about how long it took the Prison Service to publish his reports, though quite why the service published the reports of an independent inspectorate remained a mystery. The inspectorate invariably took three months after an inspection to write its report: Tumim swore he needed that long, no doubt so that he could hone the language and make sure he included some quotable phrases. But the Prison Service itself had always played a delaying game, agreeing to publication only six, nine or even twelve months after the report had been completed – by which time the service could excuse deficiencies and deflect criticisms on the grounds that the report was hopelessly out of date and the problems now rectified. There were occasional spats as a result. When it looked as though publication of one of his reports was going to be unduly delayed, Tumim sent an angry message to say that he would 'expose' the Prison Service on the midday news unless the publication date was confirmed immediately. On another occasion, he told a tabloid newspaper that I had not been the first choice for the job of Director General – showing a serious misunderstanding of the selection process, as well as a streak of vindictiveness. He was sufficiently embarrassed to send me a grovelling apology, blaming his comments on the back pain that he had been suffering at the time. His relations with other members of the Prisons Board were volatile. He would be deeply offended if no members of the Prisons Board attended a public lecture he was giving, seeing this as clear evidence that we did not care about his views on prison policy. The task of keeping him reasonably on side was assigned to Tony Pearson, whose technique was to listen eagerly and provide fulsome lunches. Tumim was never known to pay.

I was touched when Joe Pilling invited me to have lunch with him at the Athenaeum Club – a generous gesture from someone who had obviously loved his job. He told me that I would recognize him as the only short, bald and bearded person in the Athenaeum. I began by saying how sorry I was that my arrival had lost him his job; he said I needn't worry and that his grieving was now done. We talked about the service, its problems, its people and the future. His affection for prisons and prison staff was evident, as well as his no-holds-barred appraisal of the strengths and weaknesses of the key people and of the issues ahead. Had Clarke been wrong to set his face against Pilling's continuation as Director General? He probably would have been the preferred choice of the selection board, dominated as it was by civil servants. There is no doubt that the service would have had someone totally committed to it and to the caring, rehabilitative aspects of the Woolf agenda. But Pilling would have been an insider, and a Civil Service insider at that.

During these early weeks the pieces of the jigsaw puzzle began to fit together to form a picture of the management of the service. It was far worse than I had been led to believe: indeed, it was difficult to find anything that was right about it. I now realized why the Conservative government and successive Home Secretaries had put the management problems of the Prison Service into the 'too difficult' category and left them for their successors to deal with – until the arrival of Kenneth Clarke.

3

Whitehall Whispers

The ending of the Cold War may have relieved the Kremlin of some of its intimidatory atmosphere, but the Home Office retains something of those bad old days. It seems to have been designed to be dark, forbidding and impenetrable. Stern-faced security guards glare at arriving visitors through the protection of dirty glass screens. They seldom smile, and a request to see the Home Secretary for a pre-arranged appointment is received without a flicker of recognition or acknowledgement. Eventually an equally severe uniformed guide emerges to escort the visitors up to the hallowed areas of the seventh floor where the Home Secretary, his permanent secretary and several junior ministers reside. Here visitors have to wait yet again, in the minister's waiting-room, a barren location with elderly uncomfortable seats. Visitors enter the Home Secretary's enormous office by a corner door, after running the gauntlet of the private secretaries in the outer office. He sits behind an enormous table at the far end, to reach which seems a long and lonely walk.

The Home Office in general was equally intimidating. As in the Prison Service, I found myself in a world which had its own private language – mysterious committees called EDH, LG or EDX; personal and private secretaries; PES; PQs, dep-secs, principals, fast-streamers, Treasury grades; minutes; bi- and tri-laterals; strange protocols about who could communicate with whom. I had to learn early on who held the power in this curious game of chess. Much revolved around the Secretary of State, but power in the Westminster game is not always related to the size of the pieces.

Private offices, staffed by quite junior civil servants, are often the most powerful.

The private secretary, or principal private secretary in the case of a Cabinet minister, is the office manager, and effectively controls the life blood of day-to-day government – the flow of information. Private office decides what the minister sees and when it is done – and often the outcome as well. A word in the minister's ear or one of the ever-present hand-written notes suggesting that the proposal might be contentious, risky or positively dangerous may well be enough. Private secretaries also control the ever-changing diary – delaying tactics or galloping indecision are powerful weapons for scuppering sensible but politically uncomfortable plans. A full diary effectively prevents a minister prying into undesirable subjects. For civil servants on the other hand, private office is the major source of information on ministerial thinking. Private secretaries can interpret their ministers' views in all sorts of ways. Unfortunately many are not that good at it, and the original intention can get lost. For someone used to a world in which managers actually talk to their bosses, working through a medium is both cumbersome and ineffective.

I encountered many private secretaries. Some were useless, others were gifted and some enjoyed the power a little too much. Joan MacNaughton, Ken Clarke's principal private secretary for a few months, fell into the latter category. Her relationship with Clarke was uneasy, and all the indications were that she would soon be on her way. She was reprieved by a Cabinet reshuffle, and survived to join forces with his successor, Michael Howard. She had been moved to private office after a controversial period in charge of prison industries, and took with her a reputation for making a virtue out of stress and hostility. In the early months her relationship with Howard also looked a little rocky. Private office was an unhappy place under her leadership, with junior private secretaries and others the frequent butt of her vitriolic criticism. Two of her assistant private secretaries were removed to other duties; another was unable to cope with the pressure and departed. Private office was driven only by the voracious appetite of the Home Secretary for paper, with the inevitable follow-up questions to which instant answers were demanded. There was little sense of oiling the wheels – suggesting alternatives to the Home Secretary, or interpreting requests in a pragmatic way – which those familiar with traditional private secretaries consider the essence of the art. No pleasure was to be had from dealing with the office. My efforts to have an occasional private *tête-à-tête* with the Home Secretary were bitterly resented. Joan explained how dangerous it was for her and for me to talk to a minister without a record being kept. Before long our informal meetings had grown to include the private secretary, the permanent secretary, a political adviser and the Prisons Minister.

MacNaughton's replacement, Ken Sutton, was like a breath of spring, professional and personable and able to walk a fine line between loyalty to the minister and helping others to do their jobs. His laid-back style concealed a good understanding of what makes people tick and how to be supportive.

Second in influence only to private secretaries are special advisers. They are party political animals, hand-picked by the minister to keep in touch with the wider political world beyond the respectable reaches of independent civil servants. Often aspiring politicians themselves, they keep a weather eye open for a safe constituency while watching over their master's fate. Clarke managed with only one special adviser, Tessa Keswick. Her style was low-key and subtle. At meetings she had a disarming habit of appearing to be asleep for most of the time. Her skill lay in waking at the critical moment to make the sort of salient comment which left everyone asking 'Why didn't I think of that?'

A third civil servant completes the triumvirate of influence surrounding the minister – the communications director, or press officer. He or she has almost total control of the minister's access to the media and vice versa. Most press officers develop close personal relationships with their ministers, exposing the myth of a non-partisan Civil Service. They have to interpret the minister's thinking to the press, fill in the gaps and correct the occasional gaffes. The advice of the press office will determine the timing, the tone and even the content of policy pronouncements. At times of crisis the minister and his press officer become like Siamese twins.

A long way behind come the other key players, led by the permanent secretary, a bevy of deputy secretaries and the half dozen or so junior ministers. The job of permanent secretary, at least at the Home Office, is something of a mystery. The department is too big and too complex for him to be sole adviser to the Home Secretary and junior ministers – work that is done directly by the deputy secretaries. Yet there is no chief executive role in the private sector sense, since most of the major executive decisions are made by the Secretary of State himself. The permanent secretary is left somewhat high and dry, occasionally dabbling in policy, looking after the department's finances and assessing the performance of the deputy secretaries – not always easy when he sees very little of their work. The key function of a 'Sir Humphrey' is holding his own among the gossips and plotters in the Whitehall corridors of power. Intrigue and manipulation are the name of the game, and although the role may seem to be an ill-defined muddle to outsiders like me, it represents the pinnacle of a high-flying civil servant's career.

I had a good relationship with Sir Clive Whitmore, my first permanent secretary. Quite apart from his role in my appointment, he remained supportive and easy to deal with, remarking at the end of my first year on how well things had gone.

Despite recent efforts to break the structure down, civil servants, as I soon discovered, live in grades, like rigid social strata. Grade 1 is the top of the tree, consisting of the permanent secretaries; Grade 2 covers the deputy secretaries, Grade 3 assistant secretaries and so on. Grade 2s only talked to Grade 2s and Grade 3s to Grade 3s, with the notable exception of the Treasury: such is its reputation and power that its senior civil servants often talk to those who are one grade higher in other departments. There were, I discovered, regular meetings of Grade 3 Home Office staff as well as of Grade 5, which more senior people attended only rarely and by invitation. It was at one of these Grade 3 meetings that I found the Civil Service at its subversive best. Philippa Drew put out a rallying call for opposition to the government's law and order policies, declaring that they had 'no intellectual foundation', while Tony Pearson declared that his mission was to 'reduce the pain of imprisonment' – hardly compatible with government efforts to ensure that prison was an austere and effective punishment.

Much power lies with the deputy secretaries, or Grade 2s, who deal directly with the Secretary of State or junior ministers. My first introduction to this élite group was the deputy secretaries' meeting, chaired by the permanent secretary. Every two weeks or so each of the second-tier civil servants crowded into Whitmore's office for two or three hours of structured gossip. Occasionally formal items of business arose, but their handling was highly discursive and any conclusions reached were always the subject of later dispute. The heart of the meeting consisted of tittle-tattle about the Home Secretary and his troubled relationships with junior ministers, whether there would be a reshuffle, the Home Secretary's prospects in legal actions coming up in the weeks ahead, and how long the government could survive with its ever-dwindling majority. The great British pastime of enjoying the misery of others, especially ministers, was much in evidence. A prospective defeat for Howard in the courts was debated with barely concealed glee, the sideways shuffle of a junior minister, Charles Wardle, to the DTI without the promotion to which he aspired was greeted with quiet satisfaction. My predecessor had strongly advised me to take the day's mail to read during these meetings. This was wise advice. Fortunately the long hours were punctuated by coffee and biscuits – vital nourishment during an otherwise intolerable ordeal. Such animation as occurred was rare and usually over in minutes. The head of immigration, Anthony Langdon, could usually be found slumped in his chair looking just like the dormouse at the Mad Hatter's tea party. From time to time something stirred him and he leapt into action, always objecting in scathing terms to whatever was being proposed.

The substance of the meetings, such as it was, dealt with the marginal and trivial. There were interminable debates over honours – who was to be recommended for the twice-yearly list, whether there was a spare knighthood, whether someone should get a CBE or an OBE, whether there were too many WRVS candidates or too few members of prison Boards of Visitors. An annual ritual consisted of 'succession planning' – deciding who should replace senior people when they left, retired or died. The candidates we identified rarely ended up getting the jobs. And then, of course, there was the matter of performance pay – allocating a few hundred pounds a year among the senior echelons for performances that ranged from the brilliant to the incompetent. When that was over we might discuss whether or not to have a smoking ban in the office: the staff all wanted one, but the cigar-smoking Clarke was opposed. Whitmore's summing-up was invariably a masterpiece of over-complication and obfuscation, peppered with his own unique pronunciations. What struck me was how little it all mattered. The most animated discussion during my time involved the vexed question of whether or not first names should be used in the office telephone directory or on office door plates. The upshot, after endless debate, was that 'Jones' had been known as 'Mr' since the beginning of his career and we had to ensure that his dignity was preserved.

The permanent secretary is a key figure when it comes to peace-making between warring ministers and acting as pacifier-in-chief to the Home Secretary. Because most of the power is vested at deputy secretary or Secretary of State level, junior ministers can become the Cinderellas of large departments, and need substantial and regular injections of tender loving care from the permanent secretary. They are on the lowest rung of political management and find themselves doing most of the Parliamentary donkey work, from MPs' correspondence and navigating bills through the Commons to deputizing at second-rate functions; and they are often propelled into the limelight over issues that might reduce a Secretary of State's shelf life, from the shackling of women prisoners to awkward immigration cases and firearms control. A few manage to break out of this straitjacket, win the ear of the Secretary of State and make their mark on policy.

★

The tortured relationships between the various members of this cast were well illustrated by the recurrent matter of my bonus payments. My own approach to such matters had always been to sit down with the person in line to receive a bonus, discuss the objectives for the year and agree on criteria for measuring success – preferably before the year began. One seldom needed more than an hour, and often much less, in which to resolve all the problems, so that everyone could get back to doing more important things. Not so in the Home Office. At the risk of jumping too far ahead, for the year ending on 31 March 1994, the Home Office finally confirmed the criteria on 16 February, only six weeks before the year-end, 'after lengthy exchanges with the Treasury'. No resolution had been reached three-quarters of the way through the following year, when I waived my entitlement.

For the third year the opening shot was fired by a civil servant in the Home Office, John Ingman, a tall bespectacled man with a permanently anxious air. His initial four-page memo to Michael Howard outlined the difficulties of finding arrangements that would satisfy Howard, the Treasury, the Office of Public Service, the lawyers and me. Before any discussion had ever taken place, it raised the spectre of a legal challenge by me if I disagreed. It seemed that I, as the person most directly affected, was to be excluded from the discussions. A protracted correspondence then followed, punctuated by various meetings. Howard asked the permanent secretary for further advice, including whether he could cut my bonus by more than half. In his reply, the permanent secretary suggested I would be justified in seeking a compensating increase in basic salary in return for a cut in bonus and guessed that I would be unlikely to agree. A month then elapsed before another Home Office civil servant wrote to one of his colleagues to say that 'The *Guardian* report today reminded me that Mr Lewis has not yet, as far as I know, got an agreed performance bonus package for 1995/96. Our papers seem to end just before the note of an important meeting that the Home Secretary was due to hold on the subject.' I was grateful for the *Guardian*'s prompting, but it produced little action. Another two months passed before any further proposals went to the Home Secretary in a five-page memo which described the timing as 'routine', despite the fact that we were now three months into the bonus year in question. What would normally be a straightforward discussion had now become a negotiation: 'I recommend that ministers agree that negotiations should be opened with Mr Lewis using the approach described above . . . We would report progress and approach ministers again if the negotiations collapsed.' Howard was unhappy, however. He wanted to be able to cancel any bonus if there was an embarrassing incident. The civil servants went back to the drawing-board and produced another proposal. This time it was decided that it should be cleared with the Treasury, and yet more correspondence ensued.

In late August, five months into the year and six months after the work on the bonus started, the Home Office wrote to me, setting out the proposed criteria. I replied a few days later agreeing – as I could have done five months earlier – to everything except the Home Secretary's arbitrary power to cancel my bonus. This triggered yet another round of Civil Service consultations, this time involving lawyers as well. A soothing response followed which indicated 'some sympathy' with the points I had made before getting to the nub of the problem: 'If, as might well be the case . . . there were questions to ministers about your bonus arrangements for this year, it would be advantageous to be able to refer to an agreed forfeiture provision.' Fed up with the exchange of correspondence, I spoke to the permanent secretary, suggested an alternative approach and provided a draft wording for the formula. Another four-page memo went to the Home Secretary recommending that he agree and saying, 'We think it highly desirable to reach an agreement with Mr Lewis on the formula to be adopted for this year's performance bonus . . . Although weaker than the formula we proposed Mr Lewis's version does provide some material for use in [Parliament]. In the circumstances, our inclination is to accept the formula now proposed by Mr Lewis rather than prolong the argument.' This brought a swift rejoinder from the Home Secretary via his private office to the effect that 'much as he would have liked to accept the revised arrangements he does not see how he possibly can . . . He finds this quite unacceptable as he must have the final say.' Obviously reluctant to admit that the Home Secretary had rejected his recommendation, the permanent secretary then wrote to me to say that 'On reflection it occurs to me [*sic*] that this formulation does not provide for what would happen in the event of disagreement. In these circumstances I think that the Home Secretary would want to decide whether to withhold all or part of the bonus.'

The story was to remain unfinished, overtaken by my ultimate dismissal. By then seven months had elapsed and virtually half of the bonus year had expired. Many meetings had taken place and twenty-seven items of correspondence had been exchanged: these included five long memoranda to the Home Secretary, eighteen assorted memos, letters between civil servants – and only four pieces of correspondence with me.

The Home Office civil servant, at least at senior levels, has been bred to a high degree of homogeneity by long years in the tradition-bound and insular culture of the department. There are ethnic minorities, but they are small. Occasionally a civil servant is transplanted from another department for a broadening experience, or private sector people appear on secondment, sent by their companies to gain knowledge of the inner workings of government. The Prison Service also sent the occasional former governor to learn about policy-making and politics in Queen Anne's Gate. Tony Pearson had done his spell there, as had Richard Tilt, who was to succeed me as Director General. Richard had already been identified as the next-in-line for a seat on the Prisons Board when I first met him late in 1993. A reticent figure, he was sound enough in his opinions without showing much enthusiasm for joining the Prisons Board or much drive to change the service. My reservations were shared by the non-executive directors, but there were no other qualified candidates who had also run prisons, and we had to replace Ian Dunbar on his retirement. If secondment to the Home Office was responsible for his compliant, laid-back style, it had much to answer for. Richard turned out to be a reliable lieutenant, good at doing what he was asked to but not a great initiator.

One of the few occasions on which Home Office ministers, their special or political advisers and senior civil servants get together is the autumn retreat to the country to consider long-term strategy. Usually it takes place at Chevening, the Foreign Secretary's country residence, redolent of a bygone imperial age. Its formal gardens, lake and rolling parkland complement the sweeping staircase, grand rooms and ornate ceilings of its interior.

The ice between civil servants and politicians always takes time to break. Over drinks before dinner on the opening day of my first visit, civil servant spoke to civil servant and politician to politician. Only a few brave souls from either side broke through this apartheid to indulge in stilted conversation among the antiques and the formidable array of weaponry and pictures that covered the walls. By the end of the meal the ice had thawed and the politicians were becoming less discreet. The civil servants, as always, remained on their guard.

Dinner was followed by a dazzling presentation of criminal statistics from the Home Office's research guru, Chris Nuttall. His quick-fire numbers game, illustrated by the latest colour graphs, is a regular after-dinner feature, almost as out of place in the elegant tranquillity of Chevening as his unceremonious arrival on a high-powered motor cycle, clad from head to toe in chilling black leathers.

Regrettably, these regular and uncomfortable insights have done little to affect policy in recent years. With the noticeable exception of homicide, crime has risen inexorably for decades, despite the remedies applied by successive Home Secretaries and governments, and the real number of crimes is four times higher than the police records. Nuttall graphically explained that the criminal justice agencies barely scratch the surface of crime, with only 2 per cent of offences resulting in a conviction. His statistics suggested that prison does indeed work, but badly. Locking more people away cuts crime, but it would take a doubling of the prison population to reduce it by a mere 4 per cent. As he hurtled on, ministerial reactions varied. Some slumbered gently on the well-padded settees, sated on food, wine and statistics, others practised their rebuttals, while a few took genuine note.

By the next morning the facts had been pushed into the background as the all-important political agenda for the coming year was discussed. I was taken aback to learn that the definition of 'long term' for complex matters of law and order was the next twelve months. The political timetable rarely seemed to coincide with the practical implications of serious change. But that year I was able to use my slot on the second day to outline the programme of change which we had started in the Prison Service, and explain why such fundamental changes would take many years to complete. Sympathetic understanding was expressed – most of which had evaporated only two years later. We talked at length about drugs, which were seriously undermining good order in prisons and were a scourge I was determined to tackle, in part by introducing compulsory drug testing and drug treatment programmes that I had seen in the US that spring. One hereditary peer, who rarely ventured beyond his country seat or the House of Lords, couldn't understand why we allowed drugs into prison in the first place. Just stop it, he demanded. Another other-worldly minister complained that prisoners smelt so awful: why couldn't we make them wash properly? Invariably such Chevening gatherings were judged to have gone well, though concrete results were always elusive.

As I made my way back to London, I reflected that I had been exposed to a world in which ministers, from Cabinet to junior, senior and well-placed junior mandarins, and political advisers were all to be found pursuing their own agendas – supposedly hidden, but conspicuously obvious.

4

Face to Face

Shouting and banging reverberated around D wing at Whitemoor maximum-security prison, making it hard to sustain my conversation with a category A prisoner serving a life sentence for murder. Not surprisingly, I hardly noticed a dark-haired prisoner approaching from the other side of the wing, brandishing a pair of scissors. Fortunately an eagle-eyed senior officer had seen what he was up to, and prisoner and scissors were soon parted. My chief press officer took a little longer to calm down: she confided afterwards that she had had a dream not long before in which I had been stabbed while visiting a prison.

When I took up my appointment I knew I had to learn the business of running prisons fast. That meant spending a large amount of time visiting prisons and talking to staff and to prisoners. Criminals are commonly regarded with a mixture of revulsion and fear – a luxury prison professionals cannot afford. Convicted prisoners are human beings, albeit ones who are being punished for committing often serious offences. The administration of punishment has to be tempered with the White Paper's philosophy, according to which 'Prisoners remain citizens even though they have been charged with or convicted of committing an offence' – not, perhaps, a politically attractive attitude at the present time.

I set myself a target of visiting every one of the 130 prisons in England and Wales within my first two years. It was a formidable but essential commitment, and one that was to absorb much of my time. My first visit took place the morning after the announcement of my appointment. Brixton was quickly followed by Aylesbury on Christmas Eve, Pentonville on Christmas Day and Whitemoor on Boxing Day, where I visited the special secure unit, shortly before it was closed for repair work, and had my first encounter with IRA terrorists.

One lesson I learned very quickly was that disaster often strikes at unexpected moments. Boxing Day ended with a minor riot at Reading Young Offender Institution – teenage vandals running amok and destroying property for lack of anything better to do.

It became clear from my first visit to Brixton that change was possible, and that good prisons could be housed even in old Victorian buildings. What was required above all was a governor with vision and leadership who understood prisoners – the circumstances that led to their offences, what made them tick, and what was likely to reduce, or aggravate, their anti-social behaviour both within prison and outside. Andrew Coyle, the governor of Brixton, fell into that category.

Coyle had earlier spent eighteen years in the Scottish Prison Service. With his doctorate in criminology, he had a reputation as the thinking man's governor: as chairman of the Institute for the Study and Treatment of Delinquency, he was much in demand by foreign governments to advise them on the development of their prison systems. He arrived at Brixton in 1991, in the wake of the notorious escape of IRA terrorists Nessan Quinlivan and Pearce Macauley, and found a prison that embodied all that was wrong with the English prison system. It regularly held up to 1,150 prisoners, over 50 per cent more than its normal capacity. The majority still slopped out, and the wings were pervaded by the stench of excreta emanating from the cells and from the recesses on the landings where prisoners emptied their pots in the mornings. The cells and wings were dark and decaying, daubed in the depressing shades of brown and green so admired by nineteenth-century prison-builders, with much of the paint flaking and peeling. Any attempts at cleaning were at best half-hearted. The notorious 'Fraggle rock' (F wing) was like bedlam: mentally ill prisoners were held together, and the barren building echoed to their cries and the drumming of fists on doors in a scene reminiscent of *One Flew Over the Cuckoo's Nest*. Many prisoners spent all but an hour a day locked in their cells, while for those who did come out there was little to do.

Coyle was a pioneer. He had taken the Brixton bull by the horns: two years and much hard work later, Brixton had been transformed. Overcrowding and slopping out had gone, the buildings had been refurbished and cleaned up. F wing had been converted for use by normal prisoners and renamed G wing, and the previous occupants of F wing re-housed in a clean, light and humane healthcare centre. Prisoners were out of their cells and more active. It was a case study in what can be done by those who take charge of the future and approach it with optimism, rather than being managed by events.

On 21 December 1993 I visited Brinsford Young Offender Institution for its official opening. Despite its chequered start, marred by a serious riot, I found a well-ordered establishment, where the governor, Bryan Payling, was doing pioneering work in the area of drugs. Many of the young offenders could hardly string two words together, but one was able to tell me that his only significant gain from being in prison had been learning how to neutralize burglar alarms.

An hour later I was listening to a highly-articulate ex-prisoner, Noel Fellowes, preaching at the chapel carol service. He had served four years for manslaughter before his conviction was quashed, and his description of life in prison is one of the most succinct and powerful I have come across:

The primary problem for any individual entering prison for the very first time is survival in a world governed by humiliation, degradation and isolation. For most of the individual's sentence there will be little direction or meaningful guidance for the future. In the majority of cases, vocational and educational training is given to the brighter inmate, and the less fortunate semi-literate or illiterate inmate will probably leave prison the way he entered.

The Victorian prison buildings and cells reflect Victorian attitudes towards its inhabitants. The prison system still deprives the inmate of any form of responsibility for himself, which traps him into being totally dependent upon the system. Throughout his sentence he is told what to wear and when to wear it, what to eat, when to eat, how much to eat, when to sleep, when to wake, when to shave, have a haircut, when to slop out, when to work, when to smoke, when to have a bath, change clothing, when and how to speak to prison officers, when he is allowed to see the chaplain, social worker, doctor, dentist, assistant governor, governor, visiting magistrate, and a host of other rules. All a man has to do is try to remain sane and survive it.

With each visit more pieces of the jigsaw fell into place. There was always something new to learn. Often praise and encouragement were needed; on other occasions poor performance required that swift action be taken.

Having started with one of the oldest Victorian locals at Brixton, I wanted to see its modern equivalent. The Wolds on Humberside was the obvious choice. Built to a completely modern design, it had been opened less than a year earlier, and was the first prison to be totally managed by a private sector company. There was none of the forbidding blackened brickwork that one sees on the outside walls of Brixton. The entrance for staff and visitors was light and gleaming. The military-style uniforms worn by prison officers in the public sector had been replaced by a corporate dress style of slacks and blazer. First impressions for arriving prisoners – then all on remand – were very different too. The dark paint, graffiti and stale smell of the reception area at Brixton were absent here. There were no sullen prison officers grudgingly taking details or removing property, stripping new arrivals of both identity and self-respect. The functional reception area was well lit and clean. Officers combined civility with discipline. Advanced technology was evident in the form of a video camera recording a digital image of each new arrival in the prison's computer. Prisoners were offered tea or coffee and, depending on the time of day, a hot meal. Some might say that all this was pampering. But a more balanced view would recognize that these people are human beings, and experience shows that if they are treated like animals during their time in prison, they are more likely to behave like animals, so increasing the likelihood that they will reoffend on release. And prisoners are at their most vulnerable during those early hours and days, when the shock of incarceration can lead to suicide.

My later visits included two other Victorian locals which endured some of the worst conditions in our prison system – Leeds and Leicester. It was perhaps no coincidence that they had some of the worst records for prisoner suicides. No one being processed through the dark subterranean reception area at Armley prison in Leeds could fail to be intimidated by the experience – and then to be transplanted into overcrowded, dark Victorian wings where the nauseous practice of slopping out still persisted could only have had a destabilizing effect on vulnerable prisoners. Little sympathy would be shown by most of the prison officers, influenced as they were by a local POA committee notorious for its tough approach to running prisons. The governor, Tony Fitzpatrick, had a mammoth task on his hands trying to turn round this antiquated prison, and it was my job to give him all the support I could.

Leicester had even more limited facilities than Leeds. Built on a very small site, it accommodated a burgeoning prison population in tiny Victorian cells. It was the last prison to hold three prisoners in many of those single cells. Standing in a space almost totally occupied by two bunk beds with another bed alongside, a desperate sense of claustrophobia overcame me. Very little light came in through the high window, and the barrel-vaulted ceiling gave it the feel of a dungeon. Conditions at Leicester were clearly unacceptable, and we had to reduce the overcrowding. Humanity, safety and security were all threatened. I ordered an immediate cut in numbers, and within a few days we had managed to eliminate the worst excesses by moving some prisoners out of the area.

Both prisoners and staff were still suffering the after-effects of a tragic suicide. A sense of failure was evident among a group of people who cared deeply about those in their charge, led by the inspired and dedicated governor, Gerry Ross. Opening a cell door in the morning to find a body hanging from a ligature attached to the window bars or an upturned bedstead is one of the worst traumas for anyone who works in prison, provoking an immediate sense of guilt, a feeling that there must have been something more that could have been done to prevent it. Over fifty prisoners a year succeed in killing themselves, but there are numberless unsuccessful attempts and instances of self-mutilation. Cutting wrists, slashing bodies and banging heads against walls often represent a frustrated cry for help and attention, but sometimes it goes tragically wrong. Other deaths may result from a deliberate or unintentional drugs overdose.

Prisons attract many inadequate people, particularly youngsters with little or no self-esteem. They find it difficult to cope at the best of times and often have little support outside. Add the shock of being in prison for the first time, facing an uncertain future and possible conviction, the threat of bullying and 'taxing', or theft, a girlfriend who goes off with someone else, parents who are indifferent – and the pressures can become too great. Most of those at risk are identified by the staff as they come into prison: the police may have reported telltale behaviour, the medical officer may see the signs when the prisoner is examined, and experienced staff may sense a problem. Such prisoners are put in a double cell with someone else to keep an eye on them or sent to the healthcare centre, where they are under continuous observation and there are fewer opportunities for self-harm. But none of these methods is infallible when it comes to identifying those at risk, or preventing the determined prisoner from taking his own life. When it does happen, the after-shocks run through the whole prison, carrying the message that someone has 'topped himself'. One self-inflicted death often leads to others in the same prison. The repercussions for staff are painful. The inevitable inquiry to find out why it had not been prevented exacerbates their sense of guilt. They may be blamed for what is often unpreventable, instead of getting the support they need and the credit for the many suicides that they have prevented.

★

Gradually I was developing a better feel for how prisons worked, and a sixth sense about whether things were running well or badly. The telltale signs of a stable, well-run establishment include prison officers who are confident and happy to talk, and prisoners who look you in the eye. Prisoners, staff on the landings and the Board of Visitors provide useful intelligence on how things are; as does a governor who has a grip on what is happening in his prison, knows the staff as he walks around, and has a clear sense of what he is trying to do. All are positive indicators that the establishment is in good health.

As my visits continued, it became clear that overcrowding was one of the recurrent problems of the Prison Service. An important cause of the Strangeways riot, it was also a major distraction for governors: it is difficult to give proper attention to security or rehabilitation if the daily priority is finding places for additional prisoners. Unlike other businesses, the Prison Service cannot turn away new 'customers'; unlike the NHS, it cannot create a waiting list. The only solutions are overcrowding, transporting prisoners to distant parts of the country where there may be spare cells, or looking to the police to accommodate prisoners in police cells – a practice that was prevalent in the northwest when I arrived in the Prison Service, but which we soon eliminated.

Cells in police stations are usually used to hold prisoners overnight before they are charged. Senior police officers hate holding Home Office prisoners, but the junior ranks who do the work often prefer being paid overtime for doing very little to being out on the beat in winter. In the wake of the Strangeways riot, when large amounts of accommodation were lost, many police officers made modest fortunes in this way.

Some prisoners enjoy it too. They can remain near their home, and they can avoid doing any work. But it is not something a civilized country should allow. I remember visiting the Main Bridewell in Liverpool, a notorious set of police cells. Three prisoners were held in each barrel-vaulted brick cell with no natural light; the cell was lit by a single dingy light bulb and was boiling hot in summer and bitterly cold in winter. The inmates stayed in their cells most of the time: they were occasionally allowed out on to an equally dingy corridor with a single television set, but had virtually no access to exercise. Punishment involved being sent downstairs to cell number 4, a Kafkaesque place with no furniture and a hole in the floor in lieu of the broken lavatory. The prisoners looked cowed and were reluctant to talk about their treatment. It felt more like a Japanese prisoner-of-war camp in the 1940s than a police station in the 1990s. It could not be allowed to continue, and I ordered an immediate halt to its use by the Prison Service.

No one in the Prison Service had much incentive to avoid using police cells. Prison governors didn't have to pay the bills out of their own budget, and the Treasury gave the Prison Service extra money from its own resources to foot the sometimes enormous charges levied by the police: in some cases, the bills worked out at over £500 per prisoner per night. Several police officers might guard one or two prisoners in a small station, relieving the boredom by buying their charges pizza or hamburgers and renting videos to entertain them. In 1993, the Prison Service had run up a bill of almost £100 million with the police services around the country. Such expenditure had attracted the attention of the National Audit Office, which presented a highly critical report to the Public Accounts Committee, alleging that the Prison Service had exercised no proper control over the spending. As so often happens, the Audit Office missed the point. They were right to allege a lack of control, but they concentrated on whether the Prison Service had properly checked the amounts being charged and had obtained the signature of the treasurer of each of the police forces on the bills. There were glaring failures by the Prison Service to do so, but in reality it would have had little effect on the amount of the bills. The police were a monopoly supplier to the Prison Service in an emergency situation, and they could charge and justify pretty much what they wanted by massaging their costs. What the Audit Office completely ignored was whether the Prison Service had done enough to avoid the use of police cells in the first place. Had they done so, they would have found a system that created and perpetuated the problem.

Overcrowding in some parts of the country contrasted with empty cells elsewhere. Local prisons in one area turned prisoners away, while training prisons for convicted prisoners up the road had empty cells as a result of inertia in moving prisoners out of the local prisons. Some governors refused to double up to accommodate new arrivals, or failed to report their maximum capacity to make life easier; Prison Service HQ steadfastly maintained that newly built accommodation could not be overcrowded by doubling up, fearing that the Treasury would otherwise insist that it be done. Category D open prisons were part-empty, while governors of local prisons tenaciously held on to category D prisoners because they were easier to manage and useful for jobs around the prison. Our subsequent success in eliminating the use of police cells despite a rising prison population demonstrated the extent to which lethargy in the Prison Service and a cosy conspiracy between governors, prison officers, police officers and the police hierarchy had cost the taxpayer. The savings in the first year alone were £90 million.

But there was no hint of such dirty washing when Sir Clive Whitmore appeared before the Public Accounts Committee of the House of Commons on 24 February 1993 to explain this apparent shambles. It was indeed regrettable, he admitted, that more effective authorization procedures had not been in place. All the necessary corrective action had been taken, and it would not happen again. No one was really responsible for what had gone wrong, and at no stage was it suggested that the use of police cells might have been unnecessary. One of the committee members complimented Sir Clive on the consummate skill with which he had re-enacted a scene from *Yes Minister*. My appreciation of the mandarin qualities of self-preservation and diplomacy grew by leaps and bounds.

The contrast between the decent and humane, if still austere, conditions at the Wolds with those prevailing at Leeds or Leicester represented a pattern that was repeated throughout the country. The difference between state-of-the-art Woodhill, the new prison in Milton Keynes, and its older counterpart in Hull was just as dramatic and fuelled the debate over whether prison conditions were too luxurious.

On 31 March 1993 I joined Ken Clarke at Woodhill for its official opening. Its brick-clad external walls owed more to a Sainsbury's or Tesco superstore than to the traditional image of a prison. The houseblocks are triangular with cells arranged in galleries along the two adjacent shortest walls. The third wall, forming the hypotenuse of the right-angled triangle, consists of a huge glass curtain window. The accommodation is light, warm and spacious, if not homely: it would be the envy of many honest but impoverished citizens, and the contrast with Brixton and other Victorian prisons has to be seen to be believed. Whereas the gym at Hull is cramped and low-ceilinged, Woodhill's is on a scale only found in the more affluent large cities. It also has an education centre with classrooms, computers and teaching aids that would be the envy of most local schools. Class sizes never reach forty here and few have more than ten.

It was hardly surprising that Clarke's hackles began to rise as he surveyed the gym from its spectator gallery before going on to meet a prisoner using an expensive music synthesizer in the education block. His comments about excessive facilities prompted his successor, Michael Howard, to condemn luxury in prisons before he had seen any evidence of it for himself.

Woodhill has the distinction of being the most expensive prison ever built in this country, and possibly anywhere in the world – £200,000 for every prisoner accommodated there. Three times the cost of other new prisons, it was a scandalous waste of taxpayers' money. Tighter controls and new methods of construction enabled me to cut the cost of subsequent prisons by two thirds.

I discovered that the vast majority of prisoners simply accept their sentences and want to 'do their bird' quietly. This same majority makes it possible to run prisons, because they operate by consensus, not coercion, with a prison staff usually outnumbered in a ratio of ten to one. But there is always the disruptive minority, the immature young offenders still innately hostile to authority or, among older groups, the heavy hitters who aim to take control of whatever prison they are in. And there is invariably a small group of highly disruptive prisoners with the potential to be extremely violent. Many of them suffer so-called personality disorders, and the Prison Service has never found a satisfactory way of dealing with them. Some are held in small CRC, or control review committee, units, where security and staffing levels are high. Others are moved around the country from one secure segregation block to another: there they are kept under very restricted conditions, until they become too much for the staff and are moved on yet again.

The existing methods for dealing with disruptives constitute a powerful case for the creation of a single super-maximum-security prison, able to handle such prisoners in a humane way that does not impose undue stress on staff. They would be held in small units with varying regimes and could progress from one to another as their behaviour and attitudes improved.

Woodhill held one of our most notoriously disruptive prisoners, Charles Bronson. He had hit the headlines after taking a teacher hostage in his cell – a governor's worst nightmare. We waited anxiously as the negotiators patiently talked to him, trying to tire him and reduce the temperature. As always, the golden rule applied – 'no concessions'. It had always worked hitherto, and there had been no fatalities in the Prison Service as a result of hostage incidents: but there could always be a first time. Bronson asked for a blow-up doll, tea and a helicopter. As he later explained to the judge at his trial, the doll was to provide company during the twenty-three hours he spent locked in his cell each day, the tea was a kind thought for his unfortunate victim, and the helicopter . . . well, everyone asked for a helicopter, didn't they?

But Bronson is a dangerous man as well as a showman. It was not long before he struck again, at the CRC unit at Hull. This time his hostage-taking was far more threatening: his victim was the deputy governor, Adrian Wallace, and we had serious anxieties throughout for his welfare. The incident ended peacefully, but left a victim who continued to suffer trauma from the experience. More than two years later, Bronson was at it again. He was being held in a normal wing at Belmarsh prison in south London together with some Iranians accused of the Stansted hijacking and the publicity opportunity proved too tempting. Thankfully this incident too was brought to a successful end.

As I met more prisoners, I was surprised by how ordinary most of them were. A high proportion was not there for the first time. Most had started their prison careers in the junior prisons or Young Offender Institutions (YOIs), where I found a mixture of the pathetic, the angry and the inadequate. And, contrary to the popular fallacy that our prisons are filled with old lags, nearly two-thirds of prisoners are aged thirty or under. By that age a staggering one in three British men has a criminal record for something other than a motoring offence.

Home Office research told me a good deal about the background to the criminal behaviour of these young people. To begin with, a third of all prisoners have been brought up with only one parent or in an institution, while almost 40 per cent have spent time in local authority care. Educational failure is the norm. Nearly half left school before the age of sixteen – four times the national average. A third of those who attended school after the age of eleven played truant most of the time – ten times the national average. It is small wonder that many cannot read or write. And nearly half the prisoners have no educational qualifications whatsoever.

Not surprisingly, perhaps, it is estimated that well over half the prison population was on hard or soft drugs before entering prison for the first time. Even less surprising was the high rate of unemployment: only half the prison population was previously in regular employment. Offenders increasingly come from an environment in which work is not the normal activity, from families where neither parent works and may never have worked, and where living off the state is an accepted way of life.

Such statistics suggest the circumstances under which young people are likely to turn to crime, though not all those who are similarly disadvantaged become criminals. A pattern emerges of children who come from broken or inadequate homes, for whom the educational system has simply failed to deliver, who have no work ethic because work is neither a desirable nor a normal activity, and who have slipped into an endemic drug culture. Most of them make a conscious choice to follow a life of crime. Widely practised by those around them, it seems the natural thing to do.

Where parents and teachers have failed so miserably, others could hardly be expected to succeed. For those condemned to local authority care, benevolent child minders *in loco parentis* have little effect. Such children are rarely reached by the church or social workers. They drift into car theft, minor house-breaking or vandalism to relieve their boredom, or simply to sustain a drug habit. Some of those who take to theft may well justify their crimes on the grounds that their victims are well insured and can afford to buy replacements. For them crime has never been a moral issue.

They often start young. I well remember walking into a cell at Onley Young Offender Institution near Rugby. A boy in his early teens was sitting under the harsh glare of a ceiling strip light. A partially completed jigsaw puzzle on the table in front of him was in danger of floating away as the tears streamed down his childish face. A fatherly prison officer had an arm round his shoulder, trying to comfort him as he cried for his mother. How, I wondered, could such a vulnerable-looking boy be in prison. The officer supplied the answer: a succession of burglaries.

I asked a group of fifteen- to seventeen-year-olds at Wetherby YOI whether they expected to find themselves back in prison again. Without a moment's hesitation, all but one said they did, simply because they needed the money. But even if there are no jobs, surely the state would provide some financial support? 'We can't live on that,' they said. 'Not enough to buy our drugs' – which they depressingly described as their one form of pleasure.

It would be too easy to blame successive governments for this state of affairs. But while they are undoubtedly guilty of neglect and of ignoring the evidence in the naïve hope that it might go away, there are wider problems for which society as a whole must accept responsibility. Government alone cannot cure the problem of poor parenting. School governors, teachers and school administrators have some responsibility for failures in the education system. Political, business and social leaders have failed to provide the younger, more vulnerable members of society with the jobs they need, so allowing them to drift into the murky world of drugs.

Our response to these problems illustrates the worst tradition of British compromise and delay – no prevention, no treatment and definitely no cure. There has been mounting evidence for some years that overall levels of educational attainment in Britain are falling behind those of our rivals, yet we have no effective programmes designed to reach those pre-school and primary children who are most likely to drop out of the system. Effective parenting is a skill that can be learned, yet a growing number of people have neither experienced nor acquired such skills, and little effort is made to teach them. A succession of government initiatives to introduce youngsters to work has failed to make significant inroads into the problem of long-term youth unemployment.

Our response to early criminality is even more inadequate. Police warnings are followed by cautions, but seldom by any serious effort to deal with the circumstances that led to the crime. Young people may be put into local authority care or sent to a youth treatment centre – institutions that have been subject to more than their fair share of scandal in recent years. After a period in a young offender institution for fifteen- to seventeen-year-olds, they will mix with the more serious seventeen- to twenty-one-year-old criminals, often hardened, skilled and on course for a life behind bars. The first sentence in a proper prison will often be short, perhaps three or six months, with only half that time actually spent in custody: too short a time for prison staff to do anything useful with the offender, and not long enough to have any lasting deterrent effect.

By the time these young people reach twenty-one crime is their way of life, as a result of which they have become outcasts from society and part of a dangerous and divisive under-class. That is likely to be the pattern of their lives over the next fifteen years. As they grow older, they consider themselves professionals: as one prisoner put it to me, 'I am a professional burglar. It may not be a good profession, but it's the only one I have.'

One large category of prisoners, whose prison careers tend to start later in life, are sex offenders, who may be guilty of sexual assaults, rape, child-molesting or more serious paedophile offences. I soon discovered that they are despised by other prisoners. One old lag at Long Lartin complained to me about having to share a prison with 'nonces' and 'perverts'. Such prisoners suffer continual taunts, food spiked with urine or other foreign matter and occasional violence. Paedophiles, in particular, are at risk of their lives, as the murder of Leslie 'Catweazle' Bailey at Whitemoor in October 1993 demonstrated. The established response has been to allow such prisoners and others who are vulnerable to seek refuge in segregation blocks or in special vulnerable prisoner units (VPUs). This offers temporary protection, but it labels such prisoners as VPs or sex offenders (even if they are not), a stigma which they will never lose and which may make them even more vulnerable. One of our greatest fears during the riot at Wymott prison in September 1993 was for the safety of a small group of sex offenders who were no longer protected by staff. VPs cannot work with other prisoners in the workshops and often get jobs that other prisoners consider a soft option. Some pioneering prisons, such as Risley under Brendan O'Friel, have broken this vicious circle by integrating their VPs – an example that others should follow.

Childhood abuse can cause fundamental character and personality changes. The victim comes to believe that such behaviour is acceptable, with the result that most sex offenders persuade themselves that their crimes do not have a damaging effect on their victims, while others shut their minds to the consequences. Abused children grow into isolated loners, living on the fringes of society. Ultimately the effects of their childhood experiences, their sense of being rejected by society, may lead them to commit further crimes, all too similar to those from which they themselves once suffered. A classic case of history repeating itself.

The Prison Service has developed programmes that stand a real chance of changing the attitudes and behaviour of sex offenders.

Prisoners are challenged by staff and their peers to understand why they behave the way they do, and to recognize the effect on their victims. Gradually they come to realize what causes their behaviour. Talking to staff at Whatton, a prison reserved exclusively for sex offenders, I understood the traumatic effect such a programme has on the staff who run it, in that they are exposed every day to gruesome accounts of sex offences and their effect on the victims. But if it reduces the chances of prisoners reoffending after their release, it is work well done.

Fortunately we have few serial killers in this country but my first visit to Parkhurst, in August 1994, brought me face to face with one of them. Peter Maudesley had committed several callous murders on the outside and while in prison. His living conditions were unique, and not unlike those of Hannibal Lecter in *The Silence of the Lambs*. His days were spent in an isolated self-contained unit, complete with living area, bed and washing facilities. For their own protection prison officers entered in teams of four. He was a tall, sullen man with long black hair, his piercing eyes transformed his otherwise gaunt face into something menacing. Our encounter was dominated by his brooding presence and the ominous unnatural surroundings. Conversation did not come easily, but he managed to protest about the inequities of his treatment and conditions. As I walked out of his cell and heard the door slam reassuringly behind me, I felt a real sense of relief.

Maudesley is an exception among the murderers in our prisons. Very few spend the whole of their natural lives behind bars. There are over 4,000 so-called life sentence prisoners: over 3,000 of them are in prison, while the others are back in the community, and can be instantly recalled if they transgress in any way. The vast majority of murders are domestic affairs – the result of provocation, jealousy or loss of control, often brought about by drugs or drink. Others are committed in the course of burglaries or robberies, and are unplanned and unintended. Very few are callously premeditated killings. In fact, most murderers are intelligent articulate people, often providing the stability so vital to the smooth running of a prison. One of the most constructive meetings I had about the future management of the Prison Service took place at Gartree prison. The other ten participants were all murderers, but they were full of positive and innovative ideas. Domestic murderers are a world apart from IRA terrorists or serious gangland criminals.

Most people would consider Maudesley mentally disordered, a serious psychiatric case. Many others like him are shunned by the medical profession – either because they are thought to be untreatable, or because there are not enough secure psychiatric beds in the NHS. Prisons cope as best they can, but they are not equipped or staffed to provide proper care, with the result that the mentally ill are simply left to rot. The consequences can be tragic. One evening late in 1994, the telephone rang at home and I was told about a murder in my local prison at Chelmsford. Two prisoners, both mentally disturbed, had been locked in the same cell as a result of overcrowding and one had brutally murdered the other. When I visited the prison several weeks later, staff were still mortified and shocked by what had happened. The victim's parents came to see me soon after – decent, respectable, ordinary people, who were trying to come to terms, not just with the fact that their son was mentally disturbed, but with the appalling death he had suffered as the result of being locked up in the wrong place.

One other small category of prisoners is all too often neglected. Women make up only 4 per cent of the total prison population, but their tragedy and pathos can be heart-breaking. Mental disorder, crime and punishment are seldom far apart, but in a women's prison they seem inseparable. Walking down the claustrophobic corridors of Holloway – the largest women's prison in Europe, and a monu-ment to the waste of taxpayers' money through poor design – I found myself wondering whether and when madness excuses criminal behaviour. Here were women displaying all the symptoms of acute mental disorder, combined with resignation and hopelessness. Some were curled up on their beds in the middle of the day with little or no will to live, others had already tried to kill themselves several times and might try again that very night. Young women screamed and shouted, banging themselves against the walls, their staring haunted eyes suggesting that they were under sedation. How can we justify holding these people fully responsible for the crimes they had committed? Was it right that they should be locked away in a prison that can only aggravate their mental illness? We do not know what to do with these people, and can think of nothing better than putting them behind bars, well out of sight.

New Hall women's prison near Wakefield was a far cry from Holloway. Its governor, Derek England, was an inspired and caring man and his prison was a gem, striking a fine balance between the particular problems of women prisoners and their continuing obligations to family and children, and the need to punish them for their crimes.

Female offences are usually quite different from those committed by men, but drugs dominate. There are also many foreigners in the female prison population, convicted of acting as 'mules', smuggling drugs into this country. Women imprisoned for theft or burglary were usually feeding a drug-habit or providing for their children.

There has been remarkably little research into why women offend so much less than men. If we knew the answers, it might bring us closer to solving the problems of male crime. Are the differences genetic, or do they derive from the stereotypical social patterns, with the woman as the homemaker and carer of children, while the man is the hunter and provider? It may well be both, but it is an interesting commentary on our times that women are increasingly starting to commit the types of offence that were once a male preserve, including property crimes and acts of violence.

Running a women's prison can be a nightmare. Women prisoners are more likely to be first-time offenders, and they take a long time to adjust to their new surroundings. A large proportion have dependent children outside, which create enormous additional stresses, and some have young babies or toddlers with them in prison. It is difficult to maintain an austere penal environment with children around, in need of parental love and a warm, nurturing home. Lesbian relationships are rife, and constant vigilance is required to prevent relationships developing between prisoners and staff. Women can be more manipulative than men; they can inveigle staff into lapses and breaches of security. They will assert their right to be treated differently from men over matters such as the use of handcuffs. Take the notorious case of Susan Edwards, at Styal prison, who had foolishly been kept handcuffed throughout childbirth. The public was justifiably outraged. But what they did not know was that she made repeated attempts to escape and, as I discovered when I interviewed her, was expert at manipulating staff through a mixture of abuse, attention-seeking, emotion and tears.

Managing long-term female prisoners brings its own difficulties. Myra Hindley, for example, has frequently been subject to hysterical attack by the tabloid press. It is very easy for governors and prison staff to develop sympathies for a prisoner who has been incarcerated for over thirty years, and shows all the signs of remorse for what she did and a desire to live as normal a life as possible. As I talked to her alone in the governor's office at the end of my visit to Cookham Wood, she seemed intelligent, articulate, and well balanced, a far cry from the sort of person one might imagine to have been involved in horrific child murders. However, as our discussion proceeded, her speech slowed, and she showed every sign of falling asleep on the governor's sofa. Alarmed by this development, I was relieved to be told that it was the result of the medication she was taking.

Remand prisoners – men and women who had been kept in custody for as long as a year and sometimes more without being convicted or sentenced – were another cause for concern. Some 10,000 in all, they accounted for about 20 per cent of the total prison population and cost the taxpayer £300 million or more each year.

The blame for these delays lies with our painfully slow and creaking system of criminal justice and recent improvements have done little to change practices that are rooted in the nineteenth century. But prisoners and their defence lawyers compound the problem. Prisoners expecting a prison sentence drag their heels, preferring to serve time on remand, where they are not required to work and enjoy better conditions, than in the more punitive environment experienced by convicted prisoners. Defence lawyers spin out cases to increase their fees, often at public expense through the generous and widely exploited legal aid system.

And while the guilty benefit from manipulating the system, the innocent suffer. One in five remand prisoners is acquitted after serving time for a crime he or she did not commit. While on remand they may have lost their jobs, their homes and their families, but most will receive no compensation.

Talking to prisoners, hearing about the circumstances that led them to make such a mess of their lives, was often a dispiriting business. But the occasional success stories made it all worthwhile – youngsters who had learned to read and write and discover self-respect, adults who had acquired new skills inside and found employment 'on the out', giving them a real chance of leading law-abiding lives in the future. Even more remarkable, perhaps, were those that had benefited from the sex offender treatment programme.

I remember an early visit to Everthorpe on Humberside, a dismal, low-security prison which looked even more depressing in darkness and driving rain. After hours of predictable exchanges, I experienced one of those rare moments of surprise and hope which change the nature of the day. After ducking my head to enter one of the cramped cells on the threes (third floor) I found none of the usual untidiness. The grey Victorian walls had been covered with an array of pictures, from Formula One racing cars to landscapes. The inmate's love of art had been discovered and nurtured during his period in prison, and I felt sure it provided the key to his future life outside.

Time and again I was reminded that not all prisoners are intrinsically bad and that, although it is never easy, rehabilitation is still possible – the one thing that motivates prison staff on even the worst days. A former prisoner wrote to me after I had left the service:

You won't remember me. But I remember you. About two and a half years ago you were doing a tour of Exeter prison. I was in a wheelchair when you spoke to me in the hospital wing. You sat on my bed, and we talked about ME for about twenty minutes. You showed me a great deal of compassion then, and I was so sorry to hear about your problems.

This was one of the rare but rich rewards of being involved in running prisons.

But success in the eyes of the politicians is a different matter. Commercial companies are measured in terms of growth, market share, profits and share price, all of them easily identifiable and positive yardsticks. Health services can be judged by the successful operations they perform, charities by the support they provide, the police by the number of criminals they catch. But in the case of the Prison Service, the public *expect* there to be no escapes, that prisoners and staff should co-exist safely, that there should be no drugs and that prisoners should emerge from their period behind bars totally rehabilitated. If these standards were met, the public would be quite happy never to see or hear about prisons. It is an impossible ideal, but anything else represents failure.

Those involved in the management of prisons have to accept that there is no bottom line, and that success is measured more by a reduction in the failure rate rather than anything more positive. On top of which managers have to contend with the complexity of prisons, the conflict between the demands of security and rehabilitation, and the complete lack of control the service has over the number of prisoners it is required to accommodate. The service is always at the mercy of the courts, the police and politicians.

Prisons are a minefield of difficult moral issues. Take the treatment of transsexuals. Is it right that prison should provide opportunities for sex-change treatment, even if the medical profession has recommended it? And do such people belong in male or female institutions? Do the public health arguments for issuing condoms to reduce the spread of AIDS in prison outweigh the risks of encouraging homosexual activity? Under what circumstances is it justified to run security risks for humanitarian reasons – so that a prisoner can visit a dying relative, for example.

62

Few other services or businesses – except zoos, perhaps – have to contend with the persistent efforts of some of their residents to thwart what they are doing. It makes the service exceptionally vulnerable to a careless or momentary lapse by a single employee, with consequences that can be quite horrific. The service is always vulnerable to being thrown off course by the unexpected. A governor's ill-judged decision to provide his inmates with a pitch-and-put course caused a massive political and media reaction, distracting the management for weeks on end as inquests were conducted and policy re-examined. A flawed home-leave decision can have equally far-reaching consequences.

All this has to be played out against the background of often abrupt political swings. This month's government may wish to march the soldiers up the hill of rehabilitation, while next month's may march them down again to retribution and austerity. Such dramatic swings have the effect of making the organization cynical and resistant to further change. Not surprisingly, the Prison Service all too often feels abused, victimized and unjustly treated. The subject of endless public inquiries, neglected managerially and financially by successive governments, the Prison Service I joined at the beginning of 1993 was in a poor condition indeed.

5

The Hope of Independence

Kenneth Clarke had chosen 1 April 1993 as the date on which the Prison Service would acquire agency status. Already there were over a hundred so-called executive agencies, employing around three out of four of all civil servants – nearly 400,000 in total. The Prison Service would be one of the largest and most complex.

The theory behind the 'Next Steps' initiative for the creation of executive agencies had been relatively simple. It was a myth that ministers ran major government services such as the Benefits Agency or the Passport Office: they had neither the knowledge nor the skills to do so. But as long as the myth persisted, the civil servants, who were really in charge of the day-to-day operations, were not being given the authority to get on with the job, nor were they being held responsible for the performance of the agencies. The intention was to describe more precisely the respective jobs of ministers and civil servants, and to get away from the confusion that had existed hitherto. Ministers would be responsible for setting policy, approving the agencies' plans, setting targets and monitoring performance; the civil servants in charge would be given the autonomy to get on and make it all happen. The performance of the agency and its chief executive would be closely monitored by key performance indicators. Chief executives would generally be appointed on fixed-term contracts so that if they did not achieve the targets set for them by ministers they could be removed more easily. Agency status also brought with it many other management tools that were commonplace in the private sector. The essentials were clarity of roles, operational autonomy, the delegation of decision-making and holding agencies and their chief executives responsible for results.

Some wondered whether the Prison Service was suitable for agency status: was it too sensitive for ministers to let go of day-to-day control? Clarke did not think so. He was a strong believer in delegation, in giving people the room to get on with the job and backing them. He swept aside the doubters.

Much of my early work with the Prisons Board concentrated on preparing the framework agreement and corporate and business plans in anticipation of our move to agency status. It was too late for me to have much impact on this, but there was one gap that I felt needed attention. The Prison Service had had a statement of purpose for a number of years. A model of clarity and succinctness – 'Her Majesty's Prison Service serves the public by keeping in custody those committed by the courts. Our duty is to look after them with humanity and help them lead law-abiding and useful lives in custody and after release' – it was admirable as far as it went, but it went only so far. It said nothing about what sort of Prison Service we were aiming to be, what our specific goals were, and what sort of values we would adhere to in the way we operated. Above all, we needed something that would help the more voca- tional members of staff feel good about a job that involved adminis- tering punishment. Much effort had already gone into drafting a statement of vision and values, involving large amounts of consul- tation and listening to many different opinions. But, as was so often the case, it had ground to a halt in a mire of conflicting views. This was an opportunity to concentrate the minds of the board on an important task that could help draw us together as a team. The statement became an early priority. I prepared the first draft myself to show that I wanted to get things done, and that this was more than just a job for me. Others chipped in, and eventually one member volunteered to produce the final statement. The first signs of a cohesive management team were becoming apparent – and we had created a statement that has guided the service ever since.

I also needed the directors to focus on operational issues, making sure the service did the job the public expected, rather than wasting time in philosophical debate and looking up to ministers. I decided to form an executive committee, consisting of all the executive directors, and insisted on meeting every week to review day-to-day performance on the ground and take the necessary operating decisions. Imposing the necessary discipline was a painful experience, but gradually it worked.

Management, like politics, is the art of the possible. Having been successful in bringing the board together around a statement of vision and values and creating an operational focus, my next step proved to be one too far. The organizational structure of the Prison Service at senior levels was a nightmare to anyone used to the clarity of the private sector. The three operational directors were not only responsible for the prisons in one-third of the country each, but they combined this with a variety of staff functions, setting security policy, formulating educational programmes or determining disciplinary procedures. The finance director doubled up as personnel director. It was often impossible to work out who was responsible for any particular task, and when a job was shared between more than one director, life became impossible. The solution seemed obvious: we should have two operational directors doing nothing but running the prisons, and then a set of straightforward staff functions, with one or two directors looking after policy, one dealing with finance and one with personnel. Nothing could be clearer, and such a system worked well in many other organizations, both public and private. The logic seemed compelling, but the other members of the board reacted with incredulity, emotion and obstruction. I was confronted by the accumulated baggage of history, as well as a number of hidden agendas. Operations had always been the preserve of ex-prison governors, who were not allowed to get involved in the world of policy-making, which was held to be sophisticated and beyond their abilities. In the words of the cynics, one needed to be able to 'do joined-up writing'. Even former prison governors, who traditionally loathed civil servants, had subconsciously come to accept the Orwellian mantra of 'operations good, policy better'. It was an alien philosophy to me: I had always believed that what mattered was getting the job done and achieving results, and that policy was no more than a means to that end. I came to realize that career civil servants never wanted to relinquish their involvement in policy: that was where reputations were made, through regular exposure to ministers. I had stirred up a veritable hornets' nest.

A succession of directors trooped into my office with studied looks of worry. I knew they had been co-ordinating their fight-back. The speeches were well scripted. Two of the operational directors in particular were vehement in their opposition: Philippa Drew, the Home Office mandarin, wanted to keep her hand in at policy to safeguard her future career options back in the Home Office; Tony Pearson had graduated from governing to policy, which he found a less painful experience, and did not wish to be demoted to operations alone. The urbane Tony Butler acted as ambassador and shop steward of the rebels. I was warned, Cassandra-like, that to do what I wanted would bring back the dark ages, split the service, leave staff demoralized and produce all sorts of dire consequences in terms of performance.

It was a difficult choice. I could either force through my views – which I was confident were right, and subsequently proved to be so – and risk a revolt, or bide my time. I knew by reputation the formidable power of civil servants to prove that they had been right by conspiring to make things go wrong. Discretion, I concluded, was the better part of valour for the time being, so I settled for an interim change by splitting finance and personnel between two directors.

Before long the profligate way in which taxpayers' money is treated in the public sector provided further evidence of the need for a dedicated finance director. The next board meeting included a one-page paper asking the board's approval for that year's capital spending programme. The programme itself was summarized on a two-page schedule which listed capital projects adding up to £250 million. I had never been asked to approve so much money with so little information about what it was for. When I finally located the Prison Service official concerned, I asked him how I was supposed to know what these projects were, whether they were the highest priority requirements facing us and whether the amounts of money were justified. He calmly told me not to worry: everything had been taken care of. I wasted no time in explaining, somewhat forcefully, that that was not good enough: my job was to ensure that the taxpayers' money was properly spent and I might well have to account for it to Parliament. The system would have to change, but in the meantime I assumed that I would see the detailed proposals for the largest capital projects at least. 'Oh no,' replied the hapless official, 'you needn't worry about that either. We take care of it.' Incredulous, I insisted that all significant capital projects should come to the executive committee for approval before any money was committed.

In most organizations, there is at least the occasional pleasant surprise. I was beginning to despair of it in the Prison Service. When the first batch of capital projects appeared before the executive committee they still contained insufficient information on which to form a view about their merits. One sought approval for the refurbishment of a single Victorian accommodation wing, costing several million pounds. It sounded a lot of money to me, and I asked how many cells there were. Some basic arithmetic indicated that this 'refurbishment' was going to cost the taxpayer about £75,000 per cell – not far short of the cost of building a complete new prison including the accommodation, workshops, hospital, kitchen and perimeter wall. The reaction to my suggestion that this did not seem terribly good value for money was 'Oh, we'd never looked at it that way before.'

There was much more of the same, produced by well-meaning staff who had no sense of obligation to the public to deliver good value for money. I sent back a proposal to build a new gatehouse complex at Aylesbury Young Offender Institution, which was going to cost £35,000 for every prisoner housed there, with a note simply saying 'Too expensive'. Then there was the matter of the new kitchen at Blantyre House, a small resettlement prison for about one hundred prisoners. Expenditure of £1 million, or £10,000 per head, was proposed for a building that would have been capable of withstanding a nuclear attack. The kitchen was much needed, and we had made promises to the Board of Visitors, but I decided that only obstinate bloody-mindedness would ensure greater consideration for the taxpayer. Eventually it worked. A new plan cut costs by a third – and provided not only a new kitchen, but a dining-room as well, and conversion of the old facilities to much needed additional prisoner accommodation. Atrocities like the new kitchen at Chelmsford prison – which cost £3 million, was in the wrong location and was too big for the needs of the prison – were not to be repeated.

Learning about prisons, preparing for agency status and, above all, coping with the paperwork were making immense demands on my diary. The paper mountain had to be seen to be believed. With the move to agency status, I became responsible for personally signing all the replies to written parliamentary questions, as well as answering some 4,000 letters from MPs every year. Nor was I allowed to delegate. I groaned every morning when confronted by the heap of letters about individual prisoner complaints or staff members or how we operated various aspects of prisons. The system was so creaky that many of the letters were several months old, and I had to add an abject apology to my reply. I also battled with replies that were the very worst of Civil Service obfuscation. When we had got things wrong, which was all too often, the letters were padded out with excuses and undertakings to 'address' the issue. Manifest injustices were explained away on the basis of 'policy'. Never did I come across a letter which said, in effect, 'Sorry, we got it wrong and we'll try to make sure it doesn't happen again.' Information about private sector prisons, which the public had a perfect right to know, was refused on the grounds that it was 'commercial in confidence'. I had an uphill struggle to achieve a degree of promptness, brevity, clarity and honesty.

If my efforts did not seem to produce proportionate results, it was because almost everything took vastly longer than I expected. One month in the private sector seemed to translate into twelve months in the Prison Service and Home Office. For a start, the necessary information was never available – and if it was, gentle probing usually proved it to be wrong. I would, at least, have expected the Prison Service to know how many cells it had and how many prisoners it could accommodate, but when I asked why the total 'certified normal accommodation' for the service had changed by a few hundred places from the numbers I had seen a few weeks earlier, I was greeted by blank looks. No one knew. Further inquiries indicated that some governors had simply changed their numbers. They had forgotten to include some cells in the previous report or had decided to convert some accommodation to different purposes. How, I exploded, could we run a Prison Service if we didn't even know how many prisoners we could accommodate? It was a hard seven-day-a-week grind, where progress seemed to be measured in fractions of an inch rather than miles.

My relationship with Ken Clarke worked well. He obviously felt that he had broken the mould by setting the service on track for agency status and bringing someone in from outside to run it. We only met every couple of weeks, but it was sufficient to get the business done given his brisk style and ability to focus on only the key issues. There is an infectious warmth, enthusiasm and confidence about the man. He puts officials and visitors at their ease, and gets the best out of them. The atmosphere is always informal and open – the mugs of coffee, the addiction to small thin cigars and throw-away indiscretions, some of which are genuine, while others are calculated to relax, flatter or disarm. His characterizations of his fellow-politicians are always pithy. But he can be tough, robust and resolute when the need arises, as I discovered during the inevitable crises that occurred throughout my five months with him. I soon realized that the Maastricht Treaty was not the only document Clarke had never read. Surprisingly for a QC, he did not believe in reading much. The first page or two of a voluminous Civil Service brief was quite enough.

There had been many arguments over the key performance indicators and targets that would be used to measure the performance of the service. Neither the Prison Service nor the Home Office had experience of how they would work, of how the standards should be measured or the targets set. Despite their long-standing disdain for figures, my colleagues in the Prison Service embraced the concept zealously, wanting to create performance indicators for virtually everything and set targets for things that we could not measure. Eventually we honed the list down to eight points. Among these, the first and most important was to ensure a decline in the number of escapes from prison establishments and escorts. We committed to reversing the rising trend of assaults on staff and prisoners. Conditions were to be improved by ensuring that no prisoner was held three to a cell, by providing twenty-four-hour access to sanitation and by eliminating slopping out. And we aimed to increase the time prisoners spent unlocked and in purposeful activity. Clarke endorsed our recommendations, and the brief for the year was agreed.

Eventually, D-day arrived. Clarke formally signed the framework document giving the Prison Service agency status and, in theory at least, greater autonomy, and he breezed over to Prison Service headquarters for a quick-fire press conference. He said he would be looking to me 'to improve the performance of directly managed prisons and to increase the private sector involvement to provide competition, a fresh stimulus for innovation, and a new and more enlightened approach to imprisonment, from which we will all benefit.'

The Prison Service was now an executive agency, and I was its first Chief Executive and Director General. The White Paper had said: 'The necessary changes must be taken forward gradually over the coming years. Not everything can be implemented at once.' It was a massive understatement, and the question was where to begin. After only three months, I still had an enormous amount to learn. It was small comfort to discover that there were very few, if any, people in the Prison Service who had a comprehensive knowledge of how the organization worked. It required persistence and inquisitiveness of a high order to develop that knowledge in an organization so complex and impenetrable.

6

The Wind of Change

Armed with agency status, a new statement of our purpose and vision, corporate and business plans and key performance indicators, I now had to make it work and deliver the changes that Kenneth Clarke expected.

For there to be any chance of success, I had to follow a twin-track approach. Firstly, we had to achieve some tangible results early on. Only by meeting the targets we had been set could we earn sufficient breathing space to implement the more fundamental changes that would take many years to introduce and bed down. Secondly, we had to overhaul radically the culture and systems of the organization. The recruitment of a new finance director would, I hoped, introduce new financial disciplines and an emphasis on accurate reporting, and on achieving commitments we had made. I initiated a major review of the bloated headquarters, with the intention of introducing some clarity and accountability. We took a new look at our personnel policies so as to remedy some of the glaring omissions of the previous decade. And we had to get moving on two initiatives that, more than anything else, would spur on changes in performance and in culture – the development of private sector competition, and breaking the mould of industrial relations.

I found a model of how I wanted our prisons to be run in the Federal Bureau of Prisons in the United States. The Bureau had been built up from nothing in the early part of this century, instead of being cobbled together from a large variety of disparate prisons with regular changes in ownership. It had a single strong culture, as virtually all of its staff had spent their careers in the Bureau, starting work in prisons after a common induction training. Head-quarters staff were recruited from this same pool, and usually went back to prisons afterwards. The organization had strong professional pride, and had developed a wily sense of political reality, trimming its sails in anticipation of changing political wind to avoid being buffeted by gales. Reaching that ideal, I realized, would take many, many years.

The top priority was a change in attitude towards performance. I wanted to see more action and fewer words. Too much attention was paid to whether or not the right procedures had been followed, rather than what had been achieved. It was an attitude born of years of painful political experience. When things went wrong and when inquiries were conducted, the survivors were those who had followed the rule book and created their own alibis. An organization such as the Prison Service, where things are bound to go wrong and inquiries inevitably follow, is particularly prone to this kind of thinking. Many had forgotten what they were really there to do.

It was my task to jolt the service out of that complacency and persuade staff at every level that improved performance was possible as well as necessary. In the private sector, organization know that they have to change if they are to survive and avoid receivership or a hostile take-over. For many public organizations the catalyst is a crisis. Disasters such as the miners' strike or the King's Cross fire on the London Underground force changes to be made. Our most recent crisis had been the riot at Strangeways, but that had been over three years earlier. The opportunities are lost unless seized at the right time. And although the Prison Service was performing badly in many areas, it was not obviously 'on the brink'. Escapes were at a high level but they were accepted as a fact of life, and there had been no recent calamities. There were spasmodic disturbances, but nothing significant, and the world had become inured to a steady stream of critical reports from the Chief Inspector of Prisons. The closest the Prison Service had come to a shock was the introduction of the private sector, but no one knew how big that could or would become.

There were no quick fixes that would act as catalysts for dramatic change. The only option was the slow and often painful process of persuasion. Performance mattered, and as an organization we were not delivering. I had to start closest to home, with the Prisons Board itself. If the board could not work together effectively as a team, there was little hope for the rest of the organization. I had inherited a heterogeneous group, whose role was unclear to everyone, including its own members. We had made a little progress early on with the work on the statement of purpose and the development of a private sector policy, but it did not go nearly far enough. I had two options. I could either change the team or try to make the existing one work more effectively. Sir Clive Whitmore had given me assurances when I took the job on that changes to the board could be made if I found it necessary. It turned out to be a hollow promise. Civil Service bureaucracy made changes incredibly difficult. It took me nine months to bring in a finance director from the private sector, even though such an appointment had been recommended and agreed two years previously as a result of the Lygo Report. But, even more importantly, management development in the Prison Service had been so poor that there were not enough candidates ready to step up to the Prisons Board. I determined to make do with what I had in the short-term and attempt to turn the board into an effective decision-making team which would give clear and visible leadership.

The first task was to get the board to take decisions. Everything militated against this. Papers were submitted with no clear indication of what decisions the board was required to take. Board discussions meandered, and no one reading the minutes would have guessed what, if any, decisions had been taken. Board papers, several inches thick, were circulated to forty or fifty people, and there appeared to be no privacy about its discussions. People who were not members of the board invited themselves along to meetings. We had to impose discipline quickly. I insisted that board papers became shorter, and introduced the concept of an executive summary. We had to be absolutely clear about the decisions that were required of us. Many decisions had to be deferred after we had insisted that the preparatory work be done again. I also demanded that the board made explicit decisions, specifying what we were going to do, who was going to do it and when it was going to be done. In the early days this led to some long debates, particularly since I wanted the board to take collective responsibility. I made sure that we had feedback confirming that what had been agreed was actually being acted on. The disciplines of accountability made many people feel extremely uncomfortable. Those who were preparing recommendations for us hated it when weaknesses in their work were exposed in board meetings. They felt that their freedom to do what they wanted was being undermined. They were right, and it was very deliberate on my part. Gradually the changes began to pay off.

After my premature attempt to change the organization structure when I first joined, I had to bide my time for nearly a year until the next opportunity occurred with the completion of work on the headquarters' review. In between, I at last secured an experienced and competent finance director. But I was able to provide greater impetus for change by bringing in two more non-executives – Geoff Keeys and Sir Duncan Nichol. They would be able to challenge some of the accepted truths in the service and assure other members of the board that rapid change was indeed possible.

Perhaps the most tense battle came at the end of my first year, as we considered the results of the wide-ranging review of headquarters. If we were to make any progress the restructuring of board responsibilities could be deferred no longer. Brian Landers, my new finance director, wanted to separate responsibility for operations from the central staff functions, so that the operational directors could concentrate on running their prisons. I also wanted a separate services director who would run all the central functions providing services to the prisons. Two of the operational directors, Philippa Drew and Tony Pearson, remained bitterly opposed to losing their policy responsibilities, and the other executive directors vacillated. We had several acrimonious and hostile meetings in the few days before Christmas. Eventually, Drew and Pearson saw the writing on the wall, and we were able to go away for Christmas with agreement, albeit grudging.

★

But after the battle there had to be reconciliation. We remained a very disparate group, as was apparent whenever there were difficult decisions to be made, particularly where matters of ethics or justice were involved. I knew, for example, that governors were increasingly dissatisfied with their powers to punish prisoners for disciplinary offences. The most severe sanctions had been removed as a result of the Woolf Report. In headquarters, however, there was a general distrust of the way governors administered the disciplinary system and a feeling that it was wrong for them to be able to extend a prisoner's sentence for a disciplinary offence unless the prisoner had the full protection of court procedures. Time and again Tony Pearson and his team told us there was no need for an increase in disciplinary powers – governors were content with what they had already. To break the log jam I summoned a group of governors to a meeting with Pearson and the team. It did the trick. They confirmed that they needed greater powers, and I was able to ensure that they got what they needed.

Drug testing produced an equally powerful reaction, this time from the medical fraternity, who regarded it as an unacceptable invasion of individual liberties. Most controversial of all was my suggestion that we should consider using ankle chains for the most dangerous and violent prisoners when they were escorted outside prison. Other members of the board were horrified as we watched a demonstration of the hardware in the boardroom. 'Evidence' was quickly provided that they would not be necessary.

We were making progress nevertheless. After the organizational changes had been accepted and the emotional temperature had cooled, I invited an outside consultant, Penny Jones, in to build up teamwork within the group. She confirmed that we were one of the most diverse boards she had come across, but declared that we were working together at least as well as most boards in the private sector. Gradually she helped to identify the different strengths and perspectives of board members, and discussion became more constructive as respect for one another's contributions increased. By then we were two years into the programme of change. The top layer was working together, but we had to move on to those below.

76

For the service at large, communication was the first and most important tool. One of the lessons I have learned from my dealings with the advertising industry is that messages need to be repeated time and time again, particularly if there is conflicting noise from the media. I used every opportunity I could to communicate where we were going and what was expected. I knew that anything I did or said would be carefully scrutinized and quickly passed along the Prison Service grapevine. During prison visits I underlined the importance of results by reviewing them with the governor. I had to make sure that such visits were not the traditional 'royal tour', in which I was simply shown those parts of the prison that the governor wanted to be seen. I always had informal meetings with junior staff, from which management was excluded, as well as stopping to question officers on the landings and administrators in their offices. There had to be enough time for them to open up. I was very encouraged by the positive and enthusiastic responses from staff on the ground. They genuinely wanted to do a good job and needed to know what was expected of them. Very occasionally I was disappointed. Talking to a group of staff at Shrewsbury prison, I was appalled by their negative attitudes. Everything, it seemed, was someone else's fault and they were powerless to do anything about it. I made it clear that they would have only themselves to blame if they were selected for privatization or closure. The shock of someone being so brutally frank sent waves through the establishment.

To get still further away from the carefully planned visits of my predecessors, I started to make unannounced visits. Simply turning up at the prison gate was not always popular with governors. I remember a particularly long wait in the gatehouse of Liverpool prison, while the officer in charge informed the governor of the arrival of the Director General, only to be told that he must be joking. Some visits took place at night or over weekends. Management cannot live in a five-day-week world. It needs to know what things are like at night or on Sundays, when prisons are at their most vulnerable because of reduced staff numbers. As well as keeping staff on their toes, it is reassuring for them to know that their leaders are not working in a remote world a long way behind the front line.

An unscheduled call on a visits room at one prison soon convinced me that rumours of sex and drugs were true, and swift action followed. On a night visit to a high-security prison I drove my car under the prison walls in full view of the cameras and was shocked that it did not provoke a response. Tough questions were asked in the control room about the camera system and the vigilance of staff.

Although it was second nature to me, MBWA (Managing By Walking About) was not expected of senior management in the Prison Service. Strengthening supervision and ensuring that managers felt real responsibility was one of my key tasks.

A reluctance to give orders and ensure that they were carried out permeated the whole organization. Some governors claimed that the 1952 Prison Act gave them freedom of action and immunity from instruction by their bosses, and some area managers behaved as though they believed that to be the case. When notes to John Marriott, governor of Parkhurst, from his area manager, Peter Kitteridge, were uncovered, it was surprising to find him using such phrases as 'I think you might wish to satisfy yourself', 'I would advise', 'I would urge you' and 'I fear it is necessary for you'. Not what I expected of firm and responsible management. Time and time again I had to drive home the message that operational directors, area managers and governors were all line managers with both authority and responsibility for results.

At board level, I had a continuing battle to ensure that we were explicit in our instructions and that implementation was properly checked. The Home Office tradition of elegant essay-writing polluted even operational directives in the service, giving governors plenty of excuses. Instructions were seldom clear; and even when they were, they were often ignored. After the Whitemoor escape it was revealed that prison officers were buying luxury foods and clothing for high-security prisoners. I promised that we would eliminate such practices, and we set about doing so. I was amazed when, on a visit to Full Sutton prison, the governor said that he assumed I was not really serious about removing these privileges. I told him and his laid-back area manager I was absolutely serious.

When it came to a more complete overhaul of the system of privileges for prisoners, which had obviously grown out of control, the director in charge, Tony Pearson, favoured some vague general principles allowing individual governors to retain their discretion. I was told that we risked pushing prisoners too far, too fast, with potentially dire consequences. As far as I was concerned, such caution was a recipe for recreating the grotesque practices that had caused the service so much embarrassment – luxurious self-prepared lobster dinners, large expensive audio equipment in cells, designer clothes. Pearson conceded, knowing this was one battle he would not win. But I knew it ran counter to his personal credo – shared by many governors – of reducing the pain of imprisonment.

A powerful tool for reinforcing a performance culture is measurement. We introduced individual targets for each prison, and routinely measured the number of escapes, the amount of time prisoners spent in work, training or education, and how much each prisoner-place cost. That in itself concentrated the minds of governors, but the publication of inter-prison comparisons was even more effective. Inevitably there were protests – often justified – about unfairness, lack of comparability and inaccuracy. But the important thing was that the league tables worked, and performance improved. No measurement is perfect, and those who are measured soon find ways of manipulating the system. When that happens, it is time to move the goal posts.

I had to use *every* tool I could find. I introduced my own personal newsletter for all staff. People knew it came from me, and when asked about it I could explain exactly why I had said what I did. There was a hunger both to listen and to put their own views on the part of everyone I met.

I knew that there would be no change in the culture, either short-term or long-term, unless the majority of governors were committed to it. I had been shocked to discover how governors were appointed. Promotions were made on the basis of a short interview in front of a panel that knew little about the achievements of the individual and had no objective assessment of his or her capabilities, while the posting of governors to particular prisons took no account of their own strengths and weaknesses, or the nature of the prison itself. Hugh Taylor, the senior manager responsible for such appointments, admitted that he had 'brokered deals' to appoint a particular governor to a particular prison. All too often this involved selecting lowest-common-denominator candidates who would not provoke undue opposition from the area manager concerned, while helping HQ to place an individual whose performance might have been poor and would be even less acceptable elsewhere. The system looked after governors well enough, but ignored the expectations of the public. The results were sometimes lamentable. It became clear to me during a visit to a Kent prison that the local POA committee knew a great deal more about its performance than the incumbent governor. The governor of another prison protested that the drugs and violence that were so obviously rampant simply did not exist. Both men had to be removed.

We had to show that we would not tolerate such deficiencies. The prevailing ministerial culture would have preferred a public humiliation of the governors concerned, accompanied by summary dismissal. That would have been grossly unfair. Too often the failure had been in the original appointment by the Prison Service, and in most cases the individuals concerned had given the best parts of their lives to public service. Justice required that we find alternative employment for them, or offer them the opportunity of early retirement.

Political neglect and isolation from the public had allowed the Prison Service to develop in a closed, insular world of its own, which belittled the views of the man in the street and asserted the professional superiority of prison governors. Governors who ignored legitimate public feeling contributed to the poor reputation of the service. A prisoner who was allowed out to get married but took part in an ostentatious wedding celebration, a notorious fraudster who ran a business from inside prison, an over-enthusiastic governor who thought that a golf course would be good for his prisoners and the notorious 'stop me and buy one' ice-cream van at Parkhurst were simply unacceptable to the general public.

Civil Service bureaucracy was not alone in putting obstacles in our path. Almost everyone contributed. Escorting prisoners to and from court has always been an expensive and time-consuming business for the Prison Service and one where security is at its most vulnerable. The new maximum-security crown court was built at Woolwich, adjacent to Belmarsh maximum-security local prison, so that high-risk prisoners could be moved from prison to court and back again through a secure tunnel without having to be taken outside. But still we found trials of high-risk prisoners were being scheduled at the Old Bailey, involving a long journey by road, expensive police escorts and an insecure court building, while Woolwich Crown Court remained at best only partially used. Senior judges reacted angrily to our pressure to move more trials to Woolwich. While I was visiting the Old Bailey one day, the senior presiding judge for the area asked to see me. Judges were, he said, becoming very irritated by the amount of pressure they were under to use Woolwich. I explained the security considerations and our duty to prevent escapes. He was unimpressed. He made a weak attempt to claim that juries were more at risk of knobbling in Woolwich than in central London, and then sheepishly revealed the truth – most judges lived to the west of London and travelling to Woolwich meant they had to start a little earlier and arrive home a little later.

7

Competition as Catalyst

Real change and improvement in the poor performance of the Prison Service might never have happened had political ambition and operational needs not coincided in two vital areas: private prisons and industrial relations.

The idea of private prisons and running them for profit is not new. In the eighteenth century those who ran jails were expected to pay their way by extracting money from their charges. Prisoners were required to pay for admission and discharge, and for food and lodging, and the more they paid the better the conditions. Jails made money as tourist attractions, with notorious prisoners the principal exhibits. Entertainment and prostitution brought in extra income. Life for the affluent prisoner was more than tolerable, but for the poverty-stricken it was excruciating. The modern notion that prisons are not for profit would have fallen on deaf ears.

The revival of private prisons started in the United States, principally as a means of providing new accommodation cheaply and quickly to cope with the escalating prison population. In Britain the motivation was different. Involving the private sector was seen by the Conservative government as a way of stimulating change in a monopolistic hide-bound service, as well as being consistent with mainstream government thinking which strongly favoured competition, privatization, market testing and the contracting-out of public services. A 1988 Home Office Green Paper outlined the basis on which the private sector might be involved with remand prisoners and the escorting of prisoners to and from court. Group 4 was awarded the first management contract for the Wolds remand centre, which opened in spring 1992. A committed advocate of the private sector, Kenneth Clarke amended the 1991 Criminal Justice Act to allow the contracting-out of all new prisons, so that the private sector could also operate the new Blakenhurst prison, which was due to open in May 1993, and take both remand and sentenced prisoners. Meanwhile, the first contract for the escorting of prisoners was also awarded to Group 4, beginning in April 1993. The private sector prison industry was now a reality, but not without tenacious opposition.

The unions were predictably hostile, fearing a reduction in their own influence and pressure on staffing levels. Most staff in the Prison Service and civil servants in the Home Office were equally opposed. The private sector represented a challenge to the traditional Civil Service standards of public service, and – more importantly – it threatened job security. Many pressure groups approached it with an ideological hatred. Making a profit was disreputable in its own right, but immoral when it came from incarcerating other human beings. They mistrusted the Conservative Party's motives and its political associations with the private sector, and suspected that private companies would lobby for increases in the prison population in order to improve their profits and expand their businesses. There was an uproar when Prison Service staff started to resign to join the private sector.

The task of creating this new industry was given to a small group called the Remand Contracts Unit, led by a courageous and unconventional civil servant, Lynette Gill. Organization charts showed the RCU as part of the Prison Service, but the Prison Service would have nothing to do with Gill and her team, who were ostracized and treated as traitors. In practice the RCU reported direct to the Home Office, but even there it found little more enthusiasm.

Suspicions about the new private sector and its performance were exacerbated by the cloak of secrecy that surrounded the Wolds remand centre. Innumerable parliamentary questions were asked by the Opposition, but many were met with a 'commercial in confidence' response. When the Chief Inspector of Prisons, Stephen Tumim, published his first report on the Wolds in the summer of 1993, plenty of people were expecting or hoping for the worst. Tumim duly obliged. In a report which was highly complimentary of the Group 4 staff and what had been achieved, it was, as usual, the sound-bites of criticism that attracted attention. He complimented the ethos of the establishment, the quality of staff and their relationships with prisoners, the regime, the food and many other aspects. He criticized features that were endemic in any other prison in the country – the 'corrupting lethargy' to be found among remand prisoners who could not be required to work, and the prevalence of drugs. But his saying that he had been unable to establish whether Wolds offered value for money was taken as implying that private prisons probably cost more.

Distrust of the private sector was inflamed by the disastrous start of the Group 4 court escorting service in April 1993.

Long before I joined the Prison Service, the government had concluded that there must be a better way of transporting prisoners to and from the courts and of supervising them while they were there. The old arrangements were archaic. Individual police stations detailed officers to escort prisoners, while yet more officers supervised them at the magistrates court. Prisons provided their own escorting and supervised the crown courts with the result that police and prison vehicles often followed each other along the same routes, crocodile fashion. Escapes were commonplace.

The new concept was simple. All this work should be given to a specialist private company, the effect of which would be to eliminate duplication, develop specialist skills, save the taxpayer money, and allow prison officers and police constables to return to more important work. The idea was flawless, but the implementation could not have been worse.

Group 4 won the contract for the first area to be operated under the new system in Humberside and East Midlands. New computer systems were developed, new depots established, a fleet of cellular vehicles was purchased and over 300 new and inexperienced staff were recruited and trained. At the end of Friday, 2 April 1993, the police and the prisons stopped doing what they had always done. In the early hours of Monday, 5 April, five days after I took over responsibility for the private sector, Group 4 staff woke up to their new responsibilities.

Chaos ensued. What had seemed simple in training proved overwhelming in practice. Faxes poured in to the central control room from the prisons and the police stations, telling Group 4 which prisoners needed to be moved from where to where. Like rabbits caught in the headlights, staff and computer systems froze. When vehicles eventually arrived to collect their prisoners, often hours late, they were met by disgruntled staff, still angry that the job of escorting prisoners had been given to private companies. Further delays occurred before the vehicles set off for the courts.

Streetwise prisoners sensed that they were dealing with inexperienced staff. Some found that the emergency hatches on the vehicles had a design fault and were able to force their way out through the roofs and make their escape. Others threw their bodies from side to side in time to the supposedly soothing music provided, and swaying vehicles arrived at court in scenes reminiscent of the Keystone cops.

Demoralized and frightened Group 4 staff who arrived late and delayed sittings had to endure the wrath of magistrates and judges. Others were ridiculed when they had to ask the way to the courts or tried to deliver prisoners to county halls or public libraries. The situation went from bad to worse during that first week. As the delays compounded, staff became exhausted and confidence ebbed away in the face of a barrage of media criticism.

I faced a difficult choice. These were serious problems that were not going to be cured overnight. It was too late now to do what should have been done when the contracts were originally signed – start the whole project up on a phased basis, and learn to walk before trying to run. Should we cut our losses and give the job back to the prisons and the police? It would have been a humiliating embarrassment for a government that idolized privatization. It could have spelled the end of any private sector involvement, not only in court escorting, but also in the management of prisons, and it would have presented a huge victory to the unions and those who were opposed to change.

The only realistic alternative was to take a deep breath, back Group 4 publicly and try to sort out the mess. But I had to be sure that Group 4 had the commitment and the stomach to see it through. I decided on an urgent meeting with the top management from Group 4. They trooped into Prison Service headquarters running the gauntlet of the waiting media. We quickly got down to the nuts and bolts of what needed to be done and how long it would take. They were shaken men. Never before had they had a failure like this, or such extraordinary publicity. In the space of a week, the company had shot from being an obscure security business to a national joke.

By the end of the sombre meeting, I had decided to back them. Jim Harrower, the head of Group 4's UK operations, and his team were fighters who would not give up easily. But before they could get on with it we had another ordeal to go through – facing the press and a mass of cameras. It was uncomfortable for us all. We both had to own up to responsibility – the Prison Service for a flawed start-up plan, Group 4 for failing to implement it effectively. All we could do was promise to put it right.

I knew it would take time for things to improve significantly, and it did. Over the next couple of weeks rumours abounded that Group 4 was having second thoughts and might withdraw. I arranged a clandestine meeting in a private room at Stansted airport with Jørgen Philip-Sørensen, the Swedish owner of the company, so that I could look him in the face and obtain his personal promise to stick with it. It was clear that their failure had affected him deeply, but he made the commitment and I went away reassured.

I was equally concerned that the government might pull the rug from under me. But here I found an ally in Kenneth Clarke. I explained what had happened and why the problems had occurred. I told him I had confidence in the action Group 4 was taking to fix matters. Always ready to follow his intuition rather than get bogged down in the detail, and only too willing to go on the offensive, it took him little time to respond. His support was vital to our success, and a much needed vote of confidence in the Prison Service and Group 4.

The medicine started to work over the next six weeks. Group 4 was off the front pages, but the public relations damage had been done. Even though the company has subsequently delivered everything it promised, and more, Group 4 is still synonymous with escaping prisoners and bungling management; yet contracting out court escorting to the private sector has been one of the most remarkable successes in the government's programme of privatization, resulting in a reduction of about 80 per cent in escapes, savings of millions of pounds and a better service to the courts.

Soon after the escort service had begun to settle down, media attention was reawakened by the death of a remand prisoner, Ernest Hogg, while on his way from court to prison in a cellular vehicle. It emerged that he had died as a result of consuming large quantities of alcohol while waiting at court. One of his fellow prisoners had been taken seriously ill on his return to the Wolds. Particularly damning was the fact that the prisoners had been able to obtain alcohol while under the supervision of Group 4 officers. Hogg was obviously drunk when he left court, and he was incapable of getting out of the cellular vehicle at Wolds prison. The officers failed to notice that he was still on board, and he was taken on a further round trip to Hull prison and back to Wolds before it was discovered that he had choked on his own vomit. It was a grim reminder that the Prison Service depends on individual members of staff doing their job perfectly and completely every time. Nor was inexperience to blame: several of those involved were former police officers who had been doing identical work within the police service for years.

The media barrage continued with allegations that the Corrections Corporation of America, one of the partners in the consortium running Blakenhurst prison, had been engaged in malpractice. The television programme *Public Eye* alleged that Don Hutto, who was in charge of CCA's international operations, had been the subject of legal action for torture when in charge of the Arkansas state prison system. Ambushed with these allegations in an interview for the programme, Peter Lloyd, the Prisons Minister, was unable to respond. The programme-makers declined to allow a researched response and the programme was broadcast, raising serious questions about the fitness of CCA to be involved in the Blakenhurst contract.

I had met the CCA people, and my hunch that the allegations were unfounded was reinforced by close questioning of their executives. But the allegations were serious and out on the street, and we had to make an equally serious response. Bill Bentley, one of our non-executive directors, was commissioned to visit the United States and establish the facts. He returned two weeks later livid with rage. There was no foundation to the allegations. Far from being the villain of Arkansas, Don Hutto had been brought in to revitalize a corrupt and miserable prison system. His success in doing so had been recognized by a top award from the American Correctional Association. For once I found myself playing the part of the conservative civil servant, urging Bill to tone down the colourful and indignant language of his report for fear of legal action were it released into the public domain.

In early 1993 there were no longer-term objectives or strategy for the private sector. Strangeways prison was scheduled to reopen fully in 1994 and was already undergoing a market test in which the in-house management team was competing against private sector companies for the contract to run the prison. It was assumed that there would be further market tests of publicly managed prisons, but none had been announced and no plan existed. The new prison at Doncaster was also scheduled to open in about a year's time with a tacit assumption that it too would be run by the private sector, but again no firm plans had been made. And decisions about the future expansion of court escorting work were also needed.

But first one very important question had to be resolved. Who was going to be in charge of running the private sector and promoting its development? The existing fuzzy responsibilities were a nonsense, encouraging most people to oppose private sector development and to ignore the lessons that could be learned from it. Joe Pilling had been adamant that he wanted responsibility for the private sector to lie outside the Prison Service so that the public sector could focus single-mindedly on becoming more competitive. I thought Ken Clarke would have preferred responsibility to lie within the Prison Service, and that was my strong wish. Only that way, I believed, could we hope to continue running an integrated service, able to move prisoners around and to use the system efficiently, as well as obtaining performance benefits through detailed knowledge of competitive practice. I knew that it would be uncomfortable, and that the board and the Director General would be accused of divided loyalties or even betrayal. I believed equally strongly that time would be a great healer and that eventually the two sectors would come to live alongside each other, at least in a spirit of mutual tolerance and constructive competition. To my surprise, the board agreed with me. The proposal went to Clarke who quickly gave it his endorsement, and when the Prison Service was 'reborn' as an executive agency it assumed responsibility for the private sector.

Taking responsibility was one thing; determining the way forward in these uncharted waters was a very different matter. The board sat down to map out the future. Firstly we had to decide what our objectives were. If we weren't clear, no one else was likely to understand either. Despite his strong Civil Service loyalties, Tony Butler took the bull by the horns, suggesting that we acknowledge both internally and externally that a monopoly like the Prison Service could not expect to achieve the best possible results without the stimulus of competition. After several sessions and a great deal of anguish, heat and emotion, we achieved unanimity on a statement of objectives.

Formulating a strategy and detailed planning was easy by comparison. For competition to be effective, there had to be a private sector large enough to ensure a continued commitment of money and management by the firms involved. We decided that a minimum of twelve establishments, or 10 per cent of the total number of prisons, needed to be under private management to create the necessary critical mass. Just over half would be new prisons, six of which would not only be managed by the private sector but would be designed, constructed and financed under the new government private finance initiative. The balance would come from market testing existing public sector prisons, opening them up to private sector bids.

If we were to sell this as the way forward for the Prison Service, we, as a board, had to convince our 40,000 staff that we were fully behind it. Claiming that it had been imposed on us by ministers would have been a licence for some in the service to obstruct and disrupt. But my suggestion that the board should make a personal commitment to it was greeted with horror. According to Philippa Drew, this was not something that civil servants did: their role was merely to represent and execute the policies of ministers. The conflict between the theoretical basis of the Civil Service and the practical requirements of leadership in a large operational public service could not have been plainer. But we came to an agreement and our proposals were put before Michael Howard, the newly appointed Home Secretary, who obviously found them to his taste. They were immediately approved and returned, with strong encouragement to make an announcement as soon as possible, which we took to mean before the Conservative Party conference in October.

Our plans were announced on 2 September 1993. Press reactions ranged from 'bold policy for prisons' in the *Daily Telegraph* to 'Howard rushes prison plans' in the *Guardian*. Soon afterwards we faced governors and other senior managers to bring them up to date. There was little enthusiasm, but at least the service now had a clear understanding of where it was going.

Meanwhile the chickens were coming home to roost over the Strangeways market test. I have never discovered whose decision it was to pick Strangeways, but it was, as Sir Humphrey might have put it, 'courageous'. Not only was it one of the largest and most high-profile prisons in the system, an exceptionally busy local in the middle of Manchester with multiple functions and a uniquely complex layout on two sites separated by a public highway, but it was increasingly clear that the rapid growth in the prison population could well cause problems. It would inevitably take longer for a private sector contractor to have the prison fully operational than it would for the in-house team with access to staff already on site, and that could mean the loss of valuable places. Then, after the initial bids had been received, disaster struck. It was ruled that employment protection legislation would apply in this case, which meant that any incoming private contractor would inherit all Prison Service staff already at Manchester as well as their pay rates, pension terms and all their other contractual benefits. It would be a nightmare for us, sorting out who was going to stay and who was going to transfer, and for the private contractor, re-negotiating terms to fit their existing employment practices. We had to decide whether to abort the whole process, with much political embarrassment for the government, or to ask all of the bidders to re-bid taking the employment legislation into account. We prayed hard and opted for a re-bid.

Occasionally, even the Prison Service is the beneficiary of good luck. The in-house team turned out to have put in a stalwart proposal under the leadership of the governor, Robin Halward. He had successfully brought the unions aboard, despite objections from the POA national executive, and produced a bid that was imaginative, well researched and very competitive on cost. The sighs of relief were almost audible, as the Prisons Board found itself able to accept the recommendation of the evaluation panel that it should pick the in-house team.

The next major stepping-stone for the private sector was the new prison scheduled to open at Doncaster in the middle of 1994. It was another so-called new generation prison, designed along similar lines to Woodhill in Milton Keynes, though on a less extravagant scale. We opted to confine management bids to the private sector, so provoking the inevitable cries of 'foul' and 'unlevel playing field' from the unions and others. These were minor prob-lems compared with the dilemma we faced when the board met to consider the bids.

One company, Premier Prison Services, had submitted a bid that looked both attractive and sound but the price was dramatically lower than anything we had expected. The evaluation panel wanted us to accept it, and the National Audit Office and the Public

Accounts Committee would ask some pretty hard questions if we rejected a bid several million pounds a year lower than any of the others. On the other hand, some of us were nervous. The company was a partnership between an American prison operator with no UK prison experience and a British contractor with no prison experience at all. The costings were very tight and staffing levels looked thin. If we accepted the bid and ended up having to pay more later, or if there was a serious disaster at the prison, we would be held equally culpable and the credibility of the private sector as a whole would be undermined. We agonized over the problem. The company reaffirmed its commitment to the bid, but we were still not satisfied. Eventually I devised a way out of the impasse. Working with the new head of our private sector unit, David Ackland, we created a formula whereby we accepted the bid but could pay the company more if we considered more staff or resources were necessary. The cap we put on the extra payments meant that the deal would still be much better value than any of the competing bids, and we would announce the higher level at the outset so that there could be no question of surreptitiously bailing out the company later on.

The prison opened in June 1994 and its inmate population built up rapidly to its maximum of 700 in a matter of weeks – normal practice for the American partner in the venture, but quite exceptional in the UK. We had had reservations about the speed of the build-up, but decided to allow it as a controlled experiment. If successful, it would provide quick relief to the problem of overcrowding elsewhere, possibly helping to avoid the expensive use of police cells. Whether the rate of build-up was a significant contributor to the problems that followed is a difficult question to answer.

By August worrying signs were emerging. Rosemary Wool, our director of healthcare, reported concerns about standards of care in the hospital. The press reported violence and drug taking. There were rumours that staff turnover was unusually high. I needed to be sure how accurate these reports were, and as there was an immense amount of hostility towards Doncaster from the POA locally, as well as from the probation service and the local press, I had to see for myself and quickly arranged a visit. I did not like what I saw.

I found a prison that was tense but not volatile. Lack of discipline and control was clearly evident from the way in which the yards, association areas and cells had been vandalized. Willing but inexperienced staff were being intimidated by prisoners who had much more experience of the system than they did, and were barely keeping their heads above water. Nor did they have enough support from middle management. The director, as the governor is known in privately managed prisons, was an old Prison Service hand, but his organizational capabilities were being severely tested. He was obviously on the brink of a nervous breakdown. The Board of Visitors told me that action needed to be taken fast. It was clear that we were a few weeks late in identifying the problem – further evidence of the weakness of line management in the Prison Service – but the position was retrievable. Once stung into action, the company responded with alacrity. American staff and veterans of the Prison Service were drafted in to boost middle management. System changes were driven through. I insisted that one of our most senior area managers worked with them on the recovery plan and was on site to ensure that it was properly implemented. The original plans had been too optimistic and more staff were clearly needed. But they could be recruited and paid for without public embarrassment thanks to our foresight when finalizing the original contract.

Such storms seem to get worse before they abate. The prison was dubbed 'Doncatraz', and allegations of violence, homosexuality, rape and drugs were blazoned across the national press, aided and abetted by the unions and the probation service. Eventually the immense amount of work put in by the company began to produce tangible results. By the end of the year adverse press comment had reduced to a trickle, and in due course the prison received one of the most glowing reports ever from a Chief Inspector of Prisons, who described it as 'one of the most progressive prison establishments in the country'.

Where does the truth lie between those who argue for and against the private sector? The evidence on performance strongly favours the private sector. Levels of security, humanity and rehabilitative activity in privately managed prisons match and often exceed the best in the public sector, at costs that are 10 per cent or more below those in comparable public sector prisons.

The suggestion that private prisons are less open and accountable to the public and Parliament than those in the public sector has been laid to rest by greater access to information and by ensuring that all the normal safeguards of a Board of Visitors and Chief Inspector of Prisons apply in the private sector. In fact the state exercises greater control over privately managed prisons through two full-time controllers who monitor what goes on. There has never been any evidence for the claim that the profit motive gives private companies an incentive to lobby for growth in the prison population and the current growth in our prison population already provides ample opportunities. Probably the most serious argument is that it is morally wrong to make a profit out of imprisonment. I understand those views but do not share them. The state maintains a high degree of control through contractual requirements and daily supervision. Ultimately prisoners are held in custody by other people, and whether they are employed directly by the state or through an intermediate private company makes little difference, provided they do the job well. Large numbers of companies and people have always made profits out of prisons, starting with their construction, continuing with maintenance and support activities, and ending with their demolition. What is difficult to ignore is the powerful stimulus competition has provided to improve both the quality and the efficiency of our prison system.

Kenneth Clarke had given the development of the private sector a powerful impetus, though most of the benefits came through after he had moved on to the Treasury. But he also left the Prison Service a less welcome legacy.

Magistrates and MPs were increasingly unhappy about the consequences of the 1991 Criminal Justice Act. Unit fines were producing some nonsensical results in the courts, with those on low incomes being asked to pay sums that were well beyond their means, while the rich got off with nominal amounts; repeat offenders were receiving sentences no greater than those given to first timers; horror stories of repeat offenders committing further crimes while on bail became increasingly common, and threatened to undermine public confidence. Once again, the pendulum had swung too far.

Early in May 1993 I received an anxious call from Clarke's private secretary, summoning me to his office immediately. The meeting was already under way when I arrived. The message was clear. The parliamentary party would tolerate the situation no longer. If Clarke failed to act, many Tory MPs would support an Opposition bill. He detailed the principal changes to be made and then, apologetically, he came to the crunch: they would mean increasing the prison population by an estimated 5,000. No one had calculated the cost, but it did not take me long to do so. An average of 500 prisoners per prison meant about ten new prisons, and with new prison places costing around £120,000 each we were looking at a £600 million capital spend plus annual operating costs of over £100 million. I asked Clarke where the money was coming from, and he said that there wasn't time to discuss it then. His priority had to be the immediate announcement of a policy change – 'Buy now, pay later' at its worst. What had happened to the fabled financial discipline of the Thatcher era?

I left the meeting depressed. It had rammed home how little control the Prison Service had over its own destiny. I felt quite powerless. I could not stop the plan. Everyone in the Prison Service had been counting on a period of population stability to provide breathing space and an opportunity to introduce the reforms set out in the White Paper. It had started to seem a real possibility, but that dream was about to be shattered. Worse still, there was a chance that the money would never come. A large part of the 1991 Criminal Justice Bill, carefully crafted by Home Office civil servants to correct major failures in the criminal justice system, was being cast aside on the basis of short-term backbench pressure and a few minutes' superficial consideration.

Ironically, Clarke did not stay long enough to deal with the consequences of his financial indiscretion. After months of dithering, John Major eventually faced the inevitable and in May removed his Chancellor, Norman Lamont, who was tarred with the fiasco of the Exchange Rate Mechanism. Clarke was his replacement, and the person who would now refuse to pay the bill for the policy changes he had made as Home Secretary.

The ministerial changes were announced while I was visiting Latchmere House in south London, a small resettlement prison where prisoners at the end of their sentence are given the freedom to work in the community. They gain experience, qualifications and money that will help them on their release. It was governed by a dynamic and charming Irishman, Sean O'Neill, who was showing me his dilapidated temporary kitchens, making good use of my visit to persuade me of the need to build new and permanent buildings. Unfortunately for him, kitchens were the last thing on my mind. Not much was known about Clarke's successor, Michael Howard, except that he came from the right wing of the party and had been the front man for the poll tax as Secretary of State for the Environment. Were we in for a shift in prisons policy?

The atmosphere in the Home Office that afternoon was almost funereal. After the short-lived presence of David Waddington and the volatility of Kenneth Baker, Kenneth Clarke had been a breath of fresh air. He trusted civil servants and didn't second-guess them. He could laugh and be irreverent. Staff in his private office were shocked at his going. So was I.

8

Howard's Way

The telephone rang at home in the early hours of Monday, 6 September 1993. The voice at the other end of the phone said, 'It's the duty officer, sir. We have a major disturbance at Wymott. The incident suite's open.' Jolted from a deep sleep, I asked how serious it was. 'Difficult to say at present.' I asked him to ensure that the Prisons Minister and the Home Secretary were informed, and to call me as soon as there was any further information.

Soon after, the Gold Commander, an area manager always available to assume command when a serious disturbance occurs, called from headquarters. He had a chilling message: 'We seem to have lost control of C and D blocks. Looks as though we may lose the prison.' Losing a prison was what we all feared most. It meant the lives of staff and prisoners were at risk, and the possibility of permanent injury and trauma.

I ran through a check-list of the action that had been taken. The arrangements for handling riots, 'Operation Tornado', had been activated. Teams of prison officers equipped with riot gear had been summoned from prisons all round the area. The rapid response vehicle and emergency catering facilities were on their way. The police were throwing a cordon around the prison to secure the perimeter. There were fires in the prison and the fire brigade was standing by outside. Already a voracious media were telephoning the prison and press office demanding to know what was happening. It was pitch dark as I set out for headquarters.

Within an hour, Michael Howard's private secretary was on the telephone. 'The Home Secretary thinks he should call in the army,' I was told – all too clear evidence that this was a new Home Secretary, and this his first experience of a prison riot. The army is not trained to deal with prisoners. It would have taken them days not hours to get there. And nothing would have been more provocative to prisoners than the sight of armed soldiers on the perimeter. Even the police are ill-equipped to operate within prisons: they are hated by prisoners and do not have the understanding or rapport so vital in bringing riots to an end.

'Absolutely not,' I said. 'Bringing in the army is the last thing we want.' We appreciated the Home Secretary's offer of help, but we had well-tested plans for dealing with such disturbances, and needed to be left to get on with the job. Scarred by the experience of Strangeways, the Prison Service had improved techniques for dealing with riots and increased the available resources. Wymott was the first serious test of how effective they would be.

The service now has a sophisticated incident management unit with a duty officer standing by twenty-four hours a day, and an area manager always available as Gold Commander. When an incident like Wymott occurs, the Gold Commander's task is to take charge in the control suite at Prison Service headquarters. By the time I reached it, there was a full complement of staff – Gold Commander, an officer from the incident unit, a police adviser, a psychologist, a representative from population management, a press officer and other specialists. Gold Commander was in regular telephone communication with Silver Commander, the governor in charge at Wymott.

The job of those in the incident suite is to vet and approve plans made at the prison, ensuring that the heat of battle does not lead to poor judgements, and that all the options and their consequences are fully considered. Gold Commander also calls in the Tornado support teams from other prisons, arranges for additional supplies, and finds new prison accommodation for prisoners who are displaced. Above all, he has to make sure that the politicians are kept informed – and kept out. Every action and every event is painstakingly recorded on whiteboards in the suite.

It was clear that this was a serious incident. Some 400 prisoners, half the population of the prison, had gone on the rampage: they had destroyed their two houseblocks, and were now spilling over into other parts of the prison. Staff had been forced to retreat. There was concern that vulnerable prisoners – rapists and other sex offenders – might be attacked by the mob. Fires had been started and a great pall of smoke hung over the prison.

As yet there were far too few Tornado teams on site to contemplate trying to retake the prison. Intervention would have to come later. There is always a fine balance between taking decisive early action and letting a disturbance burn itself out. Most of the prisoners at Wymott were young hoodlums from Merseyside, and this was their way of letting off steam and getting back at the authorities. They would soon get tired of it, and not least of being out on an increasingly chilly September night.

There was nothing more that I could contribute. The operations were obviously well under control, the police had surrounded the prison, no prisoners could escape and all the necessary staff were on the way. All I could do was encourage, and hope. I went back to my office along the corridor from the incident suite, to sit the night out and wait for periodic reports – and discuss how we would handle the inevitable media circus the following day.

By the early morning it was becoming clear that the prisoners were running out of steam. They could not get out, and they could not do much more damage. As soon as we had enough staff to hand, we could go back into the prison and herd up the rioters, many of whom looked cold and disillusioned.

It was time for me to face the television cameras in their usual haunt on the lawn outside the House of Commons just down the road from Prison Service headquarters. I had to explain to an incredulous public how, with all the lessons of Strangeways behind us, we could lose control of a major prison which was only twenty years old. I knew there would be little sympathy from the interviewers, but I was thankful that I could say that we had successfully brought it under control. There would be plenty of opportunities later for the inquest on what had gone wrong.

After that there were ministers to be calmed. The Home Secretary wanted to go to Wymott immediately, but I advised against it. That was my job, later in the day. The more immediate problem was deciding who should conduct the inquiry. Politicians in a tight corner invariably set up an immediate inquiry, so deflecting all awkward questions until the inquiry has reported. Stephen Tumim was the obvious answer, in that he was familiar with prisons, independent of the Prison Service and able to work quickly. Sir Clive Whitmore and Michael Howard quickly agreed to my suggestion. Then it was time for a shower and a long helicopter ride to Lancashire to see the scene of the damage and talk to the people involved.

It was a beautiful September day. The green English countryside below us was a world away from the scenes of vandalism and devastation that awaited us. As we approached the prison, evidence of what had happened became apparent – police road-blocks, a diminishing plume of smoke and a police helicopter circling incessantly over the prison to observe and to cow the prisoners. Most were now herded into a compound in one corner of the prison, some still hurling stones at the helmeted prison officers outside. To ensure that we arrived in one piece, the police insisted that we travelled the last part of the journey in one of their armoured personnel carriers. It was incredibly claustrophobic, and I was glad to reach the prison.

A quick briefing assured me that no prisoners had escaped and that there had been no serious injuries among either staff or prisoners. The two most important objectives had been attained. Tony Pearson's determination to keep at least some inmates at the prison that night, thus not allowing the rioters the satisfaction of being able to claim that they had forced us to close the prison down completely, had also been achieved. But what greeted me as I started my tour of the two worst affected houseblocks was a scene of mindless vandalism. Wymott had been built for less troublesome prisoners. Prisoners slept in cubicles rather than cells, with security provided around groups of twenty-four cubicles. The external walls of the houseblocks were ordinary domestic cavity brickwork. The plumbing and heating systems were like those in any office building. Angry prisoners had smashed porcelain washbasins and urinals, and water had flooded the living units. Radiators and pipework had been ripped off the walls and used as battering rams to demolish doors and punch holes in the outer walls. Sheets and blankets had been made into ropes and used by prisoners to get down from cells on the upper floors. Fires had been started, televisions smashed. There was water and the acrid smell of smoke everywhere. From the outside, the houseblocks looked like giant Gouda cheeses, punctured by random-sized holes where prisoners had forced their way out.

I wondered what the reaction of staff would be now things were coming back under control. Many of the Tornado team members from other prisons were lying on the grass around the compound where the prisoners were held. They were tired but most of their work was done, and they knew they had done it well. Their morale was high, and they were pleased to have been able to show what they and the Prison Service could do. But the Wymott staff felt betrayed by prisoners who had enjoyed good facilities and a big investment by staff in education, training and care. How dared they betray that trust and embark on this orgy of destruction? Some staff were worried about what the implications might be for them. The prison might be shut down for a long period, perhaps for ever. What would happen to their jobs? Would they have to move? The governor and his team were exhausted. Their satisfaction in quelling the riot was tinged with the knowledge that there would be the inevitable post mortem. Would they be blamed, and would their careers be damaged or destroyed as a result? The uncertainties would be with them for many weeks, but for now the most important thing was to get home to their families.

As I left to return south, a bus full of prisoners emerged through the prison gates. They were callow youths, all in handcuffs. Some looked sullen and tired, others were still shaking their fists in defiance against authority and the establishment.

Several months later we had the results of the inquiry. There were few surprises, but the report highlighted the precarious balancing act involved in running prisons. Many factors were to blame, and most of them we could do nothing about. The prison had been badly designed with inadequate security and segregation of prisoners. Staff could not observe what was going on and were easily intimidated. The explosion in the prison population had required too many prisoners to be sent to Wymott too quickly, disturbing the balance and ethos of the prison. The large contingent from Liverpool had proved particularly disruptive. As is so often the case, drugs had played a major part, and a brave crackdown by staff had created extra tension.

One by-product of the riot was a request from Howard that a hot-line be installed connecting his desk with the Gold Commander in the incident suite. The last thing we needed was untrained Home Secretaries trying to direct incidents. Although only an apprentice mandarin, I decided the request should be dealt with in the time-honoured Civil Service way, by procrastination. He still does not have it.

The morning after Michael Howard succeeded Ken Clarke as Home Secretary on 27 May 1993, I had my first meeting with him. It was an anodyne affair. I was invited to sit down opposite him at the huge table which served as a desk. He said 'Good morning' and smiled formally. He made no ice-breaking small-talk about my background, nor did he ask about the state of the prisons. There was no hostility, but the meeting was devoid of warmth. He just sat and waited impassively. What a contrast with the genial Clarke! I ran quickly through a list of current issues. There was little response and no questions. We agreed he should visit a prison soon, and that we should talk further. Of course I know that prisons can be one of the most troublesome elements of a Home Secretary's portfolio. There are no votes in prisons and most ministers simply hope that there will be no disasters during their period in office. But I was still disappointed as I left the meeting that there had been no spark of interest. I sensed that this relationship would not be as easy or positive as the one with Clarke. In the days and weeks that followed Howard began to ask for detailed operational information following press articles, but as yet nothing of great substance. His immediate preoccupations were not with prisons. He had the legacy of Clarke's Criminal Justice Bill and the Sheehy Report into the police service to contend with. He had to establish his credentials as a right-wing Home Secretary and a credible candidate for No. 10.

The honeymoon with Michael Howard was a quick loveless affair, in contrast to the long stay in the sun with Clarke. The cold initial meeting was followed by a set-piece visit to Brixton, where he was uncomfortable throughout. Some VIP visitors have a natural ability to walk into a prison and be at ease, while others are on edge and tense. Howard was one of the latter. It was a very brief visit, enriched by a prisoner emptying a chamber pot from an upper landing, just missing Howard below. The ITN reporter was less fortunate but suspicions remained about the real target.

There was little personal contact in those first few months. New quarterly reports on the service's performance had been introduced with agency status, but we never met to discuss them. Virtually all communication was by memorandum. Even our recommendations on the development of the private sector elicited no discussions, merely an approving tick on the paper. And yet it was probably one of the most important policy decisions he ever made in relation to the Prison Service. It was surprising that he appeared to attach so little importance to getting to know those who were working for him.

I was concerned early on that it would be difficult to establish a good working relationship with Howard, when so much of our communication was on paper or in big formal set-piece meetings. On such occasions Howard revealed little of himself or what he was thinking. They were all displays of courtroom theatre, as the skilled QC squeezed information from his witnesses and tested the truth of their evidence. I needed to get him on his own in an informal setting, so I invited him to lunch. We met in September at a hotel round the corner from the Home Office, after he had been in the office for just four months. It was a pleasant enough affair, as we chatted about what I was doing in the service and the difficulties that stood in my way. He was encouraging, but again revealed little of himself. Five months later we met at the Carlton

Club, this time at Howard's invitation. He was late but we had a useful conversation about sex offenders as he ate his Dover sole. Howard murmured approvingly when I told him that we were now able to offer intensive sex offender treatment to all adult male sex offenders who were suitable for it, and asked me to find an opportunity to make some public relations capital out of it.

We left the dining-room and settled down in leather chairs for coffee. Howard leaned over and said that he wanted to let me know that he had 'the greatest admiration' for what I was doing in the Prison Service. I thanked him, encouraged by his comments which suggested he recognized the scale of the problem and the progress we were making. Then I asked him whether he would like my views on how things were going in the Home Office. When he said he would, I told him I thought he would get more out of Home Office civil servants, who were by nature hostile to his views, if he did more to get them on side. They needed to feel they were being involved rather than distrusted. Howard quickly disagreed. He did not think that was necessary. All he needed to do was to state the direction clearly and be consistent about it. Eventually people would follow.

The direction was unmistakably to the right, with the pendulum swinging towards greater emphasis on punishment rather than rehabilitation. One of the first signs of the changing philosophy concerned televisions. All prisoners could watch television when they were out of their cells during association time, but some prisons had allowed prisoners to have their own miniature televisions in their cells, and a few had actually gone so far as to provide them for prisoners. It was a controversial issue. Some in the service thought it was too soft, while many believed it helped to keep prisoners quiet and maintain order. The White Paper had considered the issue and concluded that there was no objection in principle to prisoners having televisions in their cells. It recommended that future policy be based on an evaluation of pilot projects in existing prisons. I believed there were some real advantages in making televisions available, provided they were earned through good behaviour and that prisoners paid for them out of money they received for work in prison. That way there would be a strong incentive to behave well and work hard, the risk of bullying, violence and suicide would be reduced; and there would be opportunities to use television for the purposes of education and information. Peter Lloyd, the Prisons Minister, agreed, and we had asked the Department of National Heritage for help in dealing with some difficult issues on licensing.

Our request upset the political sensitivities of Iain Sproat, a particularly right-wing junior minister at the Department of National Heritage. The letter he wrote to Michael Howard protesting about such pandering to prisoners touched a raw nerve in the still insecure Home Secretary. Without consulting the Prison Service or his professional advisers, Howard leapt to the defence of his own right-wing credentials. His private secretary was instructed to draft an instant reply. It overturned the carefully considered White Paper policy and ruled out in-cell television as a matter of principle, before the report on the pilot projects called for in the White Paper had even been received. I was informed the letter was being sent, but was given no opportunity to express a view, assess the possible prisoner reaction or consider what to do in prisons that already had in-cell television. Such policy-making on the hoof was a sign of things to come.

We now had to decide what to do. Around one-third of prisons allowed prisoners television in their cells or unrestricted access to communal sets. The privilege was highly valued by prisoners. Howard was adamant that he wanted them removed. I argued that we should restrict their availability, but make them earnable by all prisoners on the basis of good behaviour. I also believed that removing televisions from cells at a time when there were many other tensions, including serious industrial relations friction, was a recipe for unrest. We ended up in stalemate. Howard lacked the courage to order me to remove them, but would not agree to any extension. There were periodic meetings and occasional papers to the Home Secretary on the subject, but the issue never advanced. Howard's mood did not improve when Peter Lloyd, who remained in favour of televisions, and I visited the newly opened Strangeways and the following day's papers headlined the fact that prisoners could earn the privilege of an in-cell television. Always suspicious, Howard smelt a conspiracy. Ultimately the matter was left to be incorporated in the new policy on earned privileges for prisoners which was prepared late in 1994 for introduction in 1995. Michael Forsyth, the new Prisons Minister, was persuaded that televisions in cells made good sense as an earned privilege and was politically saleable, but he could not persuade the Home Secretary. Yet again the issue was left unresolved, with the status quo being maintained.

Soon after I was dismissed, Howard gave the order to remove the televisions. The internal instructions were leaked, picked up by the *Guardian* and reproduced the following day in that stalwart pro-Howard paper, the *Daily Mail*. But this time the political and media calculations went badly wrong. A front-page *Mail* article highlighted the risks of removing televisions and the benefits of allowing prisoners to earn them: 'Howard bans jail cell TV. "Provocation" row as prisoners lose a privilege in crackdown.' Howard panicked and denied giving any instructions for televisions to be removed. The minutes of the previous meeting were produced, clearly showing him to be the guilty party. The decision was put on hold, but the following day the *Mail* turned even more hostile in an editorial arguing the benefits of televisions in cells and telling Howard 'to think again on this one'. Two years of indecision followed by a decision and an instantaneous U-turn is a remarkable record. Two weeks later, Baroness Blatch, the Home Office minister in the Lords, told her fellow peers: '[The Home Secretary] is considering the policy: not reconsidering the fundamental policy . . . there is certainly no indecision.'

Television was a running battle, but the real bombshell for the Prison Service was contained in a memorandum from Joan McNaughton, Howard's prickly private secretary, which recorded Howard's wish to consider policy options that would be in conflict with Woolf and the White Paper. He was looking for ways of making life tougher for prisoners. It provided Howard with his first experience of how angry and unloved Home Office civil servants use leaks to exact their revenge. Some disaffected official obtained a copy of the memorandum and sent it in a plain brown envelope to David Rose of the *Observer*, who instantly recognized a scoop.

Rose contacted me and I maintained as inscrutable a position as I could. No, there had been no policy change, the White Paper had not been dumped and he should not necessarily read too much into leaked internal memoranda. Immediately after talking to him, I telephoned Howard who was on holiday in California. He was obviously disconcerted by the leak, still more so because he had not read the White Paper he was planning to overturn.

Fortunately his holiday reading pack included the thirteen-page summary of the White Paper. After he had read it, he called me back to say that there was nothing in the White Paper with which he disagreed, and that I could say so publicly. I quickly drafted a statement, read it to him and arranged for it to be given to the media. It was a direct contradiction of the memorandum.

Next day the *Observer* carried the leak as a front-page splash. Television and radio news programmes quickly picked up on it. I was in the far north of Scotland when this little crisis broke and had to make a ninety-mile journey to studios in Inverness to deny a change of policy on behalf of the Home Secretary. I was subjected to sceptical interrogation. A stream of telephone calls to journalists followed, but the media remained unconvinced.

Staff in the Prison Service recognized Howard's memorandum as something they had always dreaded – a right-wing backlash against the Woolf agenda to which they had made so big a commitment. On his return from California, Howard clashed with his private secretary. He denied that the memorandum reflected his views. She stoutly maintained that it did, and that he had seen it and not objected. The truth was never established, but it marked the beginning of a rocky period in their relationship.

The real watershed was the 1993 Conservative Party conference. Howard was understandably nervous about his first appearance in his new role, and preparation of his all-important speech had been a major diversion from other tasks in the preceding weeks. He had decided that he was going to make his name in the Home Office and, in his own words, 'make a difference'. The conference was the occasion he had chosen to nail his colours to the mast and set out his right-wing stall. It was an ambitious commitment for a man who had been in the job only five months. Others might have been more cautious.

But not Howard; this was going to be the launching pad for his now famous twenty-seven point plan dealing with the problems of law and order. He started with his basic beliefs:

That children – at home and at school – must be taught the difference between right and wrong. That criminals – and no one else – must be held responsible for their actions. And that the government's duty – above anything else – is to protect the public. That's my job. And I know what must be done.

There is a tidal wave of concern about crime in this country. I am not going to ignore it, explain it away or just meet it with a string of words. I am going to take action. Tough action. I shall spell out that action here today.

The rhetoric suggested that the twenty-seven points would produce dramatic results:

Today I am announcing the most comprehensive programme of action against crime that has ever been announced by any Home Secretary. Action to prevent crime. Action to help the police catch criminals. Action to make it easier to convict the guilty. Action to punish them once they're found guilty. And this is just the first instalment.

Closer examination revealed a strange compendium of largely unrelated actions. There was no grand design or strategy, only a sweeping up of what was lying around at the Home Office. So we had, for example, an attack on police paperwork, three anti-terrorist measures, acceptance of some Royal Commission recommendations, guidelines on cautioning, and the building of six new prisons to help cope with the legacy of population growth that his predecessor, Kenneth Clarke, had left him. But most significant for the prisons world was the new tone in which prisons were referred to.

The philosophy against which Howard had set his face had been clearly set out by successive Conservative Home Secretaries. 'Imprisonment is not a cheap way of dealing with offenders . . . Nor is it the most effective way,' William Whitelaw declared in 1981; nine years later, David Waddington suggested that 'Prison is an expensive way of making bad people worse', while in 1991 Kenneth Baker observed that 'Prison breaks up families. It is hard for prisoners to retain or subsequently secure law-abiding jobs. Imprisonment can lessen people's sense of responsibility for their actions.' But now we had a Home Secretary declaring that – in what was to become one of his trademark slogans – 'Prison works', and waging war on conditions in prison, not to make them more humane and decent but to make them more austere. 'Let us be clear,' he told the conference,

Prison works. It ensures that we are protected from murderers, muggers and rapists – and it makes many who are tempted to commit crime think twice.

This may mean that more people will go to prison. I do not flinch from that. We shall no longer judge the success of our system of justice by a fall in our prison population.

Today I make this announcement. We shall build six new prisons. They will be built and managed by the private sector. And I can tell you one thing – Butlins won't be bidding for the contract.

A rumour got out over the summer that I don't think prison should be a picnic. Well I'll let you into a secret. I don't. That is why I am determined to ensure that conditions are decent, but austere. I am particularly appalled by the drug taking in our prisons. That is not something we can tolerate. It is possible to test prisoners for drug use. We haven't been doing it up to now; we will be doing it in future.

The substance of his speech gave little cause for alarm among prison professionals, but much in the rhetoric and style caused discomfort and unease. Unlike Clarke's involuntary response to backbench pressure, Howard's advocacy of prison was a calculated act. It marked the beginning of a period when political rhetoric and its consequences made the life of those running prisons much more difficult. It had a powerful impact on magistrates and judges, who almost immediately started to remand more people to prison, increase sentences and use prison when non-custodial sentences might have been used previously. One judge told me that he had to respond to the prevailing mood; a magistrate noted with pride that he was now sending down more young offenders. Others were anticipating the legislative changes that Clarke had announced. The effect on the prison population was dramatic: from 40,000 at the beginning of 1993, it had risen to 47,000 by the end of October.

As we entered the annual ritual of negotiations for the public expenditure survey in the autumn of 1993 we faced a painful dilemma. The Treasury would give us no more money for new prisons or houseblocks to accommodate the rising population. Howard conceded, and decided not to take the battle to the Prime Minister. Did we in the Prison Service bury our heads in the sand and not build the extra accommodation? Or did we sacrifice much needed spending to improve conditions, repair security deficiencies and provide more employment for prisoners? Reluctantly I had to choose the latter course as the lesser of two serious evils.

Foremost among those who were worried by the new language on prisons and the rising population was Lord Woolf. He sensed that this meant a move away from the sparing use of prison to its being a desirable end in its own right. He decided that, as the foremost authority on prisons in the country, he needed to speak out, and he did so in October. It was the first occasion on which Howard found himself pitted against the judiciary. In what was a generally moderate speech, Woolf reserved his few biting criticisms for the new philosophy, describing plans to increase the use of prison as 'short-sighted and irresponsible'. Political and press reaction was mixed, but many people associated with the penal system supported Lord Woolf. In the face of criticism, Howard responded robustly: 'The public wants a tough, comprehensive approach to tackling crime. I'm providing it. I believe punishment deters crime.'

In Howard's view, he and Woolf were now on opposite sides of the policy table. A few weeks later a rumour reached Howard

that, in a radio interview, I had supported Woolf's views and not
Howard's policies. Apoplexy broke out. I was summoned out of a
meeting and instructed to go instantly to Queen Anne's Gate to
explain myself: a telephone call would not suffice. I had no doubt
some appalling fate had already been prepared for me. Howard was
grim-faced as he demanded to know the truth about the allegation.
Fortunately my press office, with its usual efficiency, already had a
transcript of the 'offending' interview, and I was able to show
Howard that I had managed to reconcile the irreconcilable and agree
with both of them. Apoplexy quickly turned to embarrassment.
Mumbled apologies accompanied my exit.

We now knew that prisons were supposed to be austere, and
that their use by judges and magistrates was to be applauded rather
than discouraged. The only problem was that the Home Secretary
was also telling the Prison Service that the White Paper philosophy
still prevailed. Governors were understandably confused as they
struggled with a rising prison population.

In November Howard was due in Blackpool to attend his first
Prison Service conference – an annual event which brings together
all prison governors and senior managers to discuss and exchange
views and experience. It was not an auspicious event. Late on
Sunday night, the day before my speech, I received an urgent phone
call from the Home Secretary. He had been doing his weekend
'boxes' and had only just come to my speech, which I had sent to
him the previous week. It was a tetchy conversation. He was
concerned about comments I was planning to make on the control
risks associated with a rising prison population, and I agreed to
make some minor changes.

The following morning I felt flu taking over, and began to doubt
whether I could get through a major speech that afternoon. When
I arrived at the conference hotel I revealed my plight to the press
office and mild panic set in. The national news media were already
there and expecting me to talk to them. The head of the press
office took command and the handful of staff in the know were
sworn to secrecy. I was initially despatched upstairs to recuperate,
and when that didn't work I was frog-marched outside, working

on the theory that the bracing Blackpool air would either kill or cure. Fortunately it cured enough to allow me to deliver my speech, albeit sitting down.

The mood of the conference was sober, tinged with disillusion as governors faced the unwelcome and unexpected explosion in the prison population. I spoke about our plans to build new accommodation and the back-up arrangements to use police cells, army camps and even floating prisons, or 'hulks', if the pressure became too great. I had to be honest about the effect on other priorities, and announced that we would be forced to cancel long planned capital spending to improve security, conditions and regimes so that we could afford to build the additional houseblocks:

We must accommodate those sent to prison by the courts and provide the capacity needed for current and future needs. That does not mean we should be silent. We have an equal duty to state clearly if the population, or the resources available, or any other factor make it impossible to achieve our purpose and goals. That is why I have warned that the recent *rate* of growth in the population does threaten our ability to fulfil the second part of our statement of purpose – 'to look after prisoners with humanity and help them lead law-abiding lives'. Our business is the management of risk. It cannot be eliminated. Rapid growth and over-crowding increase the risk to security and control. The incidents at Wymott, Haverigg and other establishments have given us a clear indication that there are limits to how far or fast we can push the service without incurring unacceptable risks. It is why we have argued hard in this year's spending round for funding to provide the much needed extra capacity.

The population pressures will require us to slip the timing of some of our major refurbishment programme. We must give priority to the new houseblocks within the available capital spend. And we just cannot afford to have so much accommodation out of use for refurbishment at one time. The details of what needs to be deferred will be worked out over the next few weeks – but we shall not be cancelling any projects already under construction. I regret that this has become necessary, but it is inescapable. I know that many of these projects have been awaited for a long time and are key to improving conditions for both staff and prisoners, as well as providing better security and control.

There has been comment in the media about being harsher to prisoners – abusing them, providing deliberately degrading conditions or treatment, often in the name of retribution. Those are not the policies of the White Paper nor of the government. They are not the values of this service as set out in the framework document and our statement of purpose, vision, goals and values. We know such philosophies do not work. There is no need for anxiety on this matter; and there should be no doubt where we stand. I, the board and the Home Secretary are at one on this.

The press picked up a potential prisons crisis, and reported my comments on the capital spending cuts.

One of the capital projects that had to be delayed at least temporarily was to come back and haunt us later – the installation of the geophones, or fence alarms, on the perimeter at Parkhurst. Just over a year later, in the aftermath of the security concerns raised by the Whitemoor and Parkhurst escapes, Howard was asked in the Home Affairs Select Committee whether there was '. . . any truth in the suggestion that monies have been switched within the Prison Service from, say, the installation of geophones (I take that merely as an example) because it was necessary to build further housing units within other prisons'. Although he had personally cleared my speech, Howard replied: 'No, not to my knowledge. Additional finance was provided for the building of additional houseblocks. I have always made it clear that security must be our first and overriding consideration.' Some six months later, when this apparent contradiction was drawn to his attention by the Prison Service and his own monitoring unit, we did our best to provide a figleaf to save embarrassment, but the monitoring unit concluded that it would not work. Nevertheless, he decided not to tell the Select Committee about the inaccuracy of his statement.

On the last day of the conference the Home Secretary's arrival was anxiously awaited. It was his first appearance before an audience of Prison Service professionals, and people were looking for a firm sense of policy direction. We were to be disappointed. As usual, the first draft of the speech had been written by officials in the Prison Service. Speeches drafted by civil servants are invariably boring, full of long sentences and obscure phraseology, and ministers and their political advisers then struggle to inject some life into them. This one remained crushingly tedious, as the Home Secretary realized while reading it on his private RAF jet from London to Blackpool. At the airport I presented him with another copy of the speech, prepared on the word processor in Blackpool, which did not correspond with the one he had been working on. He had further changes he wanted made, but time was short and he was starting to panic. The motorcade ground to a halt on a wet and windy Blackpool promenade. James Toon, his private secretary, travelling in another car, was summoned over the police radio and given a severe verbal mauling. We waited while the Home Secretary painstakingly transcribed his changes on to the official copy.

Howard arrived at the Imperial Hotel tense and nervous knowing that the prison governors were not well disposed towards him, and perhaps feeling less than well-prepared. He had time only to check that his tie and hair were straight before entering the auditorium. The last-minute alterations were not enough to rescue an otherwise forgettable speech, which Howard delivered without feeling, commitment or any real interest. It concentrated on the level of indiscipline and violence in prisons, promising greater disciplinary powers for governors. He also attacked the '. . . many examples of facilities which are lavish or unnecessary', none of which he had seen as yet. He made a personal commitment to the conference, saying '. . . it is my responsibility to ensure that there are enough prison places' and acknowledging '. . . that the prison system is not made of rubber with infinite capacity for expansion'. From a disenchanted audience even that drew little response, many perhaps suspecting that it would not lead to any action to slow the population explosion or provide more funds. He went on to state his full commitment to the White Paper and to endorse the vision of the service that I had set out, as well as its published aims, objectives and performance indicators.

There were a few desultory questions afterwards, and I was just about to bring things to a close when Howard said he would take one more. The final questioner was Joe Whitty, a notorious Prison Service maverick, who added a discordant note by expressing the opinion that some young offenders were 'rather decent kids . . . who are victims of social circumstances'.

While the conference may have been uncomfortable for Howard the following day's headlines must have pleased the politician in him: 'Howard promises tougher regimes', and 'Howard promises a hard time for unruly prisoners' and 'Howard acts to smash reign of jail "gangsters"'.

The opportunity to create a bridge between political rhetoric and official government penal policy had been missed. It was a failure of ministerial communication that persists to this day and has, if anything, become worse.

Nowadays the tone in which the phrase 'Prison works' is declaimed has become progressively more strident, and the cry has been taken up by others, including the Prime Minister. But at the same time ministers call *sotto voce* on the Prison Service to operate balanced regimes, combining security and rehabilitation. Little wonder that confusion has reigned, or that dedicated prison staff feel that they are between a rock and a hard place.

This ambivalence is perhaps best illustrated in the changes made to the rules for releasing prisoners on home leave. Virtually every civilized prison system in the Western world allows some prisoners nearing the end of their sentences out of prison for short periods to work, attend training colleges or visit their homes. There is plenty of research in the United States and elsewhere to show that reacclimatization through short periods of release back into the community reduces the risk of reoffending.

The Woolf Report had advocated greater use of home leave and temporary release for just these reasons, and over time practices had become more liberal. But liberal-minded governors then began to allow prisoners out for almost anything, including sporting competitions and extended periods at home. The notion of prison as punishment and the need to protect the public often seemed to have been overlooked. The Prison Service found itself moving in the opposite direction to a hardening public opinion. It took no more than a few well-publicized disasters – temporarily released prisoners committing further crimes, in some cases violent – to create political pressure for a U-turn.

To its credit, the Prison Service had recognized these problems and instituted its own review of the system. A taskforce was appointed led by Ian Chisholm, a typical Home Office civil servant, who thought that nothing could be done properly in less than twelve months. To his dismay, I wanted it done much more quickly, and we had the first results in late 1993. The taskforce unanimously recommended significant restrictions on home leave and temporary release to make sure they were used for the right purpose and that protection of the public was paramount.

Subsequently it became clear that Howard was concerned almost exclusively with public perceptions. The long-term benefits of educational programmes or maintaining ties with families were, he said, low on his scale of priorities. We had a series of disastrous discussions. The Home Secretary was generally late or had to leave early or both. Two-thirds of each meeting were spent summarizing the previous one and explaining the existing system; virtually no time was given to discussing the issues, at the end of which the Home Secretary apologized for having to rush off, and promised a further meeting. We staggered on like this for nearly twelve months, with meetings every month or so taking two steps forward and one and a half steps back. Just when we thought we were getting close to an agreement Patrick Rock, Howard's keen but unversed political adviser, who was all for eliminating temporary release completely, made yet more flawed suggestions. He thought prisoners serving over four years should be considered for home leave only when eligible for parole, and when parole had been granted – in other words, granting home leave only to those already released on parole!

Exasperation was setting in, and since politics not policy was the issue, we made a tactical retreat and returned to Michael Forsyth who listened attentively and quickly concluded that Rock's Draconian ideas were wrong. We went back for yet another session with the Home Secretary. Eventually, in the autumn of 1994, we had a new policy. A twelve-month delay could have been avoided if there had been a clear ministerial understanding from the beginning of where the balance was to be struck between political imperatives and sound long-term penal thinking.

Drawing up a new code of operating standards for the Prison Service was a similarly long saga. The Woolf Report and the White Paper had both recommended that the Prison Service should have a code of standards against which the performance of individual prisons could be measured – an eminently sensible and seemingly uncontroversial recommendation. The code was prepared and went to Howard for his approval on 1 November 1993. As was so often the case, difficult issues with no media or parliamentary interest went on to the backburner, re-entering the famous weekend box three weekends in a row. We were then asked to talk to his special adviser about it – a clear sign that he was more concerned about the political presentation than the substance. We made some cosmetic changes the adviser requested to give the document a greater feel of austerity, and waited until the New Year, when Howard wanted to know whether there had been a real commitment to publish. A big meeting followed, attended by ministers, the permanent secretary, special advisers and other officials. Howard was concerned that the code might be seen as a liberal 'charter for prisoners', but I explained that it was a vital management tool to improve the performance of the Prison Service.

One of his special advisers, David Cameron, then asked to see me in private. We talked through the difficulties we were having. Looking a bit sheepish, Cameron mentioned that Howard's wife, Sandra, had looked at the code's housekeeping standards, which concerned such matters as the frequency with which the bed linen and socks were changed, and the standards of food provided. Mrs Howard, I was told, thought that the code's prescription of a balanced and nutritious diet was giving today's offenders much more than they deserved.

Changes were made, but the balanced diet had to stay. The

revised draft went back to Howard, but still he withheld his approval. An acrimonious meeting eventually took place on 24 February. Howard had now decided, after four months, that he was unwilling to publish the code. He wanted to publish only a glossy brochure, with principles but no substance, so as to meet the White Paper commitment. All the rest, including the bits he thought might be politically embarrassing, was to be kept within the service. I was furious. I told him bluntly that he was impeding the proper management of the Prison Service by delaying the issue of the standards and that his paranoia about a media backlash was wholly unfounded. We would issue them in a low-key way which need attract no publicity. As the argument raged, I stood up to walk out. He relented and agreed. The following month we brought this five-month saga to an end and issued the standards. His fears proved groundless. There was no press comment then, and there was none of any significance in the two years that followed. Others told me afterwards that civil servants do not walk out on Home Secretaries.

By now I was beginning to understand who Michael Howard was and what made him tick. He is a dark, closed-up person who rarely relaxes and seldom shows warmth in his political capacity. Perhaps he is shy, but the result is a cold aloofness. His humour has a forced feel about it; infrequent at the best of times, it evaporates under pressure. When frustrated or angry, his face becomes tense and contorted. Honed in the art of advocacy, and probably most at home in complex planning cases where he achieved widespread recognition, the lawyer in him moves into top gear when confronted by legal issues, challenging the views of legal advisers and looking for alternative solutions. His formidable intellect, his powers of concentration and his work rate are spoken of in awed tones: he regularly works his way through eight red boxes, each six inches thick, over a weekend. Listening to him dissecting the advice of an unsuspecting civil servant, it is not hard to imagine him tearing apart the credibility of an opposing witness by repeatedly highlighting inconsistencies, errors and contradictions in their evidence. Destroying a witness may result in a courtroom victory, but in a minister's office it all too easily kills the flow of vital objective advice.

Like many of his colleagues, Michael Howard has no experience of working with or leading people in large organizations. Time and time again this showed through – in his unwillingness to invest time in getting staff on his side, in the rarity of his visits to prisons and in his apparent belief that fear is the principal tool of motivation.

He is driven by political ambition, for which he has developed the instincts of a jungle fighter. That ambition and a lack of long-term vision means that his decision-making and policy formulation are driven hither and thither by the breezes of media opinion and public mood. He is preoccupied with tactics to the exclusion of strategy, and at times appears to be cutting his suit to fit the political cloth just a little too finely. But behind the right-wing populism of his policies and rhetoric, accentuated by the pressures on a Conservative Home Secretary, lies a degree of conviction. He can be courageous and obstinate, occasionally to the point of foolhardiness. But as a political leader he is flawed.

As Home Secretaries, he and Clarke could hardly have been more different. Howard, the intellect, the workaholic detail man who carries his ambition on his sleeve, is anxious, insecure and apt to react defensively. He lacks the common touch of a 'people man'.

In the months that followed, the Home Office, true to form, provided him with a variety of headaches. The Home Secretary was blamed for miscarriages of justice, for young offenders who were sent on safari courtesy of local probation services, for prison escapes and for scrapes with the police and fire services. Add to those the judiciary's almost perverse delight in disagreeing with Howard's decisions on everything from deportation to the treatment of life sentence prisoners, and you have the perfect recipe for insecurity and neurosis. Before long Michael Howard was being labelled by some in the media as the 'serial bungler'.

9

The Changing of the Guard

Sir Clive Whitmore's relationship with Ken Clarke had been excellent, but Michael Howard did not like his laid-back style or his association with Home Office tradition. It was no surprise when Whitmore announced his intention to retire several months early. Protests that Howard had nothing to do with the decision were treated with scepticism. His letter to me at the time of his retirement said it all, with his usual understatement: 'I am grateful to you for not accusing me of having got you in on a false prospectus, even though some things have turned out differently from what you had expected! (I might say that not everything is quite as I expected it either.)'

I only appreciated how coveted the permanent secretary's red biretta is when I witnessed the fight over the succession. The favourite for the Whitmore throne, backed by kingmaker and Cabinet Secretary, Sir Robin Butler, was Sir John Chilcot, a veteran of the Home Office and then permanent secretary at the Northern Ireland Office.

Howard resisted his appointment tooth and nail – the last thing he wanted was another Home Office traditionalist, more loyal to the department than to its Secretary of State. The undignified behind-the-scenes drama was told with confidential indiscretion by Whitmore at successive deputy secretaries' meetings. In short, Howard wanted his own man and demanded that Richard Wilson, who had worked for him as permanent secretary at Environment, should be appointed. Butler, supported by Whitmore, objected as

Wilson had no knowledge of the complex affairs of the Home Office. In a characteristic display of obstinacy, Howard put his foot down and refused to take Chilcot. The matter was referred to the Prime Minister for resolution; and since Howard was one of the few publicly loyal right-wingers in the Tory Party, he eventually won the day.

Wilson arrived with enthusiasm and reforming zeal, only to be greeted with deep suspicion. Morale was low, and civil servants felt undervalued and denigrated by Howard and his junior ministers. They believed Wilson had been brought in to wield the knife to what Howard himself described to me as the last great unreformed Whitehall department.

Wilson clearly tried very hard, meeting people, throwing parties, trying to make them feel wanted and at ease. His long hyperactive face with large, highly mobile ears, soon became well known in the corridors of Queen Anne's Gate. Everyone acknowledged that he was charming, although many Home Office loyalists believed that behind that urbane façade lay a murderous heart. These fears were confirmed for some when two of the more dyed-in-the-wool deputy secretaries suddenly found themselves shunted sideways or retired to be replaced with those less loyal to the traditional Home Office style. But Wilson was lively and articulate with a good sense of humour – qualities often lacking at the Home Office. For these reasons, and perhaps because we were both 'outsiders', I found him congenial and supportive. He seemed keen to listen to those who had views on how the Home Office could and should change. I had plenty of suggestions. Achieving real change proved to be more difficult.

He replaced the deputy secretaries' meeting with a management board. The difficulty was finding anything the board could manage. Most of the big decisions – policy, organization and money – were a ministerial preserve, while deputy secretaries jealously guarded their sole right to make decisions on their patches. The board was left with little other than housekeeping tasks – personnel, honours, computer systems and office plans. We spent hours considering how and when to refurbish the Queen Anne's Gate building and its air-conditioning, which left everyone sweltering in summer and freezing in winter. The board was a bit more formal than its predecessor – even the gossip was regulated – but its functions were not much different.

After a few short months Wilson set up a major review of the department. It was ostensibly one of the government-wide senior management reviews of organization and structure, but Wilson wanted to use it to change the underlying culture and performance of the Home Office. The final document was highly critical of remote and unresponsive civil servants who ignored the policy desires of their ministers. Unable to operate effectively in the modern world of quantitative analysis and computers, the Home Office was characterized by one former minister as having the style of an 'All Souls' essay' rather than a reputation for getting things done. As one former secretary to the Prisons Board remarked, 'No one can move a file around like the Home Office' – but often the movement produced little effect.

The review's recommendations were both predictable and incapable of solving the real problems of the Home Office. They consisted in effect of a rearrangement of the organizational deck-chairs and a severe cut in the number of senior jobs. The more fundamental questions about the department's role and the sort of people and ethos it needed were beyond its competence.

Unlike Clarke, Michael Howard came with two special advisers – Patrick Rock and David Cameron. Rock was a marked contrast to Clarke's Tessa Keswick. A political Rottweiler with a grating bark, he was quick in the expression of his views, which appeared to be somewhere to the right of Attila the Hun's, and slow to hear the ideas and opinions of anyone else. Rock could be guaranteed to express the refined prejudices of the hearty right-winger. I was once accosted by him after he had been told that homosexual activity was prevalent in American prisons. 'We don't have any of that here, do we?' he asked. When I told him I was sure we did, he demanded instant action to stop such behaviour – apparently oblivious of the problems when men sleep two to a cell. Neutralizing

Patrick Rock became a key part of the policy-making game. Even Howard frequently tired of his fourth-form interjections, issuing curt instructions for him to keep quiet: but Rock was quite oblivious to his irritation, and merely came back for more.

Rock was a particular *bête noire* of Stephen Tumim, who described him as a youngster with no experience of the world. Tumim's relations with Howard deteriorated progressively. Howard was, in Tumim's view, an extremely intelligent man, but a hopeless Home Secretary because of his lack of experience of the real world or any common touch with people. He did not, according to Tumim, know how to say 'thank you'. Howard himself became increasingly irritated by Tumim: he was a 'loose cannon' with the press, criticizing the Prison Service – and, by implication, ministerial policy – without prior warning. He and Howard were on totally different wavelengths over penal matters. Nor was he one of Howard's men.

The first prisons ombudsman, on the other hand, was a Howard appointment. Both the Woolf Report and the White Paper had recommended the creation of an ombudsman to hear prisoner complaints and to help resolve situations where prisoners had been unfairly treated. The post had been advertised, and the selection board submitted its recommendation to Howard. The preferred candidate was Sean McConville, an academic criminologist. Howard was having none of it. McConville was dismissed as a left-leaning liberal who would clearly be on the side of the prisoners. None of the runner-up candidates was acceptable, so Howard ordered a new selection process with a brief to find someone tougher and less liberal. The final choice was a military man, a former admiral, Sir Peter Woodhead – just the sort of person, it was assumed, who would give prisoners firm no-nonsense treatment, while knowing how to take orders as well. Howard was to be severely disappointed. Woodhead turned out to be his own man, popping up on the media to express trenchant views about the service and even publishing his own preliminary report without clearing it with ministers. It was too much for Howard. He had a bitter altercation with Woodhead and then clipped his wings by barring him from considering any decisions on prisoners in which ministers had been involved. It was misleadingly described as a 'clarification' of Woodhead's original remit, but few were taken in.

Howard's frustrations were not over. He was apoplectic when a selection board appointed Adam Sampson, the deputy director of the Prison Reform Trust and a left-leaning exponent of prisoners' rights, as a deputy ombudsman. It was not a decision involving the Home Secretary, but Howard – who had only found out about it from the *Guardian* – demanded a blow-by-blow account of how it happened. Woodhead was now supported by two deputies of similar hue – the other was a well-known opponent of Howard from the Prison Service – both of whom pursued their own agendas.

As well as dealing with the Home Secretary, I had to work with his successive ministers of state with responsibility for prisons, or Prisons Ministers. Used well – as they were under Clarke, the arch-delegator – junior ministers can make a significant contribution, particularly in a department as big as the Home Office. Peter Lloyd, Clarke's Prisons Minister, was instrumental in helping to shape the Prison Service. But with the arrival of Howard as Home Secretary, the style changed.

Lloyd and Howard were at opposing ends of the political spectrum. Lloyd's interest was in programmes to rehabilitate prisoners and ease the stresses and strains on staff. Howard's priority appeared to be making prisons austere, to appeal to the populist vote. Their relationship gradually deteriorated. When Lloyd spoke at policy meetings, Howard's eyes glazed over in barely concealed contempt. Lloyd's support for rehabilitative treatment programmes was enough to sound their death knell with Howard, and when I confirmed that Lloyd was to make a high-profile speech in support of such programmes, Howard replied that he would have to ensure that the speech was sufficiently boring.

It was a tragedy for the service. Peter Lloyd knew prisons well, and was one of the few people who understood the delicate balance that had to be maintained and the difficulties involved in effecting real and lasting change. If two politicians from the same party could not work together, what hope did the Prison Service have? Eventually Howard had his way and Lloyd was unceremoniously returned to the backbenches. His departure was greeted with genuine sadness and he was greatly missed at every level of the Prison Service.

His replacement was the MP for Stirling, Michael Forsyth, an ardent Thatcherite. News of his arrival sent shivers through the service. He came with a reputation for calculating cold-bloodedness and naked political ambition. His legendary determination and toughness had been the cause of major upset in the Scottish Conservative Party. Early signs were not hopeful. As a shrewd political operator he knew that the Home Office had put paid to many promising careers, so when Wilson, the permanent secretary, welcomed him to the Home Office on his first day, his response was an icy stare and a monosyllabic 'Why?' My first meeting with him was longer, but little better. There were no social pleasantries, nor did he suggest that I should talk to him about prisons. I did so anyway and started a twenty-minute summary of the Prison Service and some of the current issues. There were no comments or questions from Forsyth and a painful silence followed. Since it was obvious that he was going to say nothing, I started a fifteen-minute encore. Another silence ensued, eventually broken by a desultory question or two before the meeting ended.

Inquiries elsewhere were hardly encouraging. He had come from the Department of Employment, where he had involved himself in minute operating decisions about the location of new employment offices. The chief executive of the Employment Service Agency reported a running battle to persuade Forsyth to confine himself to the big issues and leave the operational detail to him. Officials were shocked and angered by his direct, confrontational and openly critical style. His written messages were equally blunt, and curt comments like 'Outrageous' or 'Surely you don't expect me to sign this' were faithfully transmitted by his private secretary.

But gradually I came to understand that there was a powerful inquiring intellect inside, and that Forsyth was an astute politician, who understood how the relationships between agencies, ministers and Parliament could and should work. While never accepting his move to the Home Office with anything resembling good grace, he started to thaw and take an interest in prisons issues. In areas where political interests and moral principle conflicted he showed a welcome commitment to principle, taking the view, for example, that condoms should be provided in prisons because of the public health risks of homosexual activity, despite the bad political publicity this would bring. It was a refreshing breath of integrity. He also showed an unusual ability to be self-critical. He knew that his notes were intemperate – 'That was an angry note even for me,' he said on one occasion. He also welcomed a brisk no-holds-barred debate provided the opposing views were soundly based. Civil servants were expected to argue their corner, not be sycophantic yes-men.

Forsyth threw himself energetically into one outstanding piece of prisons business – reforming the Boards of Visitors, who felt put upon, undervalued and confused. He did the job with determination and decisiveness, and within a year he was being hailed as the best Prisons Minister ever by board members.

Although they came from the same wing of the Conservative Party, Forsyth's relationship with the Home Secretary was scarcely any better than Peter Lloyd's. He could never come to terms with Howard's frequent changing of decisions. Communication between the two men was conducted through curt notes exchanged between their private offices. He also objected to the covert way in which many decisions were taken at the Home Office and found its culture deeply distasteful.

I came to know Forsyth better when he and I made a whirlwind trip to the United States in the spring of 1995 to see how maximum-security prisons worked in America. I travelled ahead and met Forsyth and his private secretary at Colorado Springs, just north of the Federal Bureau of Prisons' new 'supermax' at Florence. Wondering which wag at the British Embassy had chosen it, we stayed the night at the luxurious Broadmoor resort hotel overlooking the Rockies.

Visiting Florence was a chilling experience. It had been designed to hold some 500 so-called predatory prisoners, many of whom had murdered others in prison. They were locked in their barren cells for twenty-three hours a day. All the furniture was moulded out of concrete, forming part of the cell itself, and food was pushed through flaps in the double doors. Prisoners were allowed out one at a time for solitary exercise, guarded by at least two prison officers armed with batons. After months or years of good behaviour, prisoners could earn their way back into the mainstream prison system. It was frighteningly effective.

From there we travelled to Minnesota to see another maximum-security prison before heading back east. I wanted to take Forsyth to upstate New York to show him an impressive prison drug programme I had seen the previous summer, and despite his tight schedule I persuaded him that it was worth a detour. We could get to Syracuse that night with time to visit the prison and get back to New York City for a lunch engagement the following day.

The only accommodation available in Syracuse was a grubby Holiday Inn, and by the time we arrived there were only smoking rooms available, impregnated with the stench of stale cigarettes. Forsyth was not amused, and still less so when we discovered that the restaurant had already closed and that we faced a walk through dark suburban streets if we were to get any food. By then I was beginning to wonder whether I had been right to press the issue, but the Colorado Mining Co. Diner came to our rescue. Beer, wine, enormous starters and gargantuan steaks changed the mood of the evening as Forsyth unwound. A short sleep and a two-hour journey to the prison in a minibus the following morning did nothing to destroy his good humour. The drug programme was just as impressive as I had remembered, and Forsyth was gracious enough to say that we had made the right decision to go and see it.

The Prison Service had good reason to be grateful to Forsyth. At a time when it was politically unpopular, he was prepared to be publicly supportive of me and the service, as well as being privately helpful. He argued our case with the Home Secretary on such subjects as home leave. His relationships with parliamentary colleagues were good, and he frequently discussed our performance with other MPs. Unlike the Home Secretary, he had quickly realized that there were no simple solutions in prisons, and that real and lasting change would have to take place over a long period and at a measured pace. Forsyth had barely been in the job for a year when the political merry-go-round started up again, and he headed off for the Scottish Office and Cabinet rank.

Much of my life was occupied in keeping the peace between various warring factions, and never more so than over the appointment of a new director of personnel. I had always known that it might be necessary to make changes in the top team at the Prison Service. Indeed, when accepting the job, I had made it a condition that I should have flexibility to move people out and bring new blood in. By early 1994 Tony Butler, our director of personnel, had already served over three years in the job and had gone through a bruising nine months with the POA, a court case and new no-strike legislation. He needed to move on, and I wanted to bring in someone with professional expertise in personnel management. Richard Wilson was reluctant to do so. Importing outsiders was unpopular, and he was already under suspicion as Howard's hitman. Eventually, though, he acquiesced. I proposed that we should bring someone in from the private sector on secondment. That way no job would be lost, and it would probably make the salary package easier to negotiate and the appointment quicker to put in place. The Civil Service commissioner was consulted. She said we could go ahead but only if we went through the full rigmarole of advertising the job and open competition. The Civil Service had struck again. It was bad enough that it should have taken six months to get this far: it would probably take another three or four by the time we had advertised, headhunted, selected and finally recruited.

The firm of headhunters we had chosen advised that a senior position of this nature might require a six-figure salary package, sensitive though that would be. We began negotiations with the Treasury, who would not agree. We went to the Home Secretary. He asked for the opinions of all his junior ministers. It was shortly after the Cedric Brown 'Fat Cat' controversy, and they were horrified. Howard put his foot down. After several meetings a compromise emerged, but when we went back to the Treasury they had moved the goal posts, so another round of negotiations was necessary. The advertisement was designed and ministerial views on the wording sought yet again. It only served to re-open the whole issue of salary. A junior minister protested and notes flew backwards and forwards between him and the Home Secretary. Eventually another compromise on money and words was hammered out and the advertisement appeared, ten months after the initial go-ahead had been given. I ruefully reflected on the numerous senior appointments that could have been made in the private sector during that time.

Four months later the Prison Service had its man, and we were negotiating the final details. The Home Secretary had to be consulted yet again and was asked to approve a limit to the salary. He wanted it 3 per cent lower. Eighteen months later our new personnel director was in place, performing a task which we all knew to be critical to the future success of the Prison Service. Surely the public has a right to ask why something that should have taken six months to complete took a year and a half?

10

Truly the Last Bastion

The fact that the Prison Service and its staff do not enjoy the support or admiration of the general public reflects to some extent the state it was in at the start of the 1990s. No public service with such a poor record for security, humane treatment of prisoners and operating efficiency deserves to be held in high regard, despite the heroic efforts of many individuals.

Part of the blame for this must be laid at the door of the Prison Officers' Association. Its stubborn defence of restrictive practices, coupled with its belligerent and often threatening demeanour, resulted in deep public prejudice against prison officers, and an image of a service rooted in the past. The POA must have been the last bastion of 1960s trade unionism. I had come to the Prison Service from the megaphone militancy of trade unionism in the car industry in the 1960s and 70s and the extraordinary feather-bedding of the television industry in the 1970s and early 80s, where the rules required the employment of craftsmen even if there was nothing for them to do. Whether by accident or design the POA escaped Margaret Thatcher's emasculation of the unions in the 80s. Its power and its readiness to obstruct, at the taxpayers' expense, were legendary. In a masterful understatement, the Woolf Report suggested that 'industrial relations within the Prison Service are in a sorry state'. Of all the changes which have transformed the Prison Service in the 90s, none is more significant than the transformation of industrial relations.

The POA had become so powerful because management and

ministers had lost control of the service. Both knew only too well that a serious strike or work to rule would make it impossible to continue running prisons for more than a couple of weeks. Industrial relations deteriorated with a predictable game of saying 'no' and then retreating when the POA threatened. Ministers, senior management and governors chose the easy road of acquiescence and appeasement. The result was a union caught in a 60s timewarp, enforcing unnecessary overtime, protecting excessive manning levels and successfully undermining or usurping management decisions. The POA simply filled the management vacuum. Local POA representatives would march uninvited into the governor's office, in *I'm All Right Jack* style, thump the governor's desk and tell him to abandon his plans. Nine times out of ten the governor agreed.

The 'Fresh Start' agreement with the POA in 1987 led to a major improvement in working practices. It made a start by eliminating overtime and reducing hours to a sensible level – some officers had been submitting claims for almost every waking hour – but at the price of continued overmanning, excessive costs and a commitment to abandon the direct recruiting of governors (for which, given the lack of young talent to take the prison system into the twenty-first century, the service is now paying the penalty). It did nothing, however, to tackle the root causes of so many of the service's problems: excessive union power and weak management.

The POA was so notorious that I approached my first meeting with its chairman and general secretary with a mixture of anxiety and fascination. I was only two weeks into the job, and I wanted to get the message across that there would have to be change. It was up to the POA to decide whether they wanted to be part of that change or to stand on the sidelines. The chairman of the union, John Bartell, a tough stocky Liverpudlian, had had a promising career as a prison officer before being seduced by the power of trade unionism. He had proved a despotic, even demagogic, leader, and my first encounter with him was a predictable, depressing experience. For an hour and a half he delivered an abusive monologue, in 1950s union-speak, without allowing me to get a word in. The problems of the service were caused entirely by the government and management; disaster might strike at any minute, and it would all be our fault. Bartell had the reputation of being a bully, without the intellectual capacity to get involved in anything resembling a discussion or negotiation. He was incapable of compromise: going back to his members and telling them that he had agreed concessions was clearly anathema to him.

The general secretary, David Evans, was entirely different. He came from modest Welsh roots, and becoming secretary of the POA was the great achievement of his life. He had gained a BA through the Open University, which distinguished him from the other members of the POA national executive. He was a moderate, pragmatic and thoughtful man, with a genuine concern for the interests of his members. During that first meeting, Evans spent most of the time during Bartell's tirade intensely examining his shoes. But it was Bartell's union and Evans had relatively little power. More was the pity, because he was the only one who displayed any desire for progress. We developed a good working relationship, exchanging enough information to enable us, had we been allowed, to oil the wheels effectively.

The day after my first encounter with Bartell, I had my first experience of a traditional Civil Service ritual: the Whitley Council which brings together unions and management in most government departments. These twice-yearly meetings of the POA national executive and the Prisons Board were supposed to advance the Whitley philosophy of woolly co-operation and consensus. In practice they were a propaganda show-piece for the POA. The union recited pre-prepared management-bashing allegations; the management responded with diplomatic evasions. It provided an opportunity for POA representatives to outdo each other in hostile rhetoric. We always began with a soliloquy from John Bartell, which usually took up a third of the meeting. He was followed by brief contributions from his supporting cast, with the other players muttering their assent. Like so many meetings, they accomplished nothing, and had the added disadvantage of being long, boring and unpleasant.

The previous day's diatribe from Bartell in my office turned out to have been a dress rehearsal for his public performance. He cautiously avoided attacking me personally on this occasion and instead reserved his vitriol for other members of the board – particularly the female members, with whom Bartell seemed ill at ease. He mocked Philippa Drew's rational but unemotional explanation of our decision not to issue body armour to prison officers. Did she really expect prison officers to defend themselves against maniacal prisoners with nothing more than 'inter-personal skills'?

Bartell and his national executive objected to my arrival. They feared it was a prelude to mass privatization of the service, and that it would usher in a 'slash and burn' programme of staff reduction. They were fearful of change carried through with determination, worried that they would lose their ability to block it. I had already made it clear to him that the union would not be allowed to stand in the way of progress.

During my prison visits I was, however, heartened to find that most rank and file P O A members did not share the extreme views of their national leaders, even if the local committees tended to toe the national line. But the stream of emotive and misleading propaganda from Bartell and his colleagues about privatization, job security and overcrowding was beginning to have an effect on ordinary officers. They were becoming anxious about the future. Their natural inclination was to support the P O A; it was their last defence, particularly against litigious prisoners or vindictive governors. Nor did they have much choice. The only alternative was the breakaway Prison Service Union, which professed to be more moderate and anti-strike but was still very small and weak. We considered recognizing it as an alternative to the P O A, but decided it was likely to be a wolf in sheep's clothing since its leaders were former hard-line P O A officials.

In the autumn of 1993 the P O A started to flex its muscles. We were approaching what turned out to be a watershed in industrial relations in the Prison Service. Back in the early summer the director of personnel, Tony Butler, had come to see me with that look of studied solemnity unique to the best of civil servants. He needed to brief me on a matter of extreme secrecy and delicacy, about which all new ministers and Director Generals needed to be informed. It was an embarrassing accident of history, he went on, that the Prison Officers' Association was not a proper trade union under the law. Because prison officers had the powers of a constable for the purposes of their job – similar powers to those of police officers, in other words – their union was not immune from being sued as a normal trade union would be. As he spoke, the extraordinary significance of what he was saying began to dawn on me. The POA could not call strikes or other industrial action – actions that would involve prison officers breaching their contracts of employment – without being exposed to the full force of legal action by the employer. Unlike normal trade unions they could be sued for the damage they caused, and could probably be stopped by order of the court.

When I replied that this could be just what we needed to solve the problems of industrial relations and the terrible imbalance of power, he gazed at me horror-struck. Although, he confessed, this had been known about for years and years, successive Director Generals and Home Secretaries had maintained the pretence that the POA was like any other union. No action had been taken when industrial action occurred, and agreements had been negotiated which appeared to concede the right of the POA to instigate such action. The POA and the Prison Governors' Association probably knew the real position too but, rather like sex in Victorian times, it had never been talked about in public. After so many years, it would be far too embarrassing to admit to the truth, even though it had been alluded to by Woolf. To do so would not accord with the British sense of fair play. I could hardly believe it. We were not dealing with the local Mothers' Union but with an organization that regularly exercised tyrannical power to the detriment of a key public service. The more I thought about it, the more convinced I was that here was the solution to the Prison Service's industrial relations problems. All that was needed was determined management and political will.

By September it seemed increasingly likely that this hidden

weapon would see active service. Later that month I attended my second Whitley Council meeting. It lasted less than an hour. Bartell opened with barn-storming virulence, predicting doom for the service as the result of an outbreak of so-called criminality among prisoners, and ended by demanding an adjournment. When the POA officers returned, Bartell announced that they were walking out because of the seriousness of the issues, and insisted on a meeting with the Home Secretary. It had obviously been premeditated, with careful stage-management and scripting. We expressed our regrets and let them go, relieved that we had been spared a wasted day.

I recommended that the Home Secretary saw them, which he did a few weeks later. The meeting started with a much abbreviated version of Bartell's diatribe. Howard had, as always, mastered the brief we had provided, and summarily demolished Bartell's case. Bartell then made a crude and transparent offer to save the Home Secretary's skin by offering to accommodate the growing prison population, provided market testing and privatization of prisons were abandoned. An outraged Howard told him that government policy was not negotiable. Bartell and Evans were left in no doubt that the Home Secretary and I were united, resolute and immovable.

This proved to be the last formal contact with the POA for some time. They were preparing for war and the battle lines were being drawn. With a degree of plain speaking previously unknown to Prison Service management, I made it clear that industrial action would not be tolerated. The POA may not have believed I had the will to fight, but they were wrong. A month later I met Evans at the annual Remembrance Day wreath-laying ceremony at the Home Office war memorial. Bartell, significantly, was not present. The POA wreath fell off its hook, a portent, perhaps, of events to come. Evans looked worried and muttered darkly about things getting serious. I agreed, but made sure he left with a firm impression that this time it was going to be different.

Meanwhile we kept Howard up to date with regular bulletins on developments, and revealed our secret weapon. For a naturally hawkish man, his initial reaction was surprising. He seemed to find the revelation embarrassing, and his inclination was that we should change the law to correct the anomaly and provide all prison officers with normal trade union rights. I later discovered that, as a young barrister, he had successfully defended a case on behalf of the Home Office in which access to an industrial tribunal was denied because the individual had the powers of a constable. Our secret weapon was not so new to him.

It took further meetings to convince Howard that we should make use of this legal weapon. More importantly we convinced him that there was political capital to be made from his role as the tough Home Secretary who climbed the last unconquered peak of union militancy.

The first rounds of the battle were mild enough. The POA executive sent circulars to prisons warming them up for the fray. This was followed by a ballot for industrial action. The reasons given were obscure, cloaked in industrial relations clichés. The result was a close vote in favour of action, but given the modest turnout, less than half the membership had actually voted in favour. The national executive now had a free hand to take any form of industrial action short of a strike, and instructions went out not to admit prisoners delivered from the courts by the police.

At that point we had to take the critical decision – whether we should go to the courts immediately, or hold back until there was evidence of the disruption caused. The lawyers advised us to take the first option. A public confrontation with the POA was not something the Home Secretary could decide on alone. It was, perhaps, the only time when I felt Howard and I were working together as a team. We had much in common – the same objective, albeit for different reasons, the same opponent, and the same need to persuade the Prime Minister. We discussed the pros and cons, and decided to accept the lawyers' advice.

An *ad hoc* meeting was hastily convened, to be chaired by the Prime Minister, at which Howard and I would explain our plans. It was a new experience for me. I entered No. 10 uncertain what to expect, and followed Howard into the assembly area outside the Cabinet Room. Other ministers drifted in, Howard introduced me to those I did not know and we filled the time with small talk.

Soon after we were called in and took our seats for the meeting, Howard and I opposite the PM and Sir Robin Butler. Howard set out the position and how we intended to deal with it, after which it was my turn to explain the importance of grasping the nettle. Here was a real opportunity to change the face of industrial relations in the Prison Service and remove the principal obstacle to progress. Failure to act would merely make our position weaker.

There were some worried looks around the table. All the affected ministers or their deputies were there – Treasury, Northern Ireland, Scotland, Employment. Ken Clarke was robust in his endorsement of the need for action. He had seen the POA in action, and spoke with authority. Our strategy appealed to his natural instinct to go on the offensive. Unafraid as usual to slaughter sacred cows, he told the meeting he disagreed with his Treasury officials who opposed setting up a pay review body as a *quid pro quo* for the loss of the right to take industrial action. He subscribed to the unfashionable view that it was the right thing to do. Howard bristled: he had made his opposition to such an idea very clear. Others made cautionary noises. John Major looked anxious. Concern was expressed about the consequences should we lose in the courts: it would be a political disaster. The Prime Minister commented that he did not like the smell of it, but eventually agreed that we should take the matter to court. Doing so only made sense if we were prepared to follow up with emergency legislation and Howard argued for a commitment to do so, but the Prime Minister insisted that such a commitment could not be made then. The Home Secretary protested about the danger of being left out on a limb, adding that there would be no alternative, but the Prime Minister was not prepared to countenance it. It had been a business-like meeting. The PM had chaired it with skill, ensuring that all voices were heard and summing up succinctly. I was reassured to find that Cabinet ministers were better behaved in the privacy of Downing Street than the theatre of the House of Commons. We left satisfied. We had achieved much, even though we lacked the final reassurance of a promise of legislation.

On 18 November 1993 we went to the High Court in the Strand

to seek an injunction against the POA to stop them inducing prison officers to breach their contracts of employment. There was a short hearing in chambers in front of Mr Justice May. David Pannick QC, a brilliant young public administration barrister who later came to Howard's rescue over the early release of prisoners in 1996, argued our case to great effect. The planned refusal to allow more prisoners into prison would have put up to 2,000 prisoners in police cells almost overnight at a cost of around £1 million a week. Counsel for the POA, John Hendy QC, floundered. The judge came down unequivocally in our favour and granted us an injunction barring the POA from initiating industrial action, observing that 'it seems remarkable that this point has lain dormant for so long'. We were deeply relieved. Failure would have been an enormous moral victory for the POA and, had we lost an appeal as well, would have forced the introduction of emergency legislation. The POA was devastated. Bartell and other members of the executive left chambers in a state of shock, and engaged in bitter recriminations in the public waiting area.

We had won in the courts. We now had to win in public. I went on television, soberly explaining that we had taken this action only 'with the greatest reluctance' because of the seriousness of the threat. Howard telephoned me later in the evening, full of compliments about my media interviews. It had been a big gamble, and we were both relieved and elated. Tony Butler was emotionally exhausted, exhilarated by what had been achieved but saddened by the step we had had to take. As expected, the Labour Party kept its head down, embarrassed by the antics of this antediluvian union. The press coverage the next day was a Home Secretary's delight. The POA had few friends in the media and we had a happy minister.

But that was not the end of it. The POA tried again, this time using a single prison as guinea-pig. At Preston prison the ultra-militant local committee issued instructions to its members not to admit prisoners if it would lead to overcrowding. They argued that they had the constable's independent duty to keep the peace as well as his privileges, and that this allowed them to ignore the governor's orders. There was no turning back. We returned to the High Court to seek a second injunction. The POA advanced a different set of arguments. The judge, after punctiliously disclosing a possible conflict as a result of having eaten a meal with the governor at Preston prison, granted us a further injunction. It proved an unpleasant business. Writs were served at the homes of Preston branch officials. The long arm of the law came as a rude shock to people who had become used to exercising unbridled power within their own institutions. The defeat sent shock waves through POA branches across the country.

The POA national executive was left in disarray. They must have been aware of their legal position but had been lulled into a false sense of security after so many years of power. Shocked that we would dare to use the provisions, they had no real response other than to huff and puff to the media, who were even less sympathetic to their cause than the public at large.

The war was all but won. Governors felt a great burden being lifted from them now that the POA spell had been broken. Working together, Prison Service management and ministers had given governors back their authority. Provided the pressure was maintained, they would no longer have to fight with the POA over every inch of progress. As I surveyed the industrial relations battleground part of me was sorry that it had to be done this way: it was never my intention to neuter the POA, but the abuse of power could not be allowed to continue.

We faced the daunting task of rebuilding positive industrial relations in this war-torn landscape. Legislation was needed to restore balance to pay negotiations now that prison officers had lost their ultimate bargaining weapon. We needed to overcome the bitterness that the legal action had created and persuade rank and file POA members that we wanted a constructive relationship in which their views would count. It would inevitably be a long slow haul.

Some moderate union members were deeply shocked by the severity of the action we had taken. Although they had little respect for their leaders, they were worried about the consequences, and their fears were aggravated by emotive propaganda issued by a national executive fighting for its survival. Local committees claimed that their fundamental democratic rights were being taken away.

It took almost a year to enshrine the changes in legislation, and the Criminal Justice Act received the royal assent late in 1994. We continued to face guerrilla warfare in a number of quarters. At Preston union members fought on for a while but eventually gave up, leaving a local committee of largely broken men. The banner was taken up by places like Gartree and Hull.

The final pocket of resistance was Liverpool, a large, overcrowded local prison with strong local roots, where the last serious attempt at industrial action occurred in September 1994. It took the form of an old-fashioned work-to-rule, carefully designed not to fall foul of the legal restrictions. Staff refused to work additional hours – the Prison Service equivalent of overtime, for which they received time off in lieu – and to unlock more than a few prisoners at a time. Officers unilaterally cancelled visits without the governor's agreement, because of alleged staff shortages. All this was being done, the POA claimed, by officers acting off their own bats, without any inducement from the union. It was not a credible claim, but we could find no hard evidence that the POA had been behind it, so falling foul of the law. The work-to-rule was accompanied by the traditional POA tactic of harassing the governor so as to make his life impossible: the objective was to secure his removal and bring in an innocent new governor whom they could control. We were not going to play that game. We publicly backed the existing governor, even though his failure to follow the agreed procedure to the letter had made our position difficult. We made it clear centrally and locally that we were not going to succumb to intimidation. Two hundred governor-grade staff were assembled from all over the country at Hutton Hall police college in Lancashire, and similar numbers of police were put on standby. We wanted the POA to know that whatever happened we could cope with a walkout, or lay off the staff *en masse* if they threatened the security and safety of the prison. This was strong stuff; there had never been such a concerted show of determination on the part of management at Liverpool. The POA wavered and then backed down in what it was hoped would be the last such confrontation at the prison.

It took nearly a year before the POA national executive could bring themselves to meet us formally. They had lost face among their members, having promised so much and achieved nothing. The loss of their normal trade union rights, and the bitterness they felt towards me and other members of the board, not to mention Michael Howard, was just too great. Eventually we had our first new-era Whitley Council meeting. There was the usual polemic from John Bartell, but the fire and confidence had gone. There was dissension and discomfort in their ranks. We made it clear that we would have nothing to do with the industrial relations of the past, and when the debate degenerated we very deliberately walked out of the meeting. The official side had never behaved like this before and the POA did not know how to react.

The Bartell era came to a sad, low-key ending. Early in 1995 my telephone rang at home one Sunday evening, and I found myself talking to Bartell. He was thinking of giving up the chairmanship of the POA, and wanted to know what would become of him. I wondered whether he was being pushed by other members of the national executive and had lost the will to fight on in the face of a devastating reversal, or whether – as some newspapers reported later – he was retiring on grounds of ill health.

Either way, it was a problem we had to deal with. Like other full-time members of the national executive he remained an employee of the Prison Service, and on ceasing to hold office he would expect to be re-employed elsewhere in the service. Given the years he had spent as a full-time official, and his reputation, there was no way we could post him as an officer in a working prison. Luckily we were able to offer him early retirement, on special terms of 'limited postability', a device used in other parts of the Civil Service but not applied to a prison officer before. But first I had to establish that there was no hidden sleaze factor behind his retirement.

The first opportunity to do so without risk of detection occurred at the annual Butler Trust award ceremony for prison staff at Buckingham Palace. I manoeuvred David Evans into a secluded corner behind a gilded statue in the state apartments, out of sight and out of earshot. I explained the position, much of which he had already guessed. Barely concealing his disdain for Bartell, he expressed his relief, and gave me the reassurance I needed. We worked out the terms in the greatest secrecy, cleared the plan with Howard, informed Bartell and concluded the arrangements, after which he quietly faded into obscurity.

He left behind a POA uncertain of its future and riven by a bitter leadership contest, dogged by allegations of vote-rigging. Alleged expenses frauds involving senior officials were also reported. It was tragic to see a once-proud union tearing itself apart in this way. One could only hope that a more representative and effective body would emerge out of the remains.

The transformation in industrial relations, though not completed, symbolized the degree of change that had occurred elsewhere. The tide had undoubtedly turned, but still had much further to flow.

II

Disasters Waiting to Happen

On Thursday, 1 September 1994, I started the day recording a video for staff about the need to improve performance in the service, after which I caught a train to York, where I was due to visit the Full Sutton maximum-security prison. Early that evening, shortly after I had joined a Quaker meeting for prisoners, the peace was rudely shattered by an urgent request that I should contact head-quarters. In a matter of seconds I realized that my visit was over. All hell had broken loose. Four IRA prisoners had been transferred that morning from Full Sutton to Maghaberry prison in Northern Ireland. Lord Tebbit, whose wife had been permanently disabled in the IRA bombing of the Grand Hotel at Brighton in 1984, was angrily criticizing the transfer, which had followed the previous day's announcement of an IRA ceasefire.

A new policy had been announced in November 1992 designed to make it easier for prisoners to transfer within the three principal UK jurisdictions – England and Wales, Scotland and Northern Ireland. Until then transfers to Northern Ireland had been ruled out because of the more generous remission rules obtaining there. The new policy then stalled as the three ministries wrangled over who was to pay the costs of the transfers and housing the additional prisoners: the Northern Ireland Office was not prepared to accept English prisoners unless it was paid to do so. There matters rested until Michael Howard became Home Secretary. He looked at the policy and was horrified. He instinctively took a hard line on terrorists, and questioned whether they should be allowed transfers at all. He was also worried that they might be released early or enjoy more liberal home leave arrangements if transferred to Northern Ireland.

Almost twelve months of government inactivity followed as the Home Secretary and the Northern Ireland Secretary engaged in a stand-off, exchanging occasional letters while civil servants endeavoured to oil the wheels. Sir Patrick Mayhew, the Northern Ireland Secretary, would not agree to a change in policy that would disadvantage IRA terrorists while there was any chance of peace in Northern Ireland. By a stroke of irony, in Northern Ireland serious terrorist offenders, including murderers, were let out of prison years earlier than would have been the case if their offence had been committed in England or Wales.

By the end of June 1994, with pressure mounting from the Northern Ireland Office and the knowledge that he would be legally exposed if the policy announced some two years earlier was not implemented, the Home Secretary grudgingly accepted defeat and approved the transfer of the first fourteen prisoners. The specific timing and operational details of the transfers were left to us and the Northern Ireland Office, although the Home Secretary insisted that they should be staggered.

The first four prisoners were moved a month later, after the Home Secretary's office had been informed. It attracted limited press coverage. After a couple of non-terrorist prisoners had been transferred in August, the Northern Ireland Office said it was ready to receive a second group of terrorist prisoners. The Prison Service and the Northern Ireland Office provisionally agreed that four should be transferred during the week of 29 August. The final date of 1 September was agreed with the Northern Ireland Office one week in advance.

The previous day saw the surprise announcement of an IRA ceasefire, marking the beginning of the Northern Ireland peace process. Later that same day a security group official in Prison Service headquarters telephoned the Home Secretary's private office and informed his private secretary, James Toon, that the next planned transfer was due to take place the following morning. They discussed the operational reasons for the timing and its bearing on the ceasefire. Toon decided that there was no need to inform either the Home Secretary, who was in South America at the time, or the Home Office duty minister. Officials in the Northern Ireland Office also decided not to inform any of their ministers. The following morning the transfers went ahead as scheduled, and the prisoners were soon secure in their new Northern Ireland prison.

When my press office said that all hell had broken loose, they were not exaggerating. Accusations were flying that these particular transfers had been a bribe to persuade Sinn Fein and the IRA to sign up to the ceasefire. Protestations to the contrary were equally vehement. From early evening No. 10 was briefing journalists that the Prime Minister was 'livid' that the transfers had taken place. All we could do was state the truth: there was no political significance in the timing; the policy had been agreed years earlier; transfer of the four prisoners had been approved over three months earlier; and the timing had been finalized well before the unexpected announcement of the ceasefire; there had been no ministerial involvement in selecting the date.

I was asked to talk directly to the Prime Minister's press secretary, Chris Meyer. I explained the background to him. He said the Prime Minister had given instructions that I was to get on the *Nine o'Clock News* and give a public explanation. I said I would happily try, but could not exactly force the BBC to give me air time. I then ran through the approach I would take. There was a long silence, followed by 'Well, you can try it . . .'

While my press office team in London were busy making arrangements with the main TV and radio stations, up in Yorkshire my able press office minder, Roy Webster, made contact with local studios. The original idea was that everything should be done from the Yorkshire Television studios in York. That sounded fine, until they called back to say that the studio was unmanned and they could not find the person with the key. By 8.20 p.m. the elusive keyholder was still at large, and I was faced with having to explain to the Prime Minister that I had failed to get on the *Nine o'Clock News* because Yorkshire Television were unable to find a key.

The only practical alternative was to head for the BBC studios in Leeds, some thirty-five miles away. Thirty-five miles in forty minutes sounded just about feasible. A governor gamely offered to take me there in his new Mercedes. The governor in charge, Ivor Woods, Roy Webster and I jumped into the car and left as rapidly as the double gatelock system would allow. The country lanes seemed to be clogged with every tractor in the country, but as we pulled on to the main A64 dual carriageway to Leeds, I thought the worst was behind us. Woods had called the police and asked for an emergency escort, and they were happy to oblige. But my optimism proved unfounded. A new Mercedes was a car to be pampered but not rushed. Not even a prime ministerial edict could persuade the driver to thrash it down the A64. And the promised police escort was nowhere to be seen.

It was already 8.55 p.m. as we entered the outskirts of Leeds. The transfer of IRA prisoners would be the lead story on the news, but there was no hope of getting to the studio in time. We had to activate plan B. Woods found out that the nearest police station was two roundabouts down the A64. Peering through the gloom, we saw its welcome blue light, swung round the roundabout and came to an abrupt halt in the car park. The two governors charged across the tarmac, while the press officer and I followed at a marginally more sedate pace. We all arrived breathless at the station counter. 'This is the Director General of the Prison Service and he needs a telephone to talk to the *Nine o'Clock News* immediately,' gasped the governor in charge. The constable behind the counter was singularly unimpressed. He drew himself up to his full height, solemnly announced that he would have to make inquiries, turned on his heel and left us. By now it was 8.59. After what seemed like an interminable delay he returned, told us to follow him, and led us through to a telephone in the room next door. Roy Webster frenetically dialled the BBC in London. It was 9.02. He passed the phone to me, and I found a cheery but much relieved producer at the other end. I had missed most of the news item, and went into my interview cold. It turned out to be fearsome enough. Wasn't this really a political decision? How could anyone believe that there was no political involvement? If it was not a political decision, how could anyone have chosen such an insensitive time? And so on. Still out of breath and finding it increasingly difficult to hear the BBC's questions amid the general hubbub of a busy police station, I was at something of a disadvantage. I was sandwiched between a man reporting a motoring incident and a woman complaining about a dog. I would gladly have swapped places with either or both of them. It was an interview I would never want to relive, but at least it was mercifully short.

I still had *News at Ten* and *Newsnight* to contend with, so we had to be on our way. Back in the car, we headed for the centre of Leeds, where our long-lost police escort at last caught up with us.

Installed in good time in the studios, I was able to collect my thoughts. The news programmes followed one another in quick succession – ITN, Sky, *World Tonight*, IRN. The line of attack was much the same in each case, but now I was better prepared. Remarkably enough, the Northern Ireland Office, which had responsibility for and inside knowledge of the peace process, and had suggested the original timing, suddenly seemed deserted: not a single official or minister was to be found anywhere near a camera, microphone or journalist. It was becoming increasingly clear that the story would run and run. John Hume, leader of the nationalist SDLP, weighed in with accusations that he had written to Howard about the transfer of one of the prisoners, and that Howard must have known.

My press office had arranged for me to take part in the *Today* programme the following morning: the only question was, how? It was now after 11 p.m. in a dark television studio in Leeds. I was offered the further use of the Mercedes, but felt that I could not inflict more pain on this newly acquired treasure. The answer was a taxi. The governor in charge called Leeds prison and asked them to arrange it. That's all very well, they replied, but who's going to pay? It's not going on *our* budget. I smiled wryly: maybe I had had some success in imposing a sense of fiscal responsibility on the service. With a keen eye on his promotion prospects, the governor volunteered to pay, and eventually a small, battered and smelly minicab appeared, with an empty tank. It was well after midnight by the time we had found a petrol station and set off down the M1 to London, my shattered press officer slumped in the front, while I tried to stretch out on the diminutive back seat. Some four hours and one motorway snack later, our driver delivered us to the door of the Caledonian Club in London at about 4 a.m., and I sank into bed with relief.

Two hours later, Audrey Nelson, my chief press officer, arrived with a large bundle of newspapers and we ran through them quickly. She rehearsed me on the points that I had to make and the answers to the toughest questions, and then it was off to face another round of hostile interviews. There were odd moments of relief, including an MP who observed that the Prison Service would have been damned whatever decision it had made. But most of the comment consisted of gloomy predictions about the damaging effect the transfers could have on the ceasefire. Some of the attacks became very personal. As the day progressed, however, it became clear that we were winning the main battle, that of persuading the public that the transfers and their timing had neither political significance nor political involvement.

The rest of that day was spent behind closed doors with Richard Wilson, preparing an urgent report for the Prime Minister. It went with a covering note confirming my public statements of regret about the anxiety that had been caused, and expressing the hope that the peace process would not be damaged. Wilson was very supportive. And at the end of the day we reflected on the main differences between us. I was used to taking decisions, he said, while he believed in passing the difficult decisions on to ministers. Civil servants were not paid well enough to take risks like that.

Life then started to calm down. The Prime Minister's livid mood had subsided. The peace process, with which he was so personally involved, appeared unscathed, and he was even reported to have commented that I seemed to have had 'rather a rough time'. He was right.

At my next meeting with Michael Howard he appeared surprisingly relaxed and affable. I did not remind him that the unfortunate coincidence of the transfers and the ceasefire would not have occurred had his fruitless arguments with the Northern Ireland Office not delayed the whole process by nearly a year. I explained what had happened, and said that it was arguable that things had worked out for the best. Had any of the officials involved delayed the transfer, it would almost certainly have become known and caused deep resentment on the Republican side. Had ministers been consulted, they would have had to admit political involvement. A decision to maintain the timing would have angered the Unionists; a delay in the transfer would have angered the Republicans. As it was, everyone now genuinely believed that there had been no political involvement, and there appeared to have been no damage to the peace process. Howard said that had been his initial reaction also, although he now believed ministers should have been told. He thought his principal private secretary, Joan McNaughton, would probably have informed him or the duty minister had she been in the office at the time. I was reassured when he concluded by saying that he had complete confidence in my leadership of the Prison Service, and that this incident had in no way affected it.

Howard's expressions of support did not extend to the public domain. On Friday, 9 September, just a week later, Nick Clarke on *The World at One*, asked him whether no one in the Home Office had realized – or mentioned – how sensitive the whole issue might be?

MICHAEL HOWARD: Well I think the facts of that were explained very fully at the time. The timing of that transfer obviously was completely wrong, and that was accepted* by the Director General of the Prison Service in the interviews he gave at the time. It's been made absolutely clear that no minister was informed that that transfer was to take place.

NICK CLARKE: But the transfer was discussed by politicians, wasn't it, in June, that's what Derek Lewis said. And even then perhaps it should have been realized that the sensitivity might arise and contingency plans put down?

* This is not accurate. I had accepted only that the timing was unfortunate.

HOWARD: Well the decision to transfer some of these prisoners was taken in June, the timing was left to the Prison Service, but there's a general expectation in government that where timing is sensitive ministers are informed. And very regrettably on this occasion they weren't.

It was a missed opportunity to show some public support for the Prison Service, and to make it clear that others in his private office and the Northern Ireland Office were involved.

Howard's interview had taken place in the middle of the Home Office strategy conference at Chevening. As I left it later that afternoon, I had to admit to feeling a little weary. Faced with a five-hour drive up the A1 to York for the Boards of Visitors conference dinner, I was severely tempted to take the forty-five-minute option and go home. But duty called, and I had a keynote speech to make the following morning.

As coffee was being served after the meal, I saw Deborah Hermer, one of our press officers, enter the dining-hall and walk towards me. Her expression warned me that something was seriously wrong. Other Prison Service directors noticed as well, and began reaching for their pagers. We had all received messages, but had failed to hear them in the hubbub of the dinner.

I received the news in private outside. Six exceptional-risk prisoners, including five IRA terrorists, had escaped from the SSU at Whitemoor using firearms, and one of our officers had been shot. I listened in silence as the seriousness of it hit me. By now surrounded by other anxious directors, we waited to find out more, and were slightly relieved when the news came through that four of the six had been recaptured almost immediately outside the prison wall. Two were still missing.

That was the end of my dinner and my conference. I called my driver, who was relaxing in a hot bath after the journey north, and we set off on the long trip back down the A1 to Whitemoor. On the way, I briefed the Home Secretary by telephone.

To Howard's credit, he took news of the escape calmly. Shortly afterwards we heard that the police had successfully recaptured the remaining two prisoners only half a mile from the prison. They were hiding in a ditch and were spotted by a police helicopter using sophisticated thermal-imaging equipment. There had been no risk or danger to the public. But questions were bound to be asked.

Whitemoor prison had had a chequered history from the time it first started to take prisoners in 1990, and it came to dominate the last twelve months of my time as Director General. One of many new prisons built in the 1980s, it was originally designed as a category B prison – one step down from the highest level of security. But while it was under construction, it was decided that a new dispersal prison was needed to replace one that could no longer meet modern security standards, so Whitemoor was upgraded to maximum-security dispersal status with its own special secure unit (SSU). The residents of March in Cambridgeshire expressed fears about the change at the time. Their worst fears were to prove well founded.

The last-minute change to Whitemoor's role meant that not all its buildings were ideally suited. More staff were needed, and most of them were new recruits to the service from the north of England with little experience of dealing with the most hardened criminals. From the beginning there was a running battle between staff and prisoners for supremacy. There were frequent minor disturbances, staff were intimidated, and an atmosphere of tension persisted in the living units. Things came to a head in January 1994 with a disturbance in one of the four main houseblocks. Cells were wrecked and furniture destroyed, but it was quickly brought under control by prison staff. From then on the slow process of re-establishing staff dominance began. The original governor, Andy Barclay, had moved on and been replaced in May by Brodie Clark from Woodhill. All Clark's initial attention was focused on the big dispersal wings, which were so prone to disruption.

The Chief Inspector of Prisons carried out an inspection in March 1994 and, commenting on the problems of control, complimented the action that was being taken. Meanwhile little notice was paid to the SSU, a quiet little operation housing only half a dozen prisoners. The Chief Inspector drew attention to the high level of physical security and observed that it was 'virtually impregnable'. Within six months his words were to prove tragically wide of the mark.

I arrived at Whitemoor in the early hours of the morning, and was immediately aware of a hushed air of shock. In the governor's office I was briefed on what was known so far. The police had sealed off the SSU, and the six prisoners were now back in solitary confinement in the segregation unit. One officer from the SSU had had a miraculous escape when a bullet had grazed his chest. Much of the episode had been captured on videotape by the security cameras on the perimeter, and we were able to watch it being re-run in black and white.

Disciplined, intelligent and calculating men, the six prisoners had succeeded in hiding ladders, ropes, grappling irons, wire cutters and handguns within the SSU. They had intimidated the staff into keeping out of parts of the SSU and away from the exercise yard. On a quiet evening they had pushed their equipment through a window of the SSU building into the sterile area between it and the perimeter wall, taken the wire cutters into the exercise yard and cut their way through. Scaling the wall of the SSU using one of their improvised ladders had been a simple job, but they were spotted on the television monitors in the main control room. An officer, who had been playing Scrabble at the time, rushed out into the exercise yard but was threatened and then shot at by a prisoner astride the top of the wall. The prisoners then ran across to the inner fence of the main prison perimeter, cut through it and set up their improvised climbing equipment while holding staff at bay with their firearms. More shots were fired from the top of the main wall before the prisoners slid down a rope to the outer world. Unfortunately for them, a new shift of officers was coming on duty and joined forces with those from inside the prison, who included dog-handlers and dogs. A Volvo, probably the pick-up vehicle, was seen to approach the prison, but disappeared after seeing the commotion outside the walls.

As more staff with dogs arrived, the chase up the long flank of the prison began. Two dogs fought each other and then attacked a prison officer before finally realizing it was the prisoners they were after. A dog caught up with the prisoners, who threw pepper in its face. One prisoner lagged behind the others, having fallen heavily as he went over the wall. At the far end of the prison, dogs and prison officers surrounded four of the prisoners and took them back into captivity. Two others disappeared across the Fens into the darkness but were recaptured before long. As a television executive I would have relished every moment; as the Director General of the Prison Service it was a terrible nightmare.

Not surprisingly, the media clamour was well under way. My press office team would handle everything until the morning, when doubtless all hell would break loose. I was due on the *Today* programme at 7.15 a.m., and arrangements were being made for an early morning press conference in which the governor, the police and I would take part. By now it was three o'clock and I needed to get some sleep. The prison seemed eerily still, but wherever I looked the darkness had been dispersed by the orange security lighting. I stretched out on an improvised bed of chairs in the governor's outer office and was grateful for the rough prison-issue blankets and iron-hard pillow, but managed only a couple of hours of fitful sleep. My mind was racing, and I could hear the guard dogs howling outside.

During the night Audrey Nelson, my chief press officer, arrived. She had become an indispensable part of my senior team in this high profile job; always there when needed with well judged advice in a crisis. At first light we went into the special secure unit. As we looked at the curtain shielding the hobby room where so much of the escape equipment had been made and hidden, and at the discarded ropes, grappling-hooks and clothing in the sterile area outside, the reality hit home. Audrey believed we should tell the press as much as possible: I agreed. Something had clearly gone very wrong at Whitemoor, and the IRA must somehow have managed to take effective control of this SSU.

It was a difficult press conference, but we were as well prepared as we could be and most seemed satisfied. A local journalist expressed indignation that this could have happened after all the assurances about security that had been given to the residents of March when the prison was being built.

In the hours that followed a decision was made which ultimately led to my own dismissal. It changed the course of events for the Prison Service for the next year, probably for many years to come; it cost the taxpayer tens of millions, expenditure that has been of questionable value; and it resulted in much grief for the Home Secretary. Who was to conduct the inquiry?

The Chief Inspector, Stephen Tumim, was the obvious choice, but both Richard Wilson and I were aware that his reports tended to be sensational, such as the one on Wymott. We were also conscious of the fact that his still unpublished inspection report on Whitemoor contained those prophetic words 'virtually impregnable'. He could hardly be an objective investigator. And we knew that the Home Secretary wanted to make a decisive, authoritative and independent appointment for political reasons. We discussed the possibility of a chief constable with public credibility, independence and investigative expertise. Ian Burns, head of the police department at the Home Office, suggested Sir John Woodcock, a retired former chief inspector of constabulary. It seemed a good idea at the time. The Home Secretary gave his approval and insisted on making an announcement that day to keep the press at bay. Sir John was contacted and agreed. He was asked no questions and given no interview. The fateful announcement was made that afternoon.

The result was a Chief Inspector of Prisons who felt severely jilted. Later he claimed that he was out at lunch that Saturday and could not be contacted, while the Home Secretary wanted an announcement in that day's *Evening Standard* – overlooking the fact that no one had tried to contact him, and that the *Evening Standard* is not published on Saturdays. Hostility between him and the Home Secretary rose to a new level.

Most incidents in the Prison Service lose their interest for the media after a couple of days. Not so Whitemoor. We faced two rapid aftershocks. First, Paddy Seligman, the feisty former chairman of the Board of Visitors at Whitemoor, went public. She claimed that she had warned the Home Secretary in her annual report of lax security practices in the SSU that had led ultimately to this escape. She was stretching a point. Her report had referred to control problems and excess personal property in the main parts of the prison, but a follow-up report by her successor had been complimentary about the improvements that had taken place. Nevertheless, it was enough to create panic in the Home Secretary's private office. It was being suggested that he had been warned but had taken no action – potentially a resigning matter. I was in Leeds for a governors' meeting on the morning of 13 September when these accusations were made, and had to respond to them with ten minutes' notice on the *Today* programme. Meanwhile the Home Secretary's private office insisted that I be back in London that afternoon for a meeting. I was told to hire a helicopter if necessary, and I did. Wilson and Michael Forsyth were also there, both grumbling that their plans had been quite unnecessarily disrupted. We talked briefly about the claims and the security actions we were already taking. It was an expensive way of holding a Cabinet minister's hand and reassuring him, given that the meeting lasted no more than half an hour.

A week later, on 22 September, the second aftershock was felt. A pound of Semtex had been discovered in the false bottom of an artist's paintbox belonging to one of the IRA prisoners, held in a sea container used for temporary storage within the perimeter at Whitemoor. That raised even more serious questions.

By then the service was on a high level of alert. Every governor had been told to check his security procedures and intensify his searches and all the high-security prisons were being combed by sniffer-dogs. It was a tense time for all that would stretch on for a further three months. A jumpy Home Secretary repeatedly questioned our search programmes and the action we were taking. Prisoners exploited the situation to the full. There were constant false alarms. Real guns were found at Manchester and in the process of being smuggled into Durham, but luckily they had nothing to do with the IRA.

In the meantime the flurry of paper between Queen Anne's Gate and the Prison Service had become a blizzard. After each weekend's boxes, a series of notes from the private office came through. Many concerned press stories; some questioned decisions, while yet others demanded further information or advice about policy recommendations – often for the third or fourth time. Within eighty-three working days, over 1,000 documents went to ministers, including 137 major submissions. The degree of detailed ministerial involvement was greater than most long-serving civil servants could remember in pre-agency days. It was a far cry from the 'much greater autonomy from ministers and the rest of the Home Office' that Ken Clarke had publicly promised.

After a successful but relatively obscure career as a policeman, Sir John Woodcock was about to become a star in an entirely different firmament. The highlights of his career had been as Chief Constable of North Yorkshire and South Wales, followed by a spell as Her Majesty's uncontroversial Chief Inspector of Constabulary. When I visited him the day after at his Warwickshire home to brief him on the Whitemoor escape, he had been retired for about a year but clearly relished the prospect of a return to the limelight.

The Woodcock inquiry displayed all the strengths and many of the weaknesses of our police service. Within hours Woodcock had gathered a team of serving and former police officers to conduct the inquiry, and appeared at Whitemoor prison the following day to demonstrate that no time would be lost. But the insularity and inflexibility of the police approach were soon apparent. This was going to be a police inquiry, conducted exclusively by police officers, using police techniques and practices usually reserved for criminal investigations. It would be interesting to see who ended up as the 'criminals'. The only obvious difference was that this investigation would not be conveyed in the usual turgid prose associated with police reports: they had secured the services of Superintendent Todd of the Bedfordshire police, whose literary style appeared to owe much to Jeffrey Archer.

As the inquiry accelerated into top gear, reports began to filter through of how the interviews were being conducted. It was clear that the protection normally afforded by the PACE, the Police and Criminal Evidence Act, had little part in the proceedings. In the best traditions of *The Sweeney*, Woodcock and his sidekick, Deputy Assistant Commissioner Fry of the Metropolitan police, subjected their victims to several hours of intense interrogation. The victim was trapped between a wall and a barren table in a small office, with Woodcock and Fry sitting opposite. The hardman/softman routine usually culminated in the victim being accused by Fry of dereliction of duty, while Woodcock smiled sweetly and offered the victim an opportunity to confess. It was like a courtroom from which the defence counsel and judge had been banned. Voluminous notes were taken, but no transcript was made available for the intimidated victim to check afterwards. Most of those interviewed left feeling bullied, browbeaten, unfairly treated and angry.

It soon became clear that the Woodcock Report was going to be highly controversial. We already knew that there had been serious failings at Whitemoor. A succession of newspaper reports about high living and luxury foods in the special secure unit were beginning to incense political and public opinion. The Home Secretary, with Tumim's grudging agreement, had decided to delay publication of the inspectorate's report on Whitemoor, with its embarrassingly complimentary observations on security. Soon afterwards the *Observer* carried selected leaked extracts from the report, emphasizing the few instances where Tumim had been critical. I alerted Howard to the impending article on my way to a silver wedding party on the Saturday evening, and arranged for the first edition to be taken to his country home by my driver. Howard was furious and the party was interrupted several times by lengthy phone calls, in the course of which I tried to calm him down. The leak had happened and there was little that could be done; Tumim protested that it had been nothing to do with him.

While the Woodcock Report was being prepared, Tumim began to protect his own position. His 1992–3 annual report had said:

We consider security procedures and their effectiveness as part of every full inspection . . . We had no serious concerns about the application of security procedures in the establishments we inspected in 1992–3 and, in general, levels of physical security seemed appropriate for the security category of the inmates held.

Subsequent annual reports and individual inspection reports included a disclaimer saying that the inspectorate did not perform security audits but 'where problems are identified', they were brought to the attention of management.

Howard would have dearly loved to remove Tumim. Shortly after the *Observer* leak, Howard debated the options. A knighthood had already been delayed in the forlorn hope that the carrot would make him less outspoken. He wistfully acknowledged that to silence or remove Tumim would be too politically damaging. But eventually Howard had his revenge. Tumim hoped and expected to have his contract extended. Howard was having none of it, and Richard Wilson was deputed to break the news. A few days later Tumim told me in hushed tones that he and Howard had jointly decided that it was time for him to move on, but the façade quickly crumbled and Tumim did little to conceal his anger and resentment at not being invited to stay on.

Love him or loathe him, Stephen Tumim did a great deal to ensure that prisons were a topic for public debate. I hope his place as one of the notable penal reformers in this country is assured. But no one should remain in a job too long.

As the numbers interrogated by the Woodcock team grew, individuals and unions became increasingly alarmed by the probable tone of the report itself. It was argued that those who were criticized should have the opportunity to see the draft and respond to it, so Woodcock was instructed to follow the so-called Salmon procedures and provide a formal right of reply. Reluctant at first, he eventually agreed. When we saw the first draft we understood why. A tabloid editor's dream, it would have made wonderful newspaper copy, written in an easy sensational style, punctuated by phrases that would have leapt straight into the headlines. It was highly critical of lax management at Whitemoor and of support from headquarters, as well as of many individuals. Yet it managed to conceal the main failing of the inquiry: its inability to identify how the escape had been allowed to happen by tracing how the guns vital to its success had got into the prison.

The need to follow Salmon procedures conveniently delayed publication until the day before the House of Commons rose for the Christmas recess in 1994. The report had been delivered to Michael Howard a week earlier, and he had spent an anxious few days considering how to satisfy Parliament and protect himself.

In order to protect himself, Howard was keen to accept all sixty-four recommendations in the Woodcock Report at once, before anyone had a chance to assess whether they were affordable, let alone good value for money. It was clear that great expenditure would be involved. But there was no time for such considerations. Howard was clearly showing signs of intense pressure in the forty-eight hours that preceded his statement. His voice became brittle and colder in meetings, the usual formal introductory smiles were dispensed with, private secretaries were snapped at for not having the necessary paper or person instantly available. I was asked in heavy tones how I viewed the situation at Whitemoor, as revealed in the report. I felt as though I was expected to make some sort of confession, as his private secretary waited, pen poised, to record my answer. Howard was clearly weighing the political pros and cons of attaching some of the blame to me – maybe even firing me. Would I think it reasonable, he asked, if I was put on some form of probation subject to progress in implementing the Woodcock recommendations? I said I was shocked that he should even suggest such a thing: what I and the Prison Service needed was his unequivocal support in the tough task we faced. He dropped the idea.

Howard was increasingly desperate to be in a position to announce in the Commons that he was accepting all sixty-four recommendations. A show of unequivocal, decisive action would be his salvation. We discussed how one last recommendation could be rephrased so as to allow him to do so – accepting 'in principle' without making any real commitment. His other problem was the Treasury, since he had to get Treasury agreement to fund the recommendations before making his statement. Our only estimates of costs were crude back-of-envelope stuff, but we knew that they would be huge. He presented the Treasury with an ultimatum. The Treasury Chief Secretary, Jonathan Aitken, was caught unawares, and agreed that Howard could say that no resource constraint would inhibit implementation of the recommendations. It was a mistake the Treasury soon regretted, and it poisoned future relations with the Home Office. Howard had tried one bounce too many – the price would be paid later when Aitken's successor, William Waldegrave, referring to the consequences of the Woodcock débâcle, told Howard that no more money would be available for the Learmont Report.

On Sunday, 18 December, as we prepared for the statement to the Commons the following day, Richard Wilson realized Howard might face questions about my position. We discussed the matter furtively in a dark ante-room adjacent to Howard's office but out of his hearing. Wilson had scribbled out a statement on the back of some old press cuttings and showed it to me.

Do you have full confidence in the Director General?
Yes. The task of implementing the Woodcock recommendations is an extremely onerous one. I believe that the Director General, who has made considerable progress in improving the performance of the Prison Service over the last eighteen months is the best person to take the Prison Service forward and implement the Woodcock recommendations.

I agreed the wording.

I had also decided that I needed to deal with the issue of my bonus for the year. The Treasury had been unhappy with the arrangements that Sir Clive Whitmore had made when I joined. No doubt egged on by the media criticism of my £35,000 bonus for the previous year, the Treasury wanted tougher criteria, and the argument was unresolved even though we were three-quarters of the way through the year. We were meeting or exceeding all the performance targets Howard had set for the service, and I would have been entitled to an increased bonus. In the wake of Whitemoor, however, I felt it would send the wrong signals to those who worked in the service, and I decided it would be wrong in principle for me to take any bonus for the year. Wilson seemed relieved and grateful. We agreed a form of words for Howard to use: 'Mr Lewis has authorized me to say that, following the Woodcock Report, he considers that it would not be appropriate for him to take up any bonus to which he may be entitled in the current year.' But when questioned about me in the House, Howard's reply conveyed a rather different impression: 'The Director General has agreed that there is no question of a bonus during the current year.'

In addition to accepting all of Woodcock's recommendations, Howard also announced a disciplinary investigation. He wanted someone of stature, independent of the Prison Service to conduct it. Richard Wilson dug into his own past at the Department of the Environment and came up with Sir David Yardley, a former local government ombudsman and lawyer. His legal background appealed to Howard, though he may not have realized that Yardley was an academic lawyer, not a tough QC practised in the art of cross-examination. Howard also went beyond Woodcock's recommendations: a new monitoring unit was to be set up within the Home Office to watch over the Prison Service on behalf of the Home Secretary – a function that the framework document already required of the permanent secretary. And the crowning glory of this intensely political response was to be yet another inquiry, this time into security in the Prison Service in general.

The Home Secretary need not have been so nervous about his statement to the House. It was an uncomfortable experience for him and there was a good deal of bluster and the ritual calls for resignations, but the Opposition was disorganized and largely ineffective, and the Christmas recess beckoned. He wisely refused to give media interviews afterwards. Press reports were predictably awful the following day, but it was a one-day wonder.

I decided to summon all governing governors to London the following day to brief them on Woodcock and spell out precisely what was expected of them. It was a sombre occasion: the Prison

Service was in mourning for its lost reputation, and I had some tough and unwelcome things to say about how the service had failed itself and, more importantly, the public:

The attempted escape of six prisoners from the SSU at Whitemoor on the evening of 9 September was an awful shock to me and to the Prison Service. I shall remember it for a long time to come. Something that should never happen did happen. Three months later the Woodcock Report does nothing to reduce the embarrassment.

It *is* true that in the last two and a half years the numbers of escapes from prisons and escort has been reduced by about half. In the last one and a half years the reduction has been by one-third. Those are outstanding achievements, but they are not necessarily the way the public sees us. The public keeps hearing about individual escapes. Those still add up to over 200 a year. They say that is too many. They say *they* want to be protected.

A gently declining trend is unacceptable. There must be a step change from three-figure numbers to two-figure numbers.

The choice we face is stark. Public confidence in the Prison Service is at a low ebb. We have done the research. There is a widely held public view that current security levels are not acceptable.

I intend that *we* should take the initiative – that it should be the Prison Service that shows the way in security. It is after all our first duty. For the next twelve months security will have not only to be our first priority but our second and third priorities also.

I wrote to all governors in the middle of September asking you to re-examine your physical and procedural security. I must tell you that I have watched with growing anger and frustration the number of instances where that message has not been heeded. There have been too many cases where governing governors and their senior management teams have simply failed to give enough attention to detail and exercise the vigilance that they are required to. It is inexcusable at one prison that spy holes were being blocked up and doors wedged a month after that request went out. It is unacceptable at another prison that a prisoner, who had attempted to escape and should have been recategorized, was simply *left* at the prison because no one took ownership of the problem and made sure that the move took place.

It is unacceptable at yet another prison that commitments on the searching of visitors were simply not being carried out.

In each of these incidents you have let the Prison Service down and further undermined confidence in the system. *It is the duty of every governor to make sure not only that people know what is expected of them but that they get out and see that it is happening. I expect that of each and every governing governor. And I expect area managers to make sure it is happening.*

It was a quiet group who went away to reflect on what I had said. On the whole they responded magnificently: escapes fell by a further 60 per cent in the following year, making a total reduction of 80 per cent.

The Prison Service ended 1994 in sober mood. The achievements of the year had been totally overshadowed by Whitemoor and the Woodcock Report. We went away for Christmas praying for a better 1995.

12

The Storm Clouds Gather

It was not to be. The New Year opened with one crisis after another. I was staying in Scotland and found a message from Prison Service headquarters on the answering machine as I returned to the house in the middle of New Year's day. Fred West had hanged himself in Winson Green prison in Birmingham. Few prisoners were more notorious than Fred West, and there are few days of the year when news is so thin. There was frenzied public and media interest, with our press office receiving 100 calls an hour. I had to find a way of travelling south – not easy on a Scottish New Year's day, a hundred miles from an airport and with a heavy blizzard blowing.

But first I had to calm a jittery Home Secretary, still recovering from the Woodcock Report and convinced that our systems must be fundamentally flawed or that someone must be culpably negligent. I phoned him, sitting on the stairs, with New Year celebrations going on around me, and eventually managed to persuade him that neither of his conclusions was necessarily right. We needed to have the facts. Some prisoners are determined to kill themselves and show no suicidal tendencies or symptoms of depression. Staff can do little in those situations.

By the time I had found a way of travelling south another day had passed. I thought the story was subsiding; the Home Secretary did not. We had a sharp exchange about whether I should make a public statement and give interviews. He wanted some of the media comment rebutted and thought I should do it. I felt that might simply add fuel to the fire. The decision quickly became academic as interest in Fred West was replaced by news of a riot at Everthorpe prison on Humberside. I could hardly believe our bad luck. Fortunately the Everthorpe disturbance was minor and quickly brought under control, with no injuries and only superficial damage to the prison. But it was a bitter blow to our credibility, coming hard on the heels of West's death. It was the beginning of what may rank as one of the worst weeks in the history of the Prison Service.

Over the following day, while I shuttled between studios in Swindon and Bristol explaining what had happened, dogged by a taxi that did not turn up and another that broke down, media interest in West's death and the Everthorpe disturbance began to wane. My driver, Les, picked me up but on the way home the telephone rang. It was the incident unit, reporting another outburst of rioting at Everthorpe – not serious in itself but adding to the problems of the previous days. I asked Les to head for headquarters.

In the incident suite, I was reassured that all was well in hand and that the prison would shortly be back under control. One of the governors tried to interrupt the briefing. He had other news for me. I told him I would be available very shortly.

When I returned to my office the governor followed me. His face had an anxious haunted look, suggesting something much more serious than a minor disturbance. Three prisoners had escaped from Parkhurst, a maximum-security dispersal prison. Two were category A prisoners, the third a category B. I was devastated. After all the precautions we had taken, the warnings, the extra searching, it was beyond belief that this could happen. I established the facts, such as they were, and briefed the Home Secretary. I sat for a few minutes before speaking to Michael Forsyth. I had to consider my own position. There had been two appalling escapes within four months and the media would be baying for a head to roll. Was I personally culpable? Would it help the Prison Service if I resigned? Was it actually worth enduring all the public exposure and stress? I then asked Forsyth whether he thought I should resign. He gave an unequivocal 'no': it would be the wrong thing to do and unnecessary. However difficult – even impossible – the situation seemed, I would not be able to look myself in the face if I walked away from it. With Forsyth's endorsement, I decided to press on.

Only two weeks earlier, I had appointed Richard Tilt as director of security, so I dispatched him to Parkhurst to conduct a rapid investigation. It was already becoming clear how the escape had taken place. The prisoners had used their privileged jobs in the engineering workshop to manufacture a replica key and the parts of an ingenious ladder, which had been concealed among other tools and stock in the workshop. During the regular evening session in the gymnasium they had carefully intimidated and hood-winked staff. Counts of prisoners had not been carried out, and those who were in the gym were not kept under continuous surveillance. The prisoners used their key to escape from a back door undetected. Failure to perform the routine prisoner counts meant that their absence went unnoticed for hours. Further use of the key enabled them to reach the workshop, collect the parts of the ladder and wire cutters, cut through the inner fence and scale the outer wall. The video cameras on the perimeter had been pointing in the wrong direction, because the prison had failed to put trained people in the central control room. It was a fatal combination of inefficiency and bungling by the prison, combined with cunning calculation on the part of prisoners. Three dangerous prisoners were at large on the Isle of Wight, and everybody was asking questions.

At the end of that week, on 6 January, I had a long-arranged commitment to visit Camp Hill prison, adjacent to Parkhurst, to present an award to their industrial workshops. It was an opportunity to visit Parkhurst as well. There was bound to be a media circus at the prisons, but we managed to avoid it until we arrived at Camp Hill. The plan was that we would drive straight into the gatelock without stopping to talk to the press, but fate intervened. Richard Tilt had arrived from Parkhurst immediately before us and was inside the gatelock, so I had to wait outside in the car, surrounded by yelling cameramen, while his car went through. It made for good pictures and good copy, but it was an uncomfortable few minutes, which elicited sympathy from Howard when I spoke to him later.

It was obvious that the POA was obstructing Tilt's inquiry into the escape by instructing its members not to co-operate fully. This seemed to merit a break in the public silence that I had agreed with Howard and we decided I should make a statement. He suggested this was an opportunity to 'finish off the POA for good'. I was not so sure. To prepare the ground, I talked to the governor, John Marriott, and a brief statement was drafted. Audrey Nelson told the throng of journalists and cameramen outside Parkhurst that they had to pick one of their number to do the interview, which would then be syndicated between them. They grumbled furiously, but eventually chose Channel 4. The next problem was where to do the interview. With the inquiry under way and the prison tense, we ended up in a cramped space in the gate lodge. I was perched near the end of an X-ray machine, with the cameraman squashed against the opposite wall.

I then had to do the late evening news programmes, which meant a frantic dash to the ferry, followed by a high-speed drive to the Southampton studios of Meridian Television. There were warm-up questions about the POA, but then the heat was turned on me. Was I going to resign? Why not? Would anyone take responsibility? It was the toughest interview I had faced so far. A call from Howard afterwards again expressed sympathy, but it seemed a little less genuine this time. And – just to finish the evening off – news then came through that prisoners at the special secure unit at Full Sutton had exploded aerosol cans in an oven. It was only a minor aggravation, but given the jumpy state of the press, the Prison Service and the Home Secretary, it was yet another cross to bear.

A busy weekend followed. The Home Secretary was scheduled to make a statement about the Parkhurst escape, as well as the death of Fred West and the Everthorpe riot, the following Tuesday, 10 January. We needed to gather data and draft statements. The absence of geophones was emerging as one of the critical issues. The governor of Parkhurst had identified the need over ten years earlier, and the local MP had taken up the cause with ministers. Nothing had been done, but the reasons for such inaction were shrouded in mystery. Was it really, as some claimed, because they would not work properly while Parkhurst was undergoing a major building programme, or was it that there simply was not enough money and they were too low down the priority list? John Ingman, who was heading the Home Secretary's Prison Service monitoring unit at that time, happened to have been in charge of the capital-spending programme in the Prison Service when the question of geophones had been raised. He seemed a worried man as we worked through the early hours of Sunday morning, trying to piece together what had really happened.

The usual pre-statement Sunday drafting session with Howard passed off relatively quietly, but we were still waiting for Tilt's preliminary report on the escape, which was not due until the Monday evening. When it arrived, Tilt, Philippa Drew, Tony Butler and I considered its implications. It was damning. Security procedures had not been enforced, the duty governor was often at home instead of in the prison in flat contradiction of the security manual requirements, and John Marriott had failed to implement all the corrective action on security deficiencies identified by the Chief Inspector the previous October, despite categorical assurances to me that he had. In short, it was a shambles. We quickly concluded that Marriott could not stay on as governor. He would rapidly become embroiled in the inquiry while we needed someone who could give their single-minded attention to sorting the prison out. We discussed whether to suspend Marriott and send him home on full pay, or move him to another job. The Code of Discipline, which I had the responsibility of policing, was unequivocal. If we could find an alternative job for him until the disciplinary investigation was complete, we should do so – suspension always carried with it an implication of guilt, and could affect his ability to secure a fair hearing. We decided that others should be moved as well, because of their involvement with the escape. I dispatched Drew to Parkhurst the following morning to make arrangements for Marriott's move as soon as an orderly handover of command could be achieved.

The following morning I briefed Howard ahead of his statement to the House. I told him what we had decided about Marriott and why. He exploded. Simply moving the governor was politically unpalatable. It sounded indecisive. It would be seen as a fudge. He challenged the basis of the decision. The Code of Discipline was produced, and legal advisers were called in. I told him that we had suitable alternative work for Marriott in a non-operational role. The Home Secretary was thinking of his personal safety that afternoon, and he remained adamant. If I did not change my mind and suspend Marriott, he would have to consider overruling me. His tone was menacing and I was left with no illusions about the possible implications for me. He asked me to leave the meeting and reconsider my decision, with the deadline an hour or so later.

It was the sort of reaction I had expected. Over the preceding months each new incident had provoked anxious and aggressive questioning from ministers, and from the Home Secretary in particular, about why governors or other staff were not being held accountable – a euphemism for being disciplined or, preferably, fired. This new philosophy of management by walking the plank revealed a profound ministerial misunderstanding of the way organizations work and staff are motivated – which was hardly surprising, given their limited experience of running anything involving large numbers of people. They had no understanding that positive motivation is more powerful than sanctions, or that indiscriminate punishment of staff only leads to fear, inactivity and elaborate backside protection. Howard was shocked when I told him that the service provided by headquarters might suffer for a time as a result of the major restructuring and shrinkage we had announced. 'Why should that be?' he asked. 'I would have expected those whose jobs were under threat to simply work harder.' Ministers generally thought we were soft on staff, even though the number of staff dismissed in the Prison Service was proportionately much higher than in the police.

I left the meeting to consider my options and joined Richard Wilson in his office. He looked grim-faced, and said that things were getting 'white hot' and 'in danger of going nuclear'. Later he told me that Howard had said that if I did not suspend Marriott he would go down to the House that afternoon and announce that he had sacked me. The risks to my personal position were serious, but the Code of Discipline was part of Marriott's employment contract, and I had a duty to interpret it fairly. In any event, the code made it quite clear that decisions had to be made by line management in a chain which ran from me to the permanent secretary and on to the Cabinet Secretary. Intervention in the decision by the Home Secretary would have been quite improper. Further checking confirmed that we did indeed have a substantive job which Marriott could do, and I made up my mind that I would sacrifice neither principle nor a fair hearing for Marriott in the interests of my own job or political expediency.

Back in Richard Wilson's office the mood seemed to have changed a little. He showed me a paragraph that he had drafted for the Home Secretary's statement that afternoon. Its language was strident and emotive but it contained no reference to suspension. Instead, it said;

The present governor is today being removed from his duties at Parkhurst. Pending the outcome of a disciplinary investigation and any subsequent proceedings, he will not run any other prison in the Prison Service. When he has completed any assistance that he needs to give to the various inquiries now in hand, he will take up non-operational duties elsewhere.

There was no time to discuss it before we were summoned back into Howard's office. (I later discovered that the interval had been occupied with frenetic telephone calls to No. 10. Wilson had advised Howard not to overrule me on the treatment of Marriott, and Howard had eventually accepted his advice.) As we resumed the meeting the new paragraph was distributed, and Howard asked whether we had any comments. I said I had a problem with the use of the word 'today', as I had given Drew discretion to determine the exact timing. Howard raised both hands and insisted that the word must stay in. Forsyth signalled down the table for me to shut up. I made another attempt to protest about the tone of the statement, but was again overruled. There was little more that I could do. Howard had decided what he was going to say in full knowledge of what we were actually doing.

The main business done, the meeting broke up. As we left, Joan McNaughton told me with a knowing look that she had recorded in her notebook my objections to the use of the word 'today'. She obviously anticipated possible trouble. But my objections were not recorded in the official minutes, according to which: 'In later discussions, the form of words which the Home Secretary eventually used in his statement to the House was agreed, avoiding any reference to suspension . . . the proper answer to the question whether Mr Marriott was suspended was "no".' The minutes did not specify whether the 'agreement' was unanimous.

I went away to consider the consequences of what Howard had decided. Did his inclusion of the word 'today' mean that I needed to give new instructions to Drew that Marriott was to vacate the prison instantly? I decided it did not. The action had been initiated 'today', and it was immaterial whether the handover was completed that day or in the next few days: what mattered was that it should be orderly.

Meanwhile, down at Parkhurst, the text of Howard's statement had been read over the telephone to Drew. The area manager, Peter Kitteridge, suggested to Drew that the inclusion of the word 'today' meant that they must get Marriott to hand over command of the prison that afternoon. Drew agreed, and they arranged for a handover to the deputy governor. The seeds were sown of a continuing controversy involving accusations that the Home Secretary had interfered and then lied in public and to the House of Commons.

I went down to the Commons to listen to Howard's statement. He faced a noisy House. MPs, fresh from their long Christmas recess, had copious supplies of indignation and outrage available for a Secretary of State in trouble. The smell of blood was in the air, and the vultures were hovering on the benches opposite. The Home Secretary was challenged by Gerald Kaufman about whether he or anyone else would take responsibility for events at Parkhurst. 'Where does the buck stop?' he was asked.

After an indecently short interval, and without mature reflection, Mr Howard uttered his now famous mantra for the first time: 'I am responsible to Parliament for policy. The Director General . . . is responsible for operational matters.' He went on to say that 'In his report Mr Tilt has not indicated any policy decision of mine that can be held to have caused in any way the breakout from Parkhurst.' I was grateful when he added that since I had become head of the Prison Service 'a great deal of progress had been made'. The Prison Service, he told the House, 'is clearly going through a difficult time. The Director General is the best person to take it through that difficult time.'

The reference to Marriott had been delivered with considerable venom and had the Conservative backbenches cheering. It caused a flurry of media interest that evening, with both Howard and I denying that Marriott had been suspended or sacked, and making it clear that the decision to move him had been an operational one that I, not the Home Secretary, had taken. The following morning's press reflected none of those corrective statements. Someone, presumably Howard's special advisers, had been briefing the lobby correspondents. The result was a rash of headlines, which talked of 'dismissal', 'sacking', 'firing' and 'axing'. No mention was made of suspension, still less of his being moved to other duties. It was an outrageous misrepresentation which had staff in the Prison Service up in arms. They looked to me for a lead, and I quickly wrote to all governors in order to 'clarify the decisions which were taken within the Prison Service for operational reasons about staffing at Parkhurst'. I went on to say:

We concluded that the very serious events at Parkhurst and the pending inquiries made it necessary for there to be a change in governor at the prison. John Marriott is rightly noted and appreciated for his dedication, humanity, courage and innovation. I am, therefore, appalled by the misleading and inaccurate reporting there has subsequently been in the media. John Marriott has not been 'sacked' or 'suspended'. There is no prejudgement of any disciplinary proceedings which may follow the disciplinary investigation and there is no ban on John governing prisons subsequently.

It was a timely letter. The Prison Governors' Association had a long-standing meeting with me later that afternoon, and its members arrived in a state of high indignation. We were heading for serious trouble with our most important group of staff. I brought the letter to the meeting, and they departed at least a little mollified. The same could not be said of the Home Secretary when he read the front-page headlines in the *Daily Mail* the following morning, describing a row between us. He told me that both my letter and the *Mail* article were most unfortunate. People would think there was a rift between us, but it was too late to do anything now. I reflected ruefully that the rift had been caused by political spin-doctoring.

The suspicion that Marriott had been shabbily treated lingered on. Appearing before the Home Affairs Select Committee a week later, I was pressed on the subject by Chris Mullin, who asked whether the Home Secretary had told me to make sure that Marriott was off the premises by the afternoon. Gerry Bermingham wanted to know if Marriott's treatment was the result of political interference. Fortunately I was able to answer 'no' to both questions. I was not asked whether I had been pressed to suspend Marriott, nor whether I had agreed to the inclusion of the word 'today' in Howard's statement. The rules governing evidence by civil servants to select committees precluded me from going beyond the question to explain what had been discussed in Howard's office. That would be up to him when he appeared in front of the same committee the following week. He did not take the opportunity to answer more fully.

SIR IVAN LAWRENCE QC MP (CHAIRMAN): Was it your decision; was it the Director General's decision; was it a decision of both of you taken together; whose decision was it that the governor of Parkhurst should, pending the outcome of the investigation, be removed as governor?

MICHAEL HOWARD: The Director General's.

LAWRENCE: Is that an operational decision; or is it a policy decision?

HOWARD: It is an operational decision.

JOHN GREENWAY MP: ... have you made it your policy to suggest to the Director General, Mr Lewis, that where incidents as grave as this do occur he should look to see whether people should be transferred to other duties pending the internal inquiries?

HOWARD: ... there was no need therefore for me to talk to him or make the suggestion which you have indicated.

While all this was going on, the general inquiry into prison security had been getting under way. It was a strong indication of things to come that Howard only told me about it after he had sold the idea to the Prime Minister, when all the arrangements had been put in place. He had instructed Wilson to find him someone to do the job: his only requirement was that it should be a general. Wilson produced a list. The first two declined. The third, General Sir John Learmont, accepted. Once described as an expert on billets and blankets, the only candidate got the job on the first interview. Howard eventually told me of his plans shortly before the announcement of Woodcock. He introduced the subject sheepishly, presumably unaware that I already knew. I told him that it was a great mistake. The last thing the Prison Service – or, indeed, the Home Secretary – needed was another inquiry. But the Home Secretary's political concerns were paramount: inquiry addiction had taken hold. Nothing less, he said, would satisfy the Commons. He little understood the impact of such inquiries on organizations like the Prison Service.

At our first meeting General Learmont began by saying: 'You should know something about me. Started in the ranks, rose to become a four-star general.' He was a big man, with a bull neck, a propensity to bark orders and an attention span measured in seconds rather than minutes. His KCB and CBE were so important to him that, when they were omitted from the inquiry's first letterhead, he carefully inscribed them on each letter in his own hand. Known as 'Raging Bull' by his former army colleagues, he displayed his prejudices openly, seeming to believe that it was the misfortune of any organization not to be the army, and that the best he could do was re-shape it along military lines. As a former quartermaster general, he believed that most problems resulted from government underfunding, and in the early stages offered to do all he could to secure extra money for the Prison Service.

Spirits in the Prison Service sank to a new low when Woodcock was appointed one of his deputies. We feared a re-run of the Woodcock prejudices, and the call to arms of the same scriptwriter. The other members of the Learmont quartet were Gary Dadds, a well-meaning but ineffectual former regional director of the Prison Service, and Major-General Mike Heath, described as the general's right-hand man. We faced the prospect with gloom – an inquiry led by a general of firm opinions who knew nothing of prisons but already had all the answers.

Learmont soon revealed the approach he would be taking. A posse of hastily recruited policemen was to report directly to Woodcock on the Parkhurst investigation. Learmont and Woodcock meanwhile would roam the Prison Service, dipping into the issues that interested them with a few foreign visits to see how things were done overseas. Back in the Home Office Major-General Mike Heath would do much of the donkey work.

Reports began to filter back about Learmont's visits. He was good with the troops. As befits a former private, he held those at the bottom of the hierarchy in the highest esteem, but had less time for management. His inquiry was highly complimentary about much of what was happening in prisons but bitterly critical of headquarters, yet although the team visited thirty-nine prisons it never set foot in Prison Service headquarters, against which it directed much of its fire.

We were prepared for some systematic data-gathering, but requests for information were sparse. Though dealing with security, they asked for no information on the numbers of escapes or how they had happened – an obvious starting point given their task of finding ways to reduce them, and one which Learmont later acknowledged he had simply 'missed'. Major-General Heath had been briefed to examine the organization of the Prison Service. He called for the telephone directory and pored over staff numbers and job functions from this uniquely unhelpful source. The style of the inquiry was to listen to oral and written views from a variety of individuals and organizations. Views which accorded with those of the inquiry team were incorporated, often verbatim; alternative opinions were rarely debated let alone included in the final report.

John Bartell turned out to be a man after Learmont's own heart. His protestations that the POA only wanted to help were taken at face value, despite similar protestations to every previous inquiry and decades of obstruction and subversion. I was also intrigued by a reference in the first draft to 'a body of psychological research' which had confirmed that disciplined work in prison reduced reoffending rates. Further inquiry revealed the body to be one psychologist whom the team happened to meet during a visit to Barcelona. Another reference in the first draft to 'an independent consultant [who] was examining the management and leadership of the service during this inquiry' turned out to be someone who had never been employed by the service but had met a few governors while touting for business – which, he admitted to me, was why he had been to see Learmont. I suppose I should not have been surprised when my own suggestions were enthusiastically received, or that I was once asked by Learmont to 'give me a paragraph on that and I'll put it in the report'. He duly did – verbatim.

The thoroughness and openness of the Woolf inquiry contrasted sharply with the superficiality and covertness of Learmont. Woolf made his agenda widely known, provided plenty of opportunities for formal submissions and open discussion, and reported evidence from all shades of opinion before drawing his conclusions. Learmont's agenda evolved on the hoof as he happened to stumble across issues that took his fancy, such as televisions or home leave. Evidence was given in secret and only published selectively, with no opportunity to cross-examine its validity. It was not an impressive way to conduct a major public inquiry.

Tumim could barely disguise his contempt for Woodcock, whom he considered a stupid man. He was slightly more charitable towards Learmont, judging him 'decent but naïve'. A few days after he had had dinner with them both, I received a letter from the inquiry team to the effect that they would be recommending that Tumim should be given a specific role during inspections to review security and the extra staff to go with it. Had they troubled to find out they would have learned that the Chief Inspector had always had such powers, and had reported on security in his individual prison inspections and annual reports, though after Whitemoor a disclaimer was added to the effect that the inspectorate did not perform security audits. The public might justifiably want to know why not.

In February 1995 Sir David Yardley had concluded the disciplinary investigation into the Whitemoor escapes. It cleared me of any negligence and recommended no disciplinary action against anyone, including Barclay. Howard was outraged – concerned that he might look a fool after announcing the disciplinary inquiry with brave words about tracking down those who were to blame. Yardley, in his view, had completely failed in his job and fudged the difficult decisions. Howard's guns now turned on Barclay, whom he person-ally blamed for the lax regime in the special secure unit at Whitemoor that had led to the escape. Under the Code of Discipline the decision on what to do about Barclay fell to Tony Butler, the director of personnel. After proper deliberation, he decided to accept the Yardley recommendation but Howard wanted Barclay to be fired – even though he had left the prison four months before the escape happened.

Home Office legal advisers were summoned. We were subjected to Howard's intense courtroom-style cross-examination as he tested to destruction the advice he was being given – an experience with which many in the Home Office had become familiar. The lawyers stuck to their guns, telling him he could do it but would have to pay compensation, perhaps in the region of a quarter of a million pounds. Howard would have none of this. He was sure that there might be some chink that would allow Barclay to be dismissed without a proper hearing and at no cost to the taxpayer and he insisted they get senior counsel's opinion. Home Office officials trod the well-worn path from Queen Anne's Gate to the Middle Temple chambers of David Pannick QC, the recipient of many briefs from the Home Office. Pannick repeated the internal lawyers' view, leaving a frustrated and angry Howard robbed of his vengeance.

The case of Private Lee Clegg provided another cause of tension in the spring of 1995. Clegg was being held at Wakefield in the early stage of his life sentence for the murder of a girl while on checkpoint duty in Northern Ireland. The public, political and media campaign to have his sentence overturned was growing stronger by the day. In theory it was a matter for the Northern Ireland Secretary, Sir Patrick Mayhew, but Howard wanted to be seen to respond to public opinion, even if it meant upstaging Mayhew's decision on Clegg's release.

Wakefield was a big austere Victorian prison – the very model of a Howard institution, but too unpleasant for an allegedly wrongly convicted soldier of the Crown, regarded by some as a folk hero. A meeting was called. The Home Secretary said he wanted Clegg moved to an open prison so that he would be more comfortable. I explained the consequences of giving preferential treatment to Clegg over other life sentence prisoners. His safety could not be guaranteed in an open prison, we would be powerless to prevent a media circus, and a legal challenge would almost certainly follow. I could not agree to such exceptional treatment and would only do it if given a specific order by the Home Secretary. The discussion raged backwards and forwards. The legal adviser counselled caution, Howard argued the political advantage of action. The special adviser, my operational director and the permanent secretary all weighed in. Eventually Howard found himself isolated. He realized that the odds were stacked against him and that if the decision backfired his head would be on the block. The matter was not raised again.

Perhaps the lesson had been learned. When Clegg was eventually released, a message came from Howard's office to say that he regarded the handling of it as entirely an operational matter. If anything went wrong it would be down to me. Fortunately it was one of our successes. Clegg was spirited out of Wakefield in the early hours in a high-security van and on to the army camp for which he was destined, without the press corps assembled outside the prison even realizing that he had gone.

Market testing public sector prisons also occupied some of my time with Howard. We had been planning to put the management of some of our worst prisons out to competitive bids, but, with the rapid rise in the prison population and attention focused on new prisons, we delayed an announcement of the market testing programme until August 1994. Initially we identified a short-list of the worst performing prisons in the public sector as potential candidates. It was suggested that it would be helpful to delay announcing the selected prisons until after the Conservative Party conference.

But then the POA showed that it had not lost its guerrilla skills entirely: we were accused of failing to provide all the necessary information required by law for collective bargaining. The union put in an application to the Central Arbitration Committee. We remained confident, since this was not a matter, like pay, over which we had an agreement to bargain. But whatever the ultimate outcome, the POA had secured a powerful means of delay. The natural inertia of the committee, combined with the calculated inability of the POA to be available on the suggested dates, resulted in a six-month delay before the hearing in early 1995. The outcome was extraordinary. The employer representative said that this was clearly not a matter for collective bargaining; the labour representative said that everything was subject to collective bargaining; the chairman, Solomon-like, agreed with them both, dismissing most of the POA claims, but informing us that we ought to provide more information anyway – which we duly did.

By then our selection of the worst performing prisons was out of date and we needed to think again. In the previous six months, the service had initiated some of its most ambitious programmes in decades – radically cutting back on home leave, introducing mandatory drug-testing and drug treatment programmes, severely curtailing prisoner privileges and tightening security. The prison population was still rising inexorably, and the system was approaching bursting point. Could we afford the distraction and potential disruption of a market test as well? In our opinion we could not.

Michael Forsyth quickly saw our point. He was as keen an advocate of the private sector as anyone else, but had the political nous to realize that proceeding against the advice of the Prison Service would leave ministers exposed if anything went wrong. Howard was less easily persuaded. He had been a staunch supporter of the development of the private sector since his arrival at the Home Office and did not relish anything that might look like a backing off, and still less so if it might be construed as a victory for the POA. He wanted to know what had changed, why we could not, for example, remove all prisoners from the prison concerned so that there was no risk of disruption, and what guarantee there was that things would be different in a few months' time. During those meetings it was hard to believe that everyone was trying to protect Howard's skin, such was the hostility with which they were interrogated.

One of the final meetings was particularly stormy. We rehearsed all the arguments and heard all the counter-arguments. Much spleen was vented against the Central Arbitration Committee and other departments who were being unhelpful. Then Philippa Drew, the operational director who had joined me for the occasion, threw an unforeseen grenade in our midst. The whole point of market testing, she announced, was not to actually do it, but to use the continuing threat of it to stimulate better performance. Nowhere had this been suggested in any of our submissions to Howard, nor was it the agreed Prisons Board view. Howard exploded: how dare she come to a meeting and introduce new arguments that were not part of the briefing? Drew spluttered apologetically, and totally withdrew her remarks. Perhaps they had helped to persuade Howard to accept the prudence of our recommendation, but they did serious damage to his relationship with Philippa Drew, already injured by the escapes at Whitemoor and Parkhurst, both of which fell within her area of responsibility.

Richard Wilson confided later that Howard had flatly vetoed his plans to move Drew to a senior position responsible for equal opportunities, dismissing her as a 'broken reed'. But he did not allow for the humanity of the Civil Service when it came to looking after its own. I was in Wilson's office one day when the question of a new head of personnel for the Home Office came up. Names were being bandied about and I mentioned hers. Wilson reacted instantly: 'She'd be excellent for the job.' There was a short pause and then he asked, 'Does she know anything about personnel?' Needless to say she got the job.

Our recommendation of a delay for a few months was eventually accepted. Nearly two years later there has still been no move to market test an existing prison. There will be no effective long-term competition unless market testing can be shown to work and contracts moved between public and private sectors, and vice versa. Otherwise the development of the private sector will simply have created a number of smaller monopolies.

For all his advocacy of the private sector, we had been completely unsuccessful in persuading Howard to visit any private prisons during his first two years in office. Indeed he was reluctant to visit prisons at all and 'press the flesh' with staff. Had he done so more, he might have been regarded with less suspicion and hostility. He had visited only eleven in his first year as Home Secretary, and a further five in his second year.

As Learmont continued his investigations other elements of the final denouement were beginning to fall into place. Richard Wilson had persuaded Howard that he should tackle the vexed question of my contract, which was due to expire at the end of 1995 unless extended for up to another two years. Discussions had been deferred because of the Woodcock Report, but now something had to be done. Questions were being asked by MPs and the press, and there were no easy answers. Initially it was proposed to defer a decision by several months until August, but then Wilson said he had persuaded Howard that the contract should be extended and changed to a conventional one-year rolling agreement. I agreed since in theory it provided the greater certainty we all needed. But like so many things that year, even this went sour.

The ink was hardly dry on my new contract when I took off for

America on the fact-finding visit with Michael Forsyth referred to earlier. While Forsyth and I were being briefed at the Oak Park Heights maximum-security prison in Minnesota, a call came through from a jumpy and angry Wilson. He told me that both *The Times* and the *Guardian* had printed positive stories about the extension of my contract, and I guessed that Howard had learned of the contract extension from the papers, which would not have pleased him. Wilson had initially suspected me of leaking the details, but the inaccuracies in the reports convinced him that I had not done so.

Howard obviously did not like the positive tone of the articles, and insisted on responding instantly with an arranged parliamentary question. He was offered two draft answers by his chief legal adviser, Michael Saunders. One said that my contract was now subject to twelve months' notice; the other, which he chose, did more to confuse than clarify the issue: 'His contract has, however, been varied so that as from 22 April 1995, he continues to serve as Director General for a period of twelve months, which may be rolled forward on a month-by-month basis.' The choice of such obscure wording was clearly deliberate: it gave the impression that I was on a month's notice.

Forsyth was as livid about it as I was, but he was unable to persuade Howard to change his mind. My staff were in despair at this calculated piece of treachery, but we quickly drafted a message to governors which said that I had 'agreed to continue for a further period of up to two years and that included in the agreement with the Home Office was a provision that either side must give twelve months' notice'. Saunders's subsequent legal advice to Howard confirmed that my explanation was correct.

Other areas of business seemed to be going well. We had introduced the biggest policy changes on home leave for prisoners in forty years, and the numbers of prisoners going out had been slashed by half. We were worried that it might provoke disruption, particularly as it had been introduced with very little notice: after a year spent debating the policy, Howard wanted it in place within a few weeks. Our success was not a matter of luck but of excellent planning, with better training and preparation than ever before. We had also introduced drug testing, another potential source of provocation, but once again the new-found management skills in the service ensured that this was done without disturbances. Escapes continued to fall sharply, and we were holding our own in accommodating the rising prison population without having to use police cells.

In the meantime I had to make changes in the Prisons Board. Philippa Drew succumbed to the pressure of the previous six months, and wanted to get out of the Prison Service as fast as possible. I was fortunate in being able to recruit Alan Walker, who had been number two in the much smaller Scottish Prison Service but was retiring early as a result of their restructuring. He offered just the mix of energy, determination and management discipline we needed. It was good to find an ally who was a pragmatist and shared my desire to make things happen. I had planned to appoint a deputy director general at about this time because I needed some assistance in order to provide breathing space and thinking time. Richard Tilt was a candidate, but I did not feel comfortable about appointing him and Wilson considered him unsuitable. He thought Walker would be a more likely candidate once he had spent some time as an operational director. Drew's departure provided an opportunity to complete a piece of unfinished business: I decided to strip out the last remaining bits of policy responsibility from the two operational directors. The other operational director, Tony Pearson, was resigned to the inevitable.

Learmont had originally promised his report for the end of March. But he found the Prison Service more complex than expected, and the first draft was not ready until mid-May. He was then forced to adopt the Salmon procedures that had so frustrated Woodcock, giving those featured in the report a chance to respond. Initially, I was the only person who received a complete copy of the draft report. The covering letter started innocuously enough:

In the interests of natural justice I am letting you know that the report of my inquiry into security in HM Prison Service and independent assessment of the circumstances leading to the escape of three prisoners from Parkhurst prison on 3 January will, based on current evidence, be critical of some procedures, practices and aspects of the command structure not only at Parkhurst but throughout the service.

I would emphasize that my inquiry has no disciplinary function and no information gleaned from you can be used in any future proceedings without your consent.

A cursory reading of the draft showed this to be an understatement – the report was emotively critical, repeatedly singling out individuals, including myself, for pointed criticism. The criticisms clearly implicated other members of the board, and I insisted that Learmont should give them complete copies, to which he agreed. A state of shock descended on the board. Indignation was expressed about the lack of understanding and objectivity, and the secrecy concerning sources of evidence. I talked it through with Richard Tilt, who thought it was a travesty and grossly unfair to many people, myself included.

We got down to work to prepare our response. It was difficult to deal with conclusions when the evidence on which they were based was not disclosed, but a request to Learmont to provide us with the necessary details was met with a blank refusal. We considered legal action. This was not the way the Salmon procedures were supposed to work. At that point the board hit a difficulty. Home Office lawyers were already advising Learmont, but Michael Saunders, the head of the legal advisers branch, was sympathetic to our plight. He arranged to divide his forces so that one half advised Learmont and the other half, across a Chinese wall, advised us. The advice we received was unequivocal: the way Learmont was proceeding – not providing us with access to the evidence on which he based his criticisms – was contrary to natural justice. The Home Office sought the advice of counsel on behalf of the board – yet again from the ubiquitous David Pannick QC. He sympathized with our views, but advised that it would be difficult to make a case stick in the courts. Meanwhile, Wilson had been alerted to our legal inquiries and was becoming very worried. He asked me for an assurance that we would not launch legal action without giving him prior warning.

Wilson had, in fact, received a private copy of the Salmon draft of the Learmont report, even though he was not the subject of any criticism. It was quite improper of Learmont to have given the Home Secretary's principal Civil Service adviser a copy before the Salmon process had been completed and the document finalized, since it created a risk of allegations being made about Wilson or even the Home Secretary having influenced the final report. From my point of view it was quite helpful, in that it gave me an opportunity to discuss the report with Wilson and talk about tactics. He was obviously shocked by its tone, and urged me to make sure that the board's Salmon response was robust and effective. He foresaw trouble if we were unable to change the tone of some of the comments.

The Whitemoor escape had once again raised the question of whether very dangerous prisoners – the exceptional-risk category A prisoners held in special secure units – should be restricted to closed visits, with armour-plated glass separating prisoner from visitor. It is commonplace in America, and prevents the smuggling of weapons, drugs and other contraband. But here the issue was intertwined with humanitarian principles and political anxieties, still more so since most of the highest-risk prisoners were IRA terrorists, and the Republicans already suspected Howard of deliberately making their lives more difficult. Woodcock had ducked this politically explosive issue, and Howard specifically asked Learmont to make a recommendation. The Salmon draft of his report in May had accepted the humanitarian arguments, and concluded that there should be no policy of mandatory closed visits:

4.26 The Inquiry's terms of reference required a specific examination of closed visits in respect of SSUs (more recently re-designated High Security Units). The only way to totally eradicate infiltration of goods during visits would be to instigate closed visits and searching of all visitors, prisoners and prison staff. Having given very careful consideration to the views expressed by Lord Woolf, HM Chief Inspector of Prisons, Prison Reform Groups and others, it is clear that the humanitarian argument requires that some physical contact should be allowed between inmates and family, in particular where children are involved.

4.27 In view of this, *mandatory closed visits are not recommended even in SSUs* but the option should be available in all prison establishments, to be used at the Governor's discretion for those prisoners suspected of or found misbehaving. [My italics]

I knew that closed visits were the only way to guarantee maximum security, and early in the summer I recommended to Howard that, if security was the overriding priority, such visits be introduced without delay, even though Learmont was coming to the opposite conclusion. Howard agreed: we went ahead, and he wrote to Learmont to tell him so. Learmont acknowledged Howard's letter with gratitude. When the final report appeared in September it had a very different recommendation to make. Instead of rejecting mandatory closed visits, the report now recommended them, in line with the policy already put into effect:

4.26 The Inquiry's terms of reference required a specific examination of closed visits in respect of Special Security Units (SSUs). The only way to eradicate infiltration of goods during visits is to instigate closed visits and the searching of all visitors, prisoners and prison staff. Having given very careful consideration to the views expressed by Lord Woolf, by HM Chief Inspector of Prisons, by Prison Reform Groups and by others, the Inquiry is clear that, *in most cases*, some physical contact should be allowed between inmates and family, in particular where children are involved.

4.27 *Mandatory closed visits are therefore recommended only for Exceptional Risk Category A prisoners.* By removing all physical contact between prisoners of this category and their visitors, the opportunity for passing illicit items should be eliminated. *The Inquiry feels that the absence of such measures of control poses a significant and unacceptable risk.*

4.28 In all other cases, the option of closed visits should be available in all secure prison establishments, to be used at the Governor's discretion for those prisoners suspected of or found misbehaving. [My italics]

Howard could now point to Learmont, so deflecting any accusations from the IRA or Sinn Fein. He used Learmont's revised recommendation to justify his decision to the House of Commons on 16 October, when he said that:

One particular aspect which I asked Sir John to consider was the extent to which visits should be closed. He recommends that there should be closed visits for exceptional-risk category A prisoners other than in exceptional circumstances. This coincides with the policy I introduced in June this year.

In the light of Howard's repeated claims to the House of Commons that Learmont and his views had been totally independent, unsuspecting MPs may not have realized that the similarity between Learmont's recommendation and the policy that had already been introduced was no coincidence. Members might then have gone on to wonder what was discussed at the meetings between Learmont and Howard which took place while the inquiry team was preparing its report.

I was not surprised to find the Home Secretary in good humour when we met for lunch at the Goring Hotel, just round the corner from the Home Office, in June. He even paid for the privilege, although it had been at my invitation. The tables were close together so the conversation was subdued. He said that all the principal changes he wanted to see in the service had been made or were underway and that he was encouraged by our progress. So he should have been: the service had advanced further in the current year than it had in the previous five. We chatted about Learmont. He already seemed to know a fair amount about the likely style and content of the report and that it would contain plenty of anecdote and hyperbole. He spoke confidentially about the need for the two of us to rebut the anecdotes with a barrage of hard, indisputable facts. I suggested, for example, that there was plenty of evidence from the Boards of Visitors about the state of morale in the service which contradicted Learmont's assessment. Howard agreed. He spoke as though we were once again working together as a team, but the real Howard was busy considering his options, and what he might do with me, when the report was published. My sixth sense told me that all might not be as it appeared. I sent him a warm letter of thanks for lunch, and summarized our conclusions. I acknowledged that we had a 'long way still to go', but carefully recorded the fact that he had been 'encouraged by progress'. I received no reply disagreeing with my summary.

The delay to the Learmont Report caused by implementing the Salmon procedures was compounded by the need for further work on costs. I had always believed that reports which made recommendations without identifying their costs were dangerous: the Prison Service and ministers would find it difficult to reject recommendations, but the money to implement them might never be forthcoming. Wilson agreed and pressed Learmont to cost his recommendations. To begin with Learmont would have none of it, then he relented, only to change his position again a few weeks later. Eventually costing work started. Wilson seemed pleased that publication would now have to wait until after the party conference season, when Parliament returned in October. By then, he hoped, the expected Cabinet reshuffle would have produced a new Home Secretary, who would down-play and disown Learmont as a creation of his predecessor.

It was not to be. Howard failed to get the promotion to Foreign Secretary that he had so hoped for. His brave face, and determined pronouncements on the importance of the job to be done at the Home Office, did nothing to conceal his disappointment. But we lost Michael Forsyth in a well-deserved promotion to the Cabinet as Secretary of State for Scotland. His pleasure in the promotion was much increased by his relief at escaping from the Home Office. He had never wanted to be there, he hated its conservatism and he did little to conceal his dislike of the way Howard operated. For us it meant a year spent teaching him what prisons were all about had been wasted – though Scottish prisons may have been the beneficiary. We had to start all over again with a new minister – the third in just two and a half years. The new recruit was Ann Widdecombe. She came with a formidable reputation as a hard-line right-winger, a tenacious anti-abortion campaigner and a notable convert to Catholicism. Even Forsyth confessed to being scared of her. Not easily intimidated, I resolved to make the most of this new partnership.

It was quickly apparent that she was tough, incisive and determined. Waffle did not survive long in her meetings. Spades were called spades. But her sincerity and willingness to listen quickly began to win her friends. She said 'thank you', and meant it. Her office frequently rang with unbridled laughter, often at her own expense. At the end of the day she opened the drinks cupboard and relaxed with whoever happened to be there. She sent personal hand-written notes instead of messages through private secretaries. She wanted civil servants to call her Ann rather than Minister – a frightening break with tradition that many civil servants found hard to cope with. Another minister once took her to task for allowing officials to use her first name. 'But,' she replied, 'God calls me Ann.' The matter was raised again in the presence of a Conservative peer. 'God calls me Ann,' she repeated. 'And God calls me Lord,' the peer replied.

Ann Widdecombe has provided the Prison Service with the visible ministerial support in Parliament and in public that it so badly needs, and of which it has been so seriously deprived by the Home Secretary. It is no mean achievement for a Prisons Minister to have visited some 100 of the 135 prisons in the country during her first eighteen months in office.

13

Unhappy Ending

Who said capital punishment was dead? The hanging was one of Tomb-
stone's finest. In years to come, old men will spit on the verandah and
gaze down main street to the sight of the gallows. 'That Michael Howard,'
they will recall, 'he tied a mean bowline. The guy was dead in seconds.'

The trial of Derek Lewis, on a charge of abetting the humiliation of a
Home Secretary, took place at 11 a.m. last Sunday in a room in the Home
Office. All was done by the book. Present were the victim, the judge, a
prosecutor, a defence lawyer and a jury of good men and true. It being
a Sunday, however, and the Home Secretary wanting to save money, he
generously performed all these duties himself. The trial opened with the
sentence: death. There followed a conversation in which Mr Lewis
pointed out that he had been acquitted of the charge by the same Mr
Howard in April. Mr Howard simply handed him a revolver and said he
wanted him dead by five o'clock. Mr Lewis refused. Okay, said Mr
Howard, by dawn.

Mr Lewis still refused. In that case, said Mr Howard, with 'great
sadness', you hang. On went the noose, whoosh went the trap, snap went
Mr Lewis's neck.

Simon Jenkins, *The Times*, 18 October 1995

Ministers returned from their long summer holidays to face the
usual rituals – the Tory Party conference and the annual torment
of a new public expenditure round. But Howard suffered the added
worry of the Learmont Report. According to Wilson, Howard
seemed to have got over his disappointment at losing the Foreign

Office to Malcolm Rifkind and was in a more positive mood. Wilson thought that Howard and I should stand shoulder-to-shoulder over the report and ride out the storm. But he remained edgy, fearing that Howard might take the easy way out in order to protect himself when the report was published. Wilson seemed to have genuine respect for the work I was doing in the Prison Service and feared for its future and for mine. He resurrected the psychological assessment done at the time of my interview to prove to Howard that the Home Office had got exactly what had been promised, and that there were no grounds for claiming faulty goods. We discussed the possible consequences of a decision to fire me. I had made it crystal clear that I would not go quietly, although I suspect he never alerted Howard to this. He had told me several times of his private fears that Howard would not survive if it came to a public battle, particularly as he felt I was more effective at handling the media. But Wilson was in a difficult position. His prospects of succeeding Sir Robin Butler as Cabinet Secretary and head of the Home Civil Service would not be enhanced by an unseemly battle at the Home Office, as a result of which it might possibly lose its most high-profile civil servant and a Secretary of State. Small wonder that he swung between fighting on my behalf and acceding to Howard's wishes. As he later commented, it was like being a spectator at a Greek tragedy, powerless to do anything to stop it.

PES, the annual public expenditure survey, takes up an inordinate amount of officials' and ministers' time and generates a good deal of huffing and puffing by the Treasury over the need to make cuts and by spending departments anxious to emphasize the indispensability of existing and proposed spending programmes. With an election looming, the pressure to make cuts was intense. The Treasury attacked our capital spending programmes, arguing disingenuously that most of them could be switched to the private finance initiative, and demanded that operating costs be reduced at a faster pace.

In the Prison Service itself, we were preoccupied by the forecast growth in the prison population. Home Office projections were based on historical trends and known changes in policy, but made no allowance for the fact that the Home Secretary's 'prison works' rhetoric was causing magistrates and judges to send more and more people to prison for longer and longer sentences. We were already outstripping our existing forecasts, and I had persuaded Howard that we should ask the Treasury for capital and operating funds to accommodate the predicted population growth beyond the normal Home Office trend. During September Treasury pressure convinced Howard that we were not going to win. He rolled over. The prison population increased as we had predicted and emergency money had to be found a year later to catch up. How much better if it had been properly planned.

I had warned Howard of the serious consequences of agreeing to massive capital spending cuts or an increased pace of cost reductions, neither of which the service could handle, but shortly after I left he again gave way to Treasury pressure and the Prison Service found itself facing a difficult future. (A year later, in the autumn of 1996, sanity prevailed and the cuts in operating budgets were restored in yet another expedient U-turn.)

The final Learmont Report, for which we had waited so anxiously, arrived on 27 September, the day of the annual Chevening gathering. Howard's copy was accompanied by a personal briefing from Learmont himself. For fear of leaks, copies were given only to me and a handful of carefully selected others. It was little better than the draft we had seen in May. A few gross inaccuracies had been removed, but no attempt had been made to provide a solid evidential base, or any degree of balance.

The Home Secretary's first thoughts were clearly for himself. Was there anything in it that might require him to resign? The general's covering letter pointed out that criticisms contained in the report affected people in the Prison Service through to board level, but that criticism stopped there. This was hardly the case, since the report heavily criticized the ways in which ministers set the service conflicting objectives, the enormous burden of ministerial involvement in the service, and the political legacy of deficiencies in industrial relations, training, management development and many other areas. And although the Prison Service statement of purpose, vision, goals and values was strongly criticized in the report, it had been personally approved by Howard and given a ringing endorsement in his speech to the Prison Service conference two years earlier. When challenged about this inconsistency by the Home Affairs Select Committee a year later, Learmont lamely replied that he was not sure who had taken these decisions.

However perverse the report's conclusions, Howard's personal needs seemed satisfied. But that might not be enough, and he turned to his own profession for immediate advice. Dinah Rose, the counsel who was later to represent the Home Office in my lawsuit, was asked whether he could legally sack me. Not even Ann Widdecombe knew that this step had been taken.

We may never know whether counsel advised Howard of the storm he was about to unleash. However, the practical advice was probably clear: he could remove me by breaking the terms of my contract, which he had extended only five months earlier. He might also be able to invoke the age-old royal prerogative, which allowed the Crown to dismiss any of its servants at will. But Howard needed to give at least some appearance of fair play.

The day after the report had been received, Wilson came to see me at Prison Service headquarters. Permanent secretaries were rarely spotted in such places. He had come in person to deliver a letter formally requesting that I provide Howard with my written response to the report. His demeanour was grave but sympathetic, and it occurred to me that Wilson would have made a wonderful undertaker. The letter was polite enough, but Howard's possible hidden agenda was clear. It said that he came to the report 'completely fresh not having been involved in the Salmon process and not having seen any part of it before' – though he was certainly aware of its thrust. The letter continued:

He will need to reach decisions on how to handle specific recommendations and we have action on this in hand. Equally important he will need to stand back and come to his own judgement about what it all adds up to, given his duty not only to account to Parliament for what has happened but also to assure Parliament personally that what needs to be done is being done to put things right.

In this connection I think it is important that he should have from you as soon as possible – certainly no later than the middle of next week – your own personal response, as distinct from that of the board, to the very serious criticisms which the report makes of the management of the service. He needs to know whether you accept them and to the extent that you do how you propose to put them right.

I was being asked, in effect, to produce a final document in my own defence. Our discussion was obviously painful for Wilson, and I found myself trying to cheer him up and bolster his confidence. After he left, I set out yet again for Chevening. Writing my response would have to wait until the weekend.

The Chevening ritual was little changed. The judges were attacking Howard – nothing new in itself – and he was trying to decide whether to counter-attack on the *Today* programme the following morning. Widdecombe read the report that evening and we discussed it briefly next day. She quickly saw through the superficial evidence and lack of analysis. Later that morning it was my turn to speak. I had a captive audience, so I began by reminding them of what I had said at the same conference two years earlier, before going on to outline our achievements against those expectations. I outlined the dramatic improvements in security performance, except for the two high-profile escapes; achievement of virtually all the targets Howard had set us; only one riot; 12,000 more prisoners squeezed into the jails; the POA dealt with; a private sector established; and new home leave, drugs and privilege schemes successfully launched. Most notable of all was the 80 per cent reduction in escapes. I set out our plans for the future, emphasizing how much was still to be done. It was a receptive audience, with one exception. Howard sat stony-faced and glassy-eyed throughout: it was either not what he wanted to hear, or his mind was on other things.

The defence document was easy to produce. Much of the material was already in the board's response to the Salmon process. I excluded those parts that were critical of the Home Secretary – provocation was unnecessary at this stage – and composed a persuasive covering letter. Widdecombe telephoned me at the weekend to find out how it was going, and insisted on coming in to Prison Service headquarters on the Sunday afternoon to lend her support. Wilson added his comments on the Monday, suggesting I lay more emphasis on my manifesto for the future. I deleted a few passages which might be considered inflammatory and the document was ready to be delivered, on schedule, on Tuesday 3 October. I waited for a reaction, but none came.

On the Thursday evening, Wilson, Widdecombe, myself, Tilt and other officials had a meeting with Howard to discuss Learmont's recommendations. Mindful of his predilection to accept recommendations, we had identified half of the 127 that we could support and did not involve money from the Treasury. There was another one-third which we supported in principle but needed money. None of this was surprising, since half the recommendations were being put into practice already or were being planned – and others had been suggested by us. There were only about twenty with which we disagreed. Richard Tilt and I ran through a series of slides explaining our opposition to them, but Howard gave them short-shrift. The recommendation to set and enforce sensible minimum security standards would cost a fortune when it came to upgrading insecure older prisons. Not so, Howard replied: one merely set the standards at the lowest common denominator of current security levels. In that way we could say the recommendations had been accepted without having to spend any money. We were making little progress.

When it came to the recommendation on Parkhurst – that it should be taken out of the dispersal system and consideration given to a replacement – we hit greater difficulties. Our slide listed six reasons for not accepting the recommendation, including increased security and control risks and additional expenditure of £8 million with no corresponding benefits. Howard intervened impatiently – not disagreeing with any of our arguments, but because we had omitted one crucial factor. 'If the recommendation is rejected and there is another escape from Parkhurst,' he explained, 'I would have to resign.' Eleven days later Howard announced that Parkhurst would cease to be a dispersal prison and that a replacement would be identified.

The following day, 5 October, Howard had a heated meeting with Wilson and Widdecombe. Howard apparently claimed that his mind was not made up about my future, but he sounded hostile. Widdecombe did most of the talking. Wilson had given up the struggle, either exhausted by it all or too concerned about his own future, but he had at least managed to persuade Howard that he could hardly make his decision without even talking to me. No conclusions were reached, but reports from the battlefield suggested – over-optimistically perhaps – that my fate now hung evenly in the balance.

A hurried meeting was set for the following Monday before Howard went off to the Party conference in Blackpool. It was supposed to last about half an hour, but as the time ticked by I knew it would be less. We started twenty-five minutes late and had no more than fifteen minutes in all. As always, Howard sat protected behind his long table. Widdecombe, Wilson and a private secretary were there. Howard looked shifty and embarrassed and kept apologizing sombrely that these were very difficult issues to deal with. He rarely made eye contact and when he did he seemed incredibly uncomfortable. He thanked me weakly for my input, referring nervously to a briefing note, presumably from Wilson. There were, he said, several paragraphs of the Learmont Report that concerned him and on which he would like my further views in writing. One of these involved the alarm bells which, according to Learmont, 'should have been constantly ringing throughout the Prison Service'.

I explained that alarm bells had been ringing for decades, trying to draw attention to poor direction, inadequate management, waste and misdirection of resources, and unreliable information and controls. Successive ministers had clearly been hard of hearing or grossly negligent, because far too little had been done before I arrived. The organization had been in a shambles. But until many of the basic problems of management and structure had been sorted out it was inevitable that some would be overlooked. Howard made no response, but merely reeled off the other paragraphs on which he wanted my written comments, apologized that he had to go, and brought the meeting to a close.

I had my work cut out to prepare a second defence document in the few days remaining. Wilson had obviously been warned off. He said he would like a copy of the second draft, but this time offered no comments. Widdecombe was as staunchly supportive as ever. The document was prepared, and I headed for Blackpool to talk its contents through with her on the margins of the conference. I was unaware then of the dressing-down Howard had given her for helping me with the previous defence document, and of Michael Forsyth's attempts to help. I had telephoned him the previous Sunday to talk things through. He asked whether I would be all right. I said I did not know, and he promised to talk to Howard; he doubted whether Howard would pay much attention to him, since he regarded him as a 'bit of a maverick'.

Feeling like a character from an unfinished John le Carré novel, I eventually found my way to a dingy back-street hotel reserved for lesser ministers and party officials. Widdecombe was already under surveillance by Howard's political advisers. We met in a small downstairs room visible through a window to those coming in and out of the hotel. Patrick Rock and Rachel Whetstone, the Home Secretary's political bodyguards, frequently found it necessary to pass by that window, keeping an eye on proceedings. As a punishment for her earlier help, Widdecombe had been banned from seeing the document I had produced, so we resorted to my telling her about it while she made *ad hoc* comments. That done, I headed back to London, taking with me Howard's hollow assurance, albeit second-hand, that he had not yet decided what to do.

Everything depended on his conference speech. Thursday, 12 October was the big day. It was a barn-storming performance, full of populist rhetoric that had the Tory faithful roaring in the aisles. Here was a Home Secretary promising to do even more to stem the rise in crime. It was a speech full of simple headline slogans: 'Crime is caused by criminals. It should never be excused. And criminals deserve to be punished', and 'Criminals all have one thing in common. They're all volunteers', and 'Release from prison. It comes too soon', and 'If you don't want the time, don't do the crime.' Sentencing was to become tougher and there were to be mandatory minimum sentences, modelled on the American pattern. Lord Taylor, then Lord Chief Justice, had been briefed only a few days previously, and had been incensed by Howard's evasiveness. He took the unprecedented step of saying so publicly as Howard received his end of speech ovation.

Howard's political imperative was so overriding that the Prison Service had not been consulted on the implications of these far-reaching penal proposals. His distrust of senior civil servants was so great that not even his principal adviser on criminal policy was allowed to be involved. I had been given an indication the previous day, but was forbidden to inform prisons until the morning of the speech, despite the real risk of disruption.

I finished the final version of my survival document that day and sent it to Blackpool by courier. It seemed fated. The courier missed his plane, and the document became temporarily lost in the conference postal system. Anxious calls to police and security officers followed. Ann Widdecombe, worried that it might have found its way into the wrong hands, went over to the Imperial Hotel and rooted around in the mail room. Eventually it was found and delivered to a Home Secretary still flushed with the approbation of the conference.

I heard nothing for three days. But in the interim there was much to do. The four non-executive directors on the Prisons Board were all very supportive. Two of them wrote to the Home Secretary expressing their views. Sir Duncan Nichol was the most recent non-executive appointment, but he also carried the most clout in government as a former chief executive of the Health Service. He wrote two letters to Wilson for onward transmission to Howard, setting out in trenchant terms his highly critical opinion of the Learmont Report and stating the need for continuity and support rather than change in the Prison Service:

If Sir John's report caused any question to be raised about the future of the top management team, especially the Director General, non-executive members would take a very serious view. Change would be severely damaging to the future of the service. If any such changes were contemplated, we would want to meet the Secretary of State before any decision was taken, in accordance with the right of access arrangements under which we were appointed.

His request was not granted.

On the Friday morning I had a long-standing engagement to give an important speech to the annual conference of the Parole Board in Northamptonshire, attended by thirty or so of the great and the good of the criminal justice world – judges, probation staff and former prison people. It was hard to concentrate on what I had to say about the future of the Prison Service; even harder still to perform my Civil Service duty of defending Howard's policies in the question session afterwards when I knew what was being plotted.

On Saturday the second page of the *Daily Express* ominously carried a big article headlined: 'Jail chief's head on the block over Parkhurst escape'. Widdecombe suspected a softening-up exercise, and the *Express* was a favourite paper in which to plant such stories.

On Sunday morning I went over to Queen Anne's Gate to see Ann Widdecombe. Howard was in the office, ostensibly preparing his statement to the House on Learmont for the following day. Widdecombe and I discussed the prospects, about which she was gloomy. She was called in to see Howard, and I waited in the same dingy conference room that I had waited in some two and a half years earlier before going into the press conference to announce my appointment. I could sense the vultures circling overhead. Howard's chief press officer was sitting awkwardly in the outer office, peering over a pile of newspapers. As I walked into Howard's office, I felt as though I was awaiting sentence from Judge Jeffries. The case had barely been heard, but the judge's arm was already stretching out for the black cap.

Howard began to intone his well-rehearsed lines in a lawyer's unemotional, clinical phrases:

This has been a very difficult decision for me. I have considered your submissions, for which I am very grateful. But your views are not compatible with those of the Learmont Report. I believe the criticisms in the Learmont Report make your position untenable.

I would like it to be as amicable as possible. I suggest that I tell the House tomorrow that we have agreed that the best interests of the Prison Service require a change in leadership and that you are resigning with effect from the end of December. If you agree with this I shall endeavour to be as complimentary as possible about your achievements . . . I would like your answer by 5 p.m. today.

In measured tones, I told him that his decision was quite wrong and unnecessary. I could not, I said, guarantee to respond before his deadline, which was wholly unreasonable given the time that he had sat on the report, and the much longer period he had known of its conclusions. Apparently, after I left, someone said, 'He won't go quietly.' Howard disagreed: 'Oh yes, he will. Wise counsel will prevail.'

I went back to the dingy conference room to wait for Ann Widdecombe to leave the meeting. She came in shortly afterwards, tears in her eyes. I could not help being struck by the absurdity of it all. I had just been fired on the decision of one man, and here was his right-hand minister in tears. There was little chance of reversing the decision now, but it was always worth a try. She was equally disinclined to give up, so I went to appeal.

Back at Prison Service headquarters I called an emergency board meeting and explained to colleagues what the Home Secretary had decided. Richard Tilt, who was regarded as the most senior of the executive directors, immediately said that he saw no reason for me to resign, and that it would be quite wrong for me to do so. I left them to decide what they wanted to do. It was a difficult decision for career civil servants whose lives had been dedicated to obeying ministerial orders. But, with remarkable courage, they decided they needed to put their views to the Home Secretary and they marched *en masse* over to Queen Anne's Gate to face Howard in his office. Howard may have been there in person, but he was clearly beyond listening. It was a brief encounter. He said that he had had a difficult decision to make, but he had made it and expected them all to do their duty.

I had further work to do. When I returned to my office, I telephoned my wife, Louise. The news came as no great surprise to her after the events of the past few days. I then told my private secretary, Helen Crosby, my secretary, Lisa Griffiths, and the others in my office who had been so incredibly supportive during the traumas of the previous twelve months. We were a sombre group. I closed my office door and spent some time considering the options. Would it be better for the service if I accepted Howard's proposal? Resignation would be tantamount to an admission of culpability, and whatever Howard might say in public, I knew that his political allies would be briefing journalists to the contrary in the lobbies. I also knew that I had the support of the board, and there would be resignations among the non-executives if I were dismissed. Howard was deeply unpopular with large sections of the media and I had built a considerable degree of support within the service. I knew only too well what a shambles the Prison Service had been when I arrived, and that I had given an enormous personal commitment in time and energy to turn it around. There was still a great deal to be done, but so much had been achieved in such a short time: walking meekly away was something I was not prepared to do.

I was going to put up a fight, and I needed to get organized – and quickly. That afternoon I moved into overdrive. My lawyers had to be briefed, the First Division Association (FDA) – the senior civil servants' union to which I belonged – needed to gear up for action, and I required PR help. I also had to get my retaliation in first with the media. I picked the *Financial Times*, the most influential paper in the business world, and a respected journalist, Ray Snoddy, whom I had known for many years. A lengthy telephone conversation and a package of my key documents delivered to his home quickly left him in command of what was going on. 'That's good for tomorrow's front page,' he told me, and sure enough it was. The *Financial Times*'s headline read: 'Row brews on damning prison report. Head of jail service says he will defy pressure to quit.'

I had no intention of responding to Howard's five o'clock

deadline. I had to carry the battle further on the political front. He and the Prime Minister needed to know that this particular act of political cowardice was not going to be a pushover. On the Sunday evening, after the deadline had passed, I wrote to Howard, with copies for the Prime Minister and Kenneth Clarke. My letter was delivered at midnight to the Treasury, No. 10 and Queen Anne's Gate.

In the meantime I had received written confirmation from Richard Wilson of what had been said in the morning. The letter indicated that if I did not accept his resignation proposal, the Home Secretary would 'reluctantly be obliged to consider dismissal as an option'. It added that as the five o'clock deadline had passed, the Home Secretary would now like my response by nine the following morning.

Next morning I was summoned to see the Home Secretary at nine o'clock. Desperate to avoid my gaze throughout, he began by thanking me for my letter. We quickly got to the issue which irked him most: how could the Parkhurst escape have happened so soon after Whitemoor? It was clear that he held me personally responsible for his own embarrassment, and it has even been suggested that he somehow held me responsible for his being passed over for the Foreign Office in the July reshuffle. Once again I took him through the situation that had existed in the Prison Service, the pressures and alarms there had been after Whitemoor, and what I had done during that frenetic period. What else did he think I could or should have done to prevent Parkhurst? In what way was I culpable? 'I don't know,' he answered, 'that's not my job.' The deadline for my execution was delayed again. My response was now required by noon. It was the last conversation Howard and I had before my sacking, and yet for the first time he had given some hint, albeit brief, about what he was really thinking. We were past the point of no return. To change his mind now would be the sort of climbdown that few people have the stature to handle, least of all Michael Howard.

My preparations were continuing. Diana Soltmann of Millbank PR, public relations advisers with whom I had worked previously, responded to the call, and was fully briefed and ready. The First Division Association – which had so vociferously condemned the manner of my appointment, but was now proving staunch in my support – prepared itself for action. I drafted the letter to Howard that I intended to make public after he announced my dismissal. And I decided that I should go to the House of Commons that afternoon to hear him make his statement, uncomfortable though it would be.

High noon came and went, and at about 12.30 p.m. Wilson's breathless private secretary arrived in my office and sheepishly handed me an envelope. I knew that it would contain final confirmation that I would never be able to finish the job I had started. Since Home Secretaries do not perform their own executions, the letter was from Wilson, who said:

The Home Secretary has concluded with regret that, for the reasons set out in my letter of 15 October, your appointment should be terminated. He has further concluded that in the circumstances it is in the interests of the Prison Service that this termination should take effect forthwith. I am therefore notifying you that your appointment as Director General and Chief Executive of the Prison Service is terminated with immediate effect.

It was signed 'Yours ever, Richard' – a strangely incongruous ending to a letter of such instant finality. Touchingly, he had planned to give me as a leaving present a bottle of whisky and a volume of Shakespeare, but he had been ordered not to for fear of prejudicing the Home Office's position.

Encouraged by Ray Snoddy's front-page splash in the *Financial Times* that morning, the media were already speculating furiously about my future, and a mass of cameramen and journalists were gathered outside Prison Service headquarters. Richard Tilt, who had been asked to stand in as acting Director General, thoughtfully suggested we go down to the House of Commons together and we walked out to the car with Deborah Hermer, from the Prison Service press office. She was later ticked off by the Home Office press office for appearing in front of the media in the company of someone who was now an outcast. It was an occasion on which to look relaxed and wear a confident smile, but neither came easily.

I had with me my pass from Black Rod's office to admit me 'to the Space on the right of the Throne to-day during the Home Office Statement on the Learmont Enquiry' – in other words, to the officials' box in the House of Commons, where civil servants who have briefed ministers sit within easy reach to provide further notes and advice. But the Home Office had acted fast to ensure the final indignity. I was already a non-person. Richard's name and mine had both been removed from the list. Wilson approached, ashen-faced at seeing us there, and spluttered apologetically that I could not go in. We bumped into a helpful MP who wrote a note which got us speedily into the Strangers' Gallery. By the time we entered, Howard was already on his feet and well into his statement. It was not long before he came to the passage that was key to his personal survival:

I have come to the conclusion, with some sadness, that that requires a change of leadership at the top of the Prison Service. The present Director General has served in his post for nearly three years. I pay tribute to him for what he has achieved, but I cannot overlook the serious criticisms in the report. I believe the service requires a change of leadership to carry forward the programme of reforms that is needed and to increase public confidence in the security of our prisons. The Director General has accordingly ceased to hold his post with effect from today.

The exchanges that followed were relatively low-key affairs. The Home Office press office had predicted that this would be a 'one-day wonder'.

The Home Secretary's action, chosen to make his life easier, marked the beginning of a political storm which further undermined his personal credibility, and did little to enhance the standing of an accident-prone government. It was a battle for reputation, and I had a great deal to lose. Integrity and honesty have always meant a great deal to me, and I was determined to fight.

I had been so totally absorbed with the Prison Service that I had lost part of myself; the frustrations had been so enormous, and I had had to suppress so much of how I really felt: but suddenly it was as though I had been released from captivity. My sense of loss of the Prison Service and some of the people in it was, however, painfully acute – and still is. Joe Pilling had said that it was the only job he had ever desperately wanted to do. I finally understood what he meant.

14

Back on the Outside

When I left the House of Commons, my sense of loss was very powerful. Suddenly cut off from the support of the Prison Service and its press office, I now relied entirely on my lawyers, the First Division Association and Millbank PR. Millbank's Great Portland Street office became the nerve centre for our operations and was inundated with hundreds of calls. With skill, speed and good humour, the team dealt with important news programmes and journalists, juggled interviews, organized cabs and provided vital food. I stepped on to a media merry-go-round with an unending sequence of interviews. Although exhausting, they had their lighter moments – as in that evening's *Newsnight* interview. Sitting in the *Newsnight* studio, Jeremy Paxman questioned me on Marriott's removal and Howard's role. Turning his attention to Howard, who was in the Westminster studio, he reiterated the questions. Howard was evasive and Paxman returned to the attack:

JEREMY PAXMAN: Mr Howard do you think that either you or your predecessor, Mr Clarke, made a serious error of judgement in appointing Mr Lewis?

MICHAEL HOWARD: No, I think that Mr Lewis has achieved a great deal in his time in the Prison Service.

PAXMAN: That rather begs the question of why you are sacking him, doesn't it?

HOWARD: Well, I . . . I . . . I've . . . I've explained that more than once during the course of today. It is a decision that I have come to with a great deal of reluctance and some sadness, but I have had to take very seriously the findings of the Learmont Report.

PAXMAN: But Home Secretary you have just heard the man you praised only a few months ago and have today sacked, say that under the agency status available to the Prison Service he actually had less freedom than when the service was run directly by your department.

HOWARD: Well, I don't accept that but I wasn't around before it was an agency so I can't make any direct comparisons about that. So far as I'm concerned, I think there is a distinction between operational and policy matters, they do have implications the one for the other as Derek Lewis has perfectly fairly said and all those implications have to be considered, but there is a distinction between the two and I . . . (interruption)

PAXMAN: He's been sacked to save your skin, hasn't he?

HOWARD: . . . and I'm responsible for policy and, er, the Director General is responsible for operational matters.

PAXMAN: Hasn't he been sacked to save your skin, Mr Howard?

Again Howard evaded the question, referring Paxman to the report and its helpful covering letter.

I was due to address a meeting of governors at Westminster Hall on the Learmont Report and its implications on 17 October. I discussed the situation with Richard Tilt and told him that although it would be a very difficult occasion for me, I would welcome an opportunity to say goodbye to governors and wish them well before handing over to him. Other members of the board thought it a good idea, but when I spoke to Richard later, he was worried about its political consequences – perhaps at the instigation of Queen Anne's Gate. He thought I would receive a standing ovation, which would prove embarrassing for ministers at a sensitive time. I was saddened, but did not press the matter.

By all accounts, the meeting itself was an anxious and irritable affair. Widdecombe, whom I had previously invited, bravely attended and received a rough ride. She skilfully managed to agree with the Home Secretary's compliments about me, without supporting his decision, and went on to say, with characteristic warmth, that she was 'very pleased with what Derek Lewis achieved. I only worked with Derek Lewis for a short time, but in that time I was very impressed by the quite formidable and outstanding qualities of the man.'

Tilt had a difficult time. As acting Director General, he was subject to immense pressure from the media and ministers, while at the same time having to satisfy the sense of anger and betrayal among governors and others who worked in the service. His letter to staff provided welcome support:

Derek Lewis laid very firm foundations for taking the service forward. I and my colleagues on the Prisons Board all felt a very strong sense of loyalty to Derek and want to record our sense of loss at his departure. I know that there are many people in the service who have experienced the same strong feelings of gratitude and admiration for a person who was capable of leading the service, of identifying what was wrong, what needed doing and of tenaciously pursuing the changes that were necessary.

But for me it was time to be moving on to the next stage. Richard Wilson's letter had indicated a willingness to discuss compensation, but I was sceptical. The way the Home Secretary had handled the situation so far, and the political fall-out from paying a substantial amount of money, suggested that an early settlement was unlikely. I disliked the prospect of legal action, but it might well prove necessary. Legal wheels grind very slowly, and if I was going to sue, it had to be done quickly. It might be difficult to reach an acceptable settlement without access to Home Office documents; a court case with full discovery was the only sure way.

I spent time with my solicitors, who arranged for us to decamp to the offices of counsel. He agreed that we should issue a writ and, in a cramped smoke-filled room, counsel, solicitor, Liz Symons, general secretary of the FDA, and I set about drafting it. We went on working into the early hours.

By Wednesday the media blitz was beginning to have its effect, and opinion was swinging in the right direction. I released both of the detailed defence documents that I had given Howard before he fired me, so that the press and the public would have the facts.

And we decided to issue the writ before the scheduled Opposition debate on the Learmont Report in the Commons on Thursday. By all accounts the writ was unexpected and caused a flurry of anxiety in the Home Office ahead of the debate.

The Prisons Board met on the Wednesday for what must have been a difficult meeting. Geoff Keys, one of the four non-executive directors, announced his decision to resign in protest at Howard's action. A second, Bill Bentley, agreed to continue to serve only during Tilt's period as acting Director General. Next day the third non-executive, Millie Banerjee, also announced her resignation.

The Commons was packed by 4.21 p.m. on 19 October after the Speaker had ruled that the law suit did not make the whole matter *sub judice* and so prevent a debate. The Opposition was calling for Howard's resignation. They claimed that he had to take overall responsibility for the criticisms in the Learmont Report, and that he had seriously misled the House about his interference in the removal of John Marriott. The government had lined up strong backbench support to make life difficult for Jack Straw, the shadow Home Secretary, who led for the Opposition. Given that support, resignation was never really on the cards.

Jack Straw began with an excerpt from the Prisons Act 1952 which, he said, made no distinction between the Home Secretary's responsibility for the policy of the Prison Service and the operation of that policy. He added that the right hon. and learned gentleman was following a constitutional fiction in seeking wholly to separate the two, and claiming that he was responsible only for his policy towards prisons but not for operational matters, for which he was accountable but not responsible. This was the famous 'operations versus policy' debate that became synonymous with Michael Howard and has continued ever since. Straw went on to say that Howard had 'on numerous occasions taken decisions and otherwise interfered with the operation of the Prison Service, but because of the fiction that he is not involved in it, or that he is not responsible for operational matters he has at all times had to avoid any admission that he has been so involved'. He accused Howard of giving explanations to the House and to the Home Affairs Select Committee about the Marriott affair 'which are uncorroborated and wholly at variance with other evidence that is now available'. Thereafter the debate turned into an uproarious shambles, with intervention after intervention; and Straw seemed to be caught out when asked whether he would have dismissed me.

Gerald Kaufman then intervened, quoting the Home Secretary's January statement that 'The Prison Service is clearly going through a difficult time. The Director General is the best person to take it through that difficult time. What has changed since then other than the Home Secretary's need for a scapegoat?' he asked.

The debate became bogged down over the Marriott affair. Howard refused to respond to Straw's claims that he had put pressure on me to suspend Marriott and on the timing of his move, and remained resolutely in his seat. He was eventually provoked and Straw was subjected to shouts of 'Give way, you coward' when Howard tried to intervene. Straw eventually brought his speech to a conclusion, and then it was Howard's turn.

His justification for the distinction between policy and operations went as follows: 'I am personally accountable to the House for all matters concerning the Prison Service. I am accountable and responsible for all policy decisions relating to the service. The Director General is responsible for the day-to-day operations.' He went on: 'When I received Sir John's report, I studied it very carefully. If the criticisms in it had been made of me, I should not be standing at the dispatch box.'

The pressure then focused on Howard's handling of the Marriott affair. In response to other questions he made a number of statements which were, at best, 'economical with the truth'. He claimed, for example, that 'There was no question of overruling the Director General.' In fact, as we have seen, he told me that he would have to consider intervening to overrule me if I did not suspend Marriott. He was later persuaded by Richard Wilson not to do so. And he told the House:

On Tuesday, the Leader of the Opposition made three allegations: that I personally told Mr Lewis that the governor of Parkhurst should be suspended immediately; that when Mr Lewis objected as it was an operational matter, I threatened to instruct him to do it; that when Mr Lewis further objected, I told the operational director of the Prison Service, by fax, that I would announce it in the House of Commons that day. Each and every one of the allegations is untrue.

These allegations were not wholly untrue. Howard had certainly told me that the governor of Parkhurst should be suspended, and had threatened to overrule me.

At this point, Tony Blair, the Leader of the Opposition, who had been visibly uncomfortable during Straw's speech – repeatedly trying to remove a speck of dust from his trousers and passing messages along to Straw – made a surprising intervention, pressing the question about Marriott for the seventh time. But Straw's position had been severely undermined by all the interruptions and heckling. Howard continued to side-step the question and went on to complete his speech with a masterly peroration. He had done enough to secure his job.

Gerald Kaufman then vigorously attacked Howard, saying that 'What we heard this afternoon was a shyster lawyer defending a shifty client with the Home Secretary being the shyster lawyer and the shifty client,' and was taken to task by the Speaker for use of the word 'shyster'. He refused to withdraw it, but allowed the Speaker to overrule him.

Sir Peter Lloyd, the first Prisons Minister with whom I had worked and now a respected backbencher, entered the fray with a statesman-like speech which ended:

I realize that the Home Secretary had a difficult decision to make. He is usually admirable in refusing to be guided by reports that are insufficiently cogently argued to the point in question. I am sorry that he did not show that same characteristic here. I believe that, to achieve the kind of efficient Prison Service that this country deserves, the Home Secretary should have backed the Director General and his board.

Ann Widdecombe, the current Prisons Minister, concluded the debate in gutsy combative tones:

Do the Opposition want to debate the single biggest prison-building programme of the century? No – because the Conservatives introduced it. Do they even want to consider improvements in the prison system, such as the reduction in overcrowding? In 1987, 5,000 prisoners were living three to a cell; none is doing so today. No, the Opposition do not want to talk about that. Do they even want to mention the 75 per cent reduction in the number of escapes over the past two and a half years? No. Do they want to talk about the improved value for money in our system? No, they do not even want to do that.

prompting a predictable response from her opposite number, George Howarth, the shadow Prisons Minister: 'The Hon. Lady is issuing a catalogue of praise for the former Director General of the Prison Service. If the service was run so wonderfully, why was he sacked?'

It was good knockabout House of Commons theatre, but it had shed little light on the issues facing the Prison Service, and even less on questions of accountability, responsibility and culpability, or of policy versus operations. The new Howard doctrine that he could only be held responsible for policy decisions he had made entered the history books, and the inconsistency of a report which criticized ministerial decisions but absolved them of responsibility went largely unchallenged.

The most extraordinary week of my life was over. As if by magic I had been transformed from a fairly typical 'conservative' business-man into a controversial figure, tackling the political establishment head-on. At times it felt almost like an out-of-body experience, as if someone else was at the centre of all the media attention. Eventually the press pack and their outside broadcast vehicles stopped besieging our home, and my family and I were able to return from the friends that had kindly provided a safe house for us.

Although it had been a rough ride, it had achieved almost everything I had hoped for. But it was only the first round, and there were many more to come. I had no illusions: I knew I would be facing a wounded and bitter Home Secretary, and that I had to pursue a difficult campaign against the powerful legal, public relations and political machine of the Home Office.

There were the inevitable follow-up interviews for the Sunday newspapers and for think pieces by journalists looking for new or under-exposed angles. Debates continued to rage about ministerial responsibility, and the split between policy and operations. (The papers were also full of scare stories about government warnings over the safety of some types of contraceptive pill, and the Department of Health denied rumours that the announcement and its timing had been deliberately designed to distract attention from Howard's difficulties.) That Sunday I faced Sir Ivan Lawrence, chairman of the Home Affairs Select Committee, on Jonathan Dimbleby's lunchtime TV programme. He had been put up as Howard's representative, but his performance lacked bite or conviction: perhaps he was aware of having written me a glowingly complimentary letter a few days earlier about my achievements in the service.

I wanted to write letters to all 130 governors and to many other senior managers in the Prison Service, saying thank you, farewell and good luck for the future. And there was a speech to be given to the annual conference of the Criminal Law Solicitors' Association, a commitment I had made while still at the Prison Service. What would normally have been a low-key conference was transformed into a major media event with a phalanx of cameramen and journalists. My relatively mild criticisms of the Home Secretary, peppered with compliments about his support in tackling problems such as industrial relations and drugs, were seized upon by the press as a 'coruscating attack' and helped to fill an otherwise quiet evening of radio and television news. If Howard had thought it would all die down quickly, he must have been very disappointed.

I needed to know how Howard would play the law suit. My solicitors, Russell, Jones and Walker, expected the Home Office to settle quickly. As far as they were concerned it was an open and shut case; it seemed inconceivable that the Home Secretary would contemplate incurring the costs or the damaging publicity likely to accompany a court hearing. The first shot was a letter from Home

Office solicitors complaining, somewhat impudently, that the writ was unnecessary. It was followed by their defence which, while not admitting that the Home Secretary had been in breach of contract in dismissing me, offered to pay compensation as if I had been wrongfully dismissed.

An amiable government lawyer called Solomons was acting for the Home Office. He readily confessed that his expertise lay in judicial review, rather than employment law, and his inexperience quickly showed. As the weeks passed my solicitors found it hard to understand why the Home Office hadn't adopted the standard government practice of paying a lump sum compensation payment into court, and making me sweat for a while: were I to decide not to accept the money, and to pursue the case through the courts, I could have had to pay costs if lower damages were eventually awarded by the court. A relatively modest amount paid in at an early stage would have left me with a very difficult decision. The First Division Association had been extremely supportive and were bearing the legal costs, but they would have had to consider the best interests of their members if faced with such a choice. Various sources within the Home Office confirmed that the Home Secretary had been advised to settle, and that it would need to be a fairly full payment. But for some reason he could not bring himself to do it.

Desultory correspondence followed. We agreed a timetable for the conduct of the case, and waited. We wondered whether their tactic was to come to a shotgun settlement in the run-up to Christmas, which could then be announced at a time when Parliament was not sitting and the newspapers were little read – so minimizing Howard's political embarrassment.

Howard was also under pressure to find a permanent successor to me. Despite ministerial denials, several people outside the Prison Service were asked if they would do the job. They gave a frosty reply. They were certainly not going to risk similar treatment. The *Daily Mail* reported 'senior Home Office sources' as saying that candidates 'wouldn't touch the job with a bargepole'. What Howard had hoped would be seen as a decisive political act looked increasingly like a piece of bungling, where no forethought had been given to how things would be handled afterwards. Headhunters were asked to make proposals for handling the recruitment. One came to me for advice on how they should approach it, and even wondered whether it was worth doing given that the salary was to be cut by half. Howard eventually decided to appoint none of the headhunters and to abandon the normal open competition – presumably because it was obvious that there would be embarrassingly few, if any, suitable candidates. Instead, on 1 April 1996, after an interregnum of five and a half months, Tilt was confirmed in the job. Howard promised to set up an advisory board with a part-time chairman – a promise which was still unfulfilled a year after Learmont.

The question of the constitutional relationship between the Prison Service and the Home Office was also kicked into the long grass. In a statement on 16 October 1995 Howard said that an in-depth study, as recommended by Learmont, was under way, and that he would report when it was complete. The following day Ann Widdecombe confirmed that it was being undertaken by Kate Jenkins. Were Jenkins's later conclusions unpalatable? In a written parliamentary reply a month later, Widdecombe's description of Jenkins's role had been considerably watered down ('The initial work has been assisted by Miss Kate Jenkins'), while according to a further written parliamentary reply in March 1996, 'no in-depth study as recommended by Sir John Learmont has been commissioned'. When announcing Tilt's appointment, Howard said that he had 'concluded that the terms of the framework document which established the Prison Service as an executive agency of the Home Office in 1993 would benefit from some clarification. I propose to ask the advisory board further to consider the need for such clarification and to make recommendations.' The delay in forming the board conveniently postponed action on this issue and any challenge to the now comfortable protection of the operations/policy distinction.

The issues raised by my sacking would not go away. There were regular parliamentary questions about it, and even the notoriously deferential Sir David Frost, who provides sympathetic opportunities for Cabinet ministers to invade the peace of Sunday morning, had been unable to resist a jibe when he interviewed Howard in December 1995. Quoting the *Daily Express*, which had said that I was to receive a £200,000 golden handshake, approximately £50,000 of which was for good performance, he asked Howard the obvious question: 'If that's so, why did you sack him?' Howard ducked the issue, saying: 'There are negotiations under way about the extent to which Derek Lewis will be paid compensation and I'm not going to comment on those negotiations . . .'

At best it was a half-truth. No one could describe odd requests for information as anything remotely resembling negotiation – as the Home Office solicitor confirmed three months later, when he telephoned to say that he had only then been instructed to enter into negotiations.

Early in the New Year both Howard and I were asked by Radio 4's *World Tonight* to take part in their series on prisons, to be broadcast at the end of January. Howard had originally agreed to appear on Friday but had switched to Thursday, asking that it should be the last in the series so that he would have the last word. I delayed confirming whether I would appear, worried that I might get caught up in an unconstructive debate with Michael Howard. The first two programmes went ahead, and on the Thursday the *World Tonight* telephoned the Home Office press office to tell them that they would possibly be interviewing me on the Friday evening. The next morning Diana Soltmann at Millbank Public Relations confirmed to the *World Tonight* that I was prepared to be interviewed that evening.

Unfortunately, Howard had not himself been told about my interview, but nevertheless heard it, and was livid. He fired off an angry letter to John Birt, the director general of the BBC, complaining that he had been misled, and that the *World Tonight* programme was dishonest. Birt's reply explained the position, but only inflamed Howard's anger. He wrote back, saying that Birt's reply had astonished him and demeaned its sender. More letters were exchanged, and the matter went to the programme complaints unit. The unit was unable to decide whether the *World Tonight* or the Home Office had been at fault, but in the end a conciliatory letter was sent to Howard, which left him feeling that he had won something from the debate. It is a sad reflection that two interviews, both of them uncontroversial, for a programme with an audience of only a few hundred thousand, should have absorbed so much ministerial time and provoked so much petulant behaviour.

The legal action crawled on. In the process of discovery those involved in a legal action are obliged to provide any documents in their possession that may be relevant to the other side. My list extended to over a hundred documents. To our surprise, the Home Office, with its much more extensive files, came up with only twenty-two documents, most of which I already had, that might be relevant to the question of whether my dismissal was a breach of contract, whether it was justified, whether the proper procedures had been followed, what my performance had been and what the level of compensation should be. Sources within the Home Office suggested that they were fearful about the consequences of opening the books to public scrutiny. I had to make it clear that I was not going to be intimidated. My solicitors issued a summons forcing the Home Office to disclose, and the First Division Association put out a press notice to ram home the point that this was not acceptable behaviour by elected officials. Fortunately the announcement coincided with the Home Secretary's speech to the annual Prison Service conference. The Home Office had chosen the occasion to announce that action would at last be taken to cut the number of fine defaulters who go to prison, filling scarce prison places, and our release proved an unwelcome distraction.

The summons was scheduled to be heard on 29 March. Surely the Home Office would not wish to be dragged through the courts, with all the costs and potential embarrassment involved? I was amazed that they had allowed it to get so far, and assumed negotiation must be imminent. Indeed, it began to look as though this might be the case when the Home Office solicitor called mine and said that he had at last been instructed by the Home Office to enter into negotiations for a settlement. That sounded hopeful, even promising. An offer was made of £175,000 compensation plus costs. It was clearly a low opening shot on the part of the Home Office and was soon rejected, but it seemed to indicate that the Home Office wanted to settle before the court hearing. But we heard not another word, beyond a reiteration of the original offer.

We arrived early at the High Court on 29 March for a private hearing in chambers in front of Master Foster at 11.30. Dinah Rose (by a strange quirk of fate the sister of David Rose of the *Observer*, not known for his admiration of the Home Secretary) was the Home Office counsel. Curiously the Home Office had no one there to deal with the media, who had obligingly turned out in force at our invitation. While my press adviser briefed the journalists, we went into chambers.

It all started conventionally enough. My counsel quickly set out the issues at stake. Dinah Rose then explained that the constitutional right of the Crown to dismiss public servants at will meant that it could not formally admit wrongful dismissal; nevertheless, the Home Office did not wish to contest the case and was willing to pay damages. Master Foster homed in on the vital issues. Would it be acceptable, he suggested, if judgement were to be entered in my favour by the court, but the Home Office would not be forced to admit liability because of the constitutional position? That would resolve the issue, and allow the case to move on to consider the level of damages. Home Office counsel looked anxiously at the Home Office solicitor who gestured uncertainly at this unexpected turn of events. Master Foster adjourned the hearing. This was exactly what I had wanted – an effective admission of guilt from the Home Office, which would then allow the proceedings to focus on money. But how could the Home Office accept a formula with such obviously damaging PR consequences? Solomons, the Home Office solicitor, scurried off to consult his client: we wondered whether he was telephoning the chief Home Office lawyer, or Richard Wilson, or even the Home Secretary himself. He returned breathless, having tracked down a telephone in another court building; and after conferring with his counsel, he nodded his agreement to us.

The hearing moved on to consider the other issue of discovery.

This was my opportunity to get my message across to the public. As the debate continued I sat at the back of the court writing a press release. The next hearing was scheduled for 7 May, and we went out to confront the media.

I read my hand-written statement to the assembled journalists. I expressed satisfaction that the Home Office had agreed to a judgement entered in my favour, and condemned the Home Office for the wholly unjustifiable delays and waste of taxpayers' money that had resulted from their handling of the case. It was a sympathetic audience. I was asked for my views on the Home Secretary's position, but declined to call for his resignation. I was asked whether the distinction between policy and operations, to which he attached so much weight, was a legitimate defence. That distinction, I said, was no more than a political fig-leaf – and one so small as to be grossly indecent. The journalists disappeared to write their copy for the Saturday morning editions, while I faced a barrage of cameras. It was one occasion on which I could allow myself a smile.

The Home Office was in disarray. There was no pre-prepared response, and it was nearly three hours before the press office issued a short statement, lamely claiming that liability had not been admitted. No one believed it. Governments don't pay out substantial damages because they are feeling generous, if there's no fault.

I could hardly have asked for more when next morning's newspapers arrived. The headlines included: 'Axed jail chief's £¼m apology from Howard', 'Howard's humbling' and 'Prison chief wrongly sacked, says Howard'. I suspect Howard wasn't having such a good day. He had been scheduled to make a keynote speech to the spring Conservative conference in Harrogate, after setting out his new sentencing proposals in a White Paper a couple of days earlier. But publication of the White Paper was deferred because of the BSE crisis. Instead he arrived with yet another 'beleaguered' label to add to his collection, and had to be propped up by a statement of support from the Prime Minister. He must have wished he had taken the advice he had been given and settled over the Christmas break.

The Home Office continued its erratic behaviour, worried

about an announcement on money. So through an intermediary, I suggested that the impending local elections on 2 May would be a good occasion on which to announce a settlement with minimum publicity: the inevitable slaughter of the Conservative vote would provide plenty of cover.

Six days later, on 4 April, £200,000 was paid into court. Six months earlier I would almost certainly have accepted. But not now. Negotiations continued. The Home Office increased the cash offer to £215,000 – still not quite enough, but very close. On 3 May, while the Central Office big guns were out making the best of the expected electoral drubbing, a deal was done that totalled some £280,000: a cash payment of £220,000, plus all my legal costs and a tax indemnity worth up to another £20,000. It was within £8,000 of the amount I had asked for. It covered the salary and pension I was entitled to, something very close to the maximum possible bonus, in recognition of the fact that eight of the nine targets Howard had set for the service had been achieved, all my legal costs of some £40,000 and most of my PR costs. The terms were to be ratified by the court the following Tuesday. The Home Office asked us to keep it confidential, which we did, but no sooner had an oral agreement been reached than the Home Office issued a brief unilateral statement giving details of the settlement.

The news was flashed through to me in Inverness. Fortunately our response was ready and went out instantly on the wires. I spent several hours on the phone explaining the deal to those journalists who were available, and countering Home Office allegations that the settlement was much less than I had requested, and that the delays were all my fault. It also gave me an opportunity to explain that part of the settlement was going to the Butler Trust. I wanted to fund a new award in the name of Lord Woolf in recognition of his contribution and – even more importantly – to highlight rehabilitative work in prisons, which is vital if prison is to have real value. Such an award seemed particularly necessary in order to counterbalance the increasing emphasis on security and punishment.

A week later I had my first encounter with Howard since he had fired me – a chance affair at a charity function at the Grosvenor

House. His name on the seating plan caught my eye, and I decided it was time to establish more normal relations. As I walked across to his table, I wondered how he would react. I shook him warmly by the hand and said I was delighted to be able to talk to him other than through lawyers. He remained seated, looking shocked and uncomfortable. His hesitant claim that he was pleased to see me carried no conviction. It was obvious that the conversation was not to be prolonged and that his wounds had not healed.

There are lessons to be learned from this sorry tale. Perhaps the *Evening Standard* put it most succinctly when it listed the fifty things that the Conservative government had got wrong and included among them getting into a public argument with the head of the Prison Service. Decisions taken on the basis of political expediency and survival can often misfire.

What happened also served to illustrate that the political neutrality and independence of the Civil Service and those in senior public service jobs is threatened unless safeguards are introduced. Decisions to remove senior officials should not be left in the hands of a single politician. Objective outsiders must play a key role, in the same way that they do when making appointments or enforcing a disciplinary process. Large and sensitive public services, such as prisons and immigration, need to be given some form of statutory separation from ministers, so that appointments are made by independent boards rather than politicians. Otherwise our top public service jobs will become politicized and will not attract the talented outsiders which the public services so badly need.

15

Reflections

The unprecedented period of change that began when the Prison Service became an agency in April 1993 has produced a service very different from that which existed in the 1980s and earlier. Journalists and others still refer to our overcrowded prisons, but they are quite wrong to do so. Since 1993 the prison population has grown from 40,000 to nearly 60,000, yet the practice of holding prisoners three to a cell has gone and 80 per cent are in uncrowded conditions. In 1992 nearly £100 million of taxpayers' money was spent on holding several thousand overflow prisoners in police cells: that – for the moment at least – is a thing of the past. In 1992 prisoners were escaping at an average of more than one a day; since then, escapes have been reduced by 80 per cent, as have the number of prisoners absconding from open prisons. The number of prisoners failing to return from home leave has also been slashed by three-quarters.

Our prisons are generally far more humane than they were. Slopping out is history. Meals are no longer served in a quick succession of breakfast, lunch and tea to suit the needs of staff rather than inmates. Being locked up for twenty-three hours is also a thing of the past, and most prisoners spend ten or more hours a day out of their cell. Excesses in the opposite direction have gone as well: privileges are more tightly controlled and more appropriate to a prison environment. After many years of rising violence prisons are becoming safer places for both prisoners and staff. Determined action is being taken to curb the presence of drugs in prison.

Our prisons have also become more positive places. The amount of time spent on work, training and education increased by 6 per cent in the first three years of agency status. Prisoners are achieving more educational and vocational qualifications than ever before. More prisoners are undergoing specific programmes designed to stop them offending again. There are programmes for all adult sex offenders, for those prone to uncontrollable anger, and for those addicted to drugs and alcohol. Work inside is becoming more like work in the community: more realistic wages motivate prisoners and enable them to contribute towards the cost of keeping them in prison, as well as to their families and to victims. Healthcare is no longer a source of universal shame. Prisoners have personal officers. There are extensive pre-release programmes to equip prisoners for life on the outside. And all this is being done for lower costs in real terms: a better service for less money.

The practical effect of all this change had been to liberate good governors, and put bad ones on the spot. Good governors found that they had the licence and flexibility to make the changes that they had long known to be needed. The effects could be stunning, as evidenced by the work of – among many others – Niall Clifford at Cardiff, Graham Clark at Wandsworth, Sean O'Neill at Latchmere House, Peter Atherton at Long Lartin, John Aldridge at Stoke Heath Young Offender Institution, Ivor Ward at Feltham YOI, Alison Gomme at Erelestoke, Harry Crew at Askham Grange open female prison, Jim Semple at Blantyre House, Sarah Payne at Bullingdon, and Brodie Clark at Whitemoor. The common theme of all these transformations was a governor with the vision, enthusiasm, courage, leadership and management skills to seize the opportunity and refuse to take no for an answer from HQ bureaucrats, the Prison Officers' Association or anyone else.

The overall effect on the Prison Service was to transform it into an organization that was capable of doing what it promised. By 1995 we faced an enormous programme of new initiatives – security changes following Whitemoor and Parkhurst, severe curtailment of home leave with entirely new criteria being applied, a major crack-down on drugs with the introduction of drug testing, and a wholesale restructuring of privileges for prisoners based on the principle of earning through good behaviour. None of these changes was popular with prisoners. In one way or another they would all make life in prison more irksome and more unpleasant. There were many Cassandras within the service and outside who said we were taking on too much, and that widespread rioting would ensue. Yet all this was accomplished on time and without any serious prisoner disruption.

That is not to say that the barriers to change were eliminated altogether. Trying to achieve anything substantial was still a Herculean task. But, encouragingly, many parts of our headquarters team had responded well to the new order. For the first time we were really in control of our accommodation, knowing how much there was supposed to be and where it was. We could plan to cope with the growth in population, and respond rapidly to unexpected spurts. And, at long last, those responsible for our building projects had taken on board the concept of value for money, and 'gold-plated' projects were replaced by functional buildings that took proper account of the needs of the taxpayer.

Of course, these accomplishments were marred by the escapes from Whitemoor in 1994 and Parkhurst in 1995. But they were symptoms of the old sloppy Prison Service, parts that had still not been reformed. As General Sir John Learmont said in his second, little-noticed report, published two months after the first: 'In a period of less than a year the Prison Service has made infinitely more headway in implementing the Woodcock recommendations than it seemed reasonable to expect, and in line with the published timetable.' It would have been unreasonable of him, or others, to expect everything that had been wrong with the Prison Service to be put right in two short years.

I was touched that so many governors and other senior managers, most of whom had been hostile when I was first appointed, felt that we had made real progress. Their comments, support and affection were a great source of strength. One governor told me in a letter:

I was devastated by your departure. For the first time in twenty-nine years I had actually begun to believe that the Prison Service finally had a leader with the vision, charisma and flair to take us through into the twenty-first century. It says a great deal for your profound impact on the service that so many people have rushed to highlight the magnificent achievements which the Prison Service made under your inspired leadership.

I cannot remember in my service such a feeling of loss across all grades of the service . . . your impact on the service may have exceeded your wildest expectations. I admired your courage, sensitivity, care and compassion, and those qualities allied to an astute and highly developed political antenna marked you out as a very special person. It seems that you always had time for people – regardless of the pressures of time or space.

Another said:

Whilst many of us initially had our reservations at 'this outsider' coming in to take charge (albeit that some of us also considered that such an appointment made a refreshing change to the career civil servants), we soon became aware of your total commitment. It has been good to have somebody provide the leadership which you have and it is with a sense of shame I feel that we governors have let you down.

While another commented:

When you took on the job of Director General in 1993 you inherited a legacy of many years of weak and ineffective management. The progress made under your leadership has been immense and I, personally, had hoped that you would lead us into the next century in an organization which other countries would strive to emulate. Regrettably, that is not to be.

But the satisfaction the many such letters gave me had to be tempered with the considerable personal cost and the disappointments involved. It had been the toughest, most personally demanding period of my life. The frustration, obstructions, hidden agendas, conspiracies, suspicion and frequent hostility were all unpleasant and unwelcome side-effects. I was bitterly disappointed not to have been able to finish the task that I started. But I have no regrets about taking the job. It was a totally absorbing period, and I learned an amazing amount about people from all walks of life. When I left I took with me the satisfaction of having been able to achieve real change for the better. The Prison Service is very fortunate to have some exceptional people in it who care passionately about its future. But experience has shown me that that is not enough – we must *all* be concerned about the future of our prisons.

16

What the Future Holds

My departure from the Prison Service and full-time return to the television industry brought into sharp focus the vastly different paces of change in the two worlds. Whereas change within the Prison Service remained frustratingly slow, television was being transformed by the growth of cable and satellite and the spawning of new channels. UK Gold had matured, become profitable and acquired a successful sister channel, UK Living. The two were on the verge of becoming part of a larger grouping, with a value many times the original investment made less than four years earlier.

But my return to television did not mean that I had lost interest in prisons. The service and its staff and the treatment of prisoners had become too important to me. As an outsider to Whitehall and the world of criminal justice who had held one of the key public service jobs in the criminal justice system, I had a unique vantage point. It had given me special insights, uninhibited by tradition, conventional wisdom or political pressures. Much of what I had seen troubled me. Now I was able to speak out freely on these issues; no longer constrained by the Civil Service rules which require employees to speak on behalf of their ministers and under their directions, rather than as their conscience dictates. I became a concerned and, when necessary, vocal observer.

I continued to be surprised by the lack of any long-term government strategy towards crime. Each branch of the criminal justice system – the Crown Prosecution Service, the courts, the police, probation and the Prison Service – ploughs its own furrow. There is little co-ordination with other departments, such as Health, Education and Environment, the responsibilities of which impinge on crime. Home Office strategy remains a matter of reacting to events like the murder of Philip Lawrence or the Dunblane massacre, and the long-term consists of twelve to eighteen months at most.

The growth in the prison population has continued relentlessly since my departure, and – not surprisingly – the performance of the Prison Service has suffered. In its first two and a half years as an agency it achieved or exceeded nine out of ten of the objectives Ken Clarke and Michael Howard had set for it, making it one of the best performing of the one hundred or more executive agencies in the public sector. In the six months after my dismissal, it met only two-thirds of its targets. The rehabilitation programmes, designed to make prisons more positive places and offer some hope of a life without crime, have suffered most. Prisoners are being locked in their cells for more hours each week, reversing the improvements of previous years. Although prisons are bursting at the seams, little has been done to deal with the unnecessarily large numbers of women and young offenders who are being imprisoned. Nor has any serious attempt been made to reduce the length of time remand prisoners are being held awaiting trial. We seem to be witnessing an inexorable drift towards the greater use of prison, in circumstances that are disturbingly reminiscent of those in the United States over a decade ago.

In the early 1980s America faced a rapidly growing crime rate. Violent crime, particularly in the inner cities, was escalating out of control, and the public – not least affluent citizens in the suburbs surrounding the major cities – became increasingly alarmed.

America's prison population was then around a quarter of a million – roughly the same per head of population as it is here now. Voters demanded tough action, so tougher sentences were introduced, and greater use was made of prison to punish and protect. Successive waves of legislation were introduced at federal and state level, imposing minimum sentences for different categories of offence. The Democrats and the Republicans competed to be the toughest party on crime. Prisons became nastier both by design and by default. A rapidly escalating prison population soon led to appalling overcrowding, with prisons often holding twice as many prisoners as they had been designed for. Worse still, correctional officials, as they are known in the States, were given an implicit licence to treat prisoners badly. Rehabilitation became a dirty word.

One of the few beneficiaries was the construction industry. Techniques were pioneered whereby new prisons could be completed in about three months. Tax-exempt bonds were created to raise the necessary finance. A new private sector flourished, able to finance, build and operate new prisons quickly and cheaply. But funding was an enormous problem. In California new prisons were built with 10,000 additional places, but the state did not have the money to open them. Prisoners were left to rot in overcrowded conditions in existing institutions, while the new prisons were mothballed.

The outcome of this frantic political competition to be tough on crime was a prison population of 1.6 million people, and costs in excess of $50 billion a year. Whether the crime rate fell as a result is a matter of debate; nor was thought given to what would happen to prison inmates when they were ultimately released into the community after twenty, thirty or forty years of institutional life. Money that could have been spent on education or health went into building and operating prisons. Rarely has so much hope and money been invested over such a long period in a programme that has produced so little benefit.

As in America ten years ago, we too have seen a divergence of views between the politicians and the criminal justice professionals. Both major political parties advocate a tough line on crime and criminals, so creating expectations that cannot be fulfilled, and the rhetoric and the expectations are amplified by the media. No politician has yet openly advocated wholesale incarceration as a means of protecting the public, but each new rhetorical flourish and each new piece of legislation moves us in that direction. If a little more prison makes sense, the logic of a lot more is difficult to resist.

In this country we have at least retained some belief in our ability to help criminals turn away from crime and lead 'law-abiding and useful lives', in the words of the Prison Service statement of purpose. While prison cannot be the cure for criminal behaviour, much more can be done to protect the public by rehabilitating prisoners before they go back into the community. Much of what happens in prison has the opposite effect. Minor offenders associate with hardened career criminals and 'learn' from them. Others are alienated and institutionalized. But a change for the better is possible. A growing number of treatment programmes have reduced the rates of reoffending. The 'therapeutic community' prison at Grendon, and similar units elsewhere, have had some success in turning serious offenders away from crime and the intensive sex offender treatment programme is equally promising. Programmes have been developed to control impulsive and angry behaviour or deter youngsters from car crime. And, of course, much hope is being placed on efforts to help prisoners break the drug habit. But little is known about what works in prison. We do not know what programmes deliver the biggest results; whether, for example, the huge investment in prison education, which so far has been largely a matter of faith and hope, is really justified, or whether the money could be better spent elsewhere.

The sacking of one Director General, the near sacking of a second over the early release of prisoners, regular rows, accusations of deception and a deterioration in relations between the service and ministers provide incontrovertible evidence that the constitutional arrangements for the service are not working effectively. Agency status has been a step in the right direction, but too often, under Michael Howard, it has left Prison Service staff unsure of where they stand or who is calling the shots. The fuzzy relationship between ministers and the Director General makes it all the easier for prisons to be used as a political pawn, whereby changes in policy are made to meet short-term needs rather than provide a better long-term service to the public. And the current constitutional arrangements are too dependent on the personal chemistry between the Home Secretary and the Director General of the day.

The monolithic national structure of the Prison Service is ill-matched with the regional structures of the police and probation services, with which it does most business. Chief constables and chief officers of probation speak publicly about the policies of the day and the impact they have on their own operations, but the Director General of the Prison Service is a civil servant and is therefore prohibited from doing so. But the public has a right to know the views of prison professionals if it is to form proper judgements on the policies being pursued by the government. Without such information, there is little to prevent ministers imposing half-baked policies or budgets and then washing their hands of the resulting disasters on the grounds that they are operational matters. That gives ministers power without responsibility, and the Director General responsibility without authority.

Determined action on five major points would create a chance of real progress.

Firstly, there must be institutional changes which would make possible a comprehensive and long-term approach to crime. We need a Ministry of Justice which would have direct responsibility for all branches of the justice system – police, prosecution, courts, prisons – and overall responsibility for reducing crime, with oversight as well as supervision of the relevant educational, social and health programmes. Unlike the Home Office, it would not be distracted by responsibilities for gambling, identity cards and dangerous dogs from its primary job of administering justice and reducing crime.

We now have 'charters' setting out our expectations for most aspects of our public services, from the Inland Revenue to the National Health Service. There is no such document offering the ordinary citizen a complete understanding of how justice should be administered, and my second requirement would be a clear statement of the government's strategy for reducing crime, and what the citizen can expect from the system of justice – and one which moved beyond the often sterile argument between liberals and hardliners. Those who advocate a tough line towards criminals and promise reductions in the crime rate merely delude the public, while the more liberal-minded professionals fail to recognize or meet the public's legitimate expectation that discipline will be enforced through punishments which are bound to be unpleasant. We need to recognize that prison is expensive, that its effectiveness as a punishment and deterrent is mixed, that it protects the public from only the tiny proportion of criminals who are actually inside, and that it is poor at rehabilitation. Improvements are possible, but prison cannot be a cure for crime.

We should aim to achieve a balance between dealing effectively with the consequences of crime – detection, prosecution, trial and punishment – and dealing with the circumstances that breed crime, such as poor parenting, child abuse, incomplete education and drug addiction. We should take a lead from programmes like 'Headstart' and the Perry Programme in the United States, which have targeted pre-school education for those disadvantaged children who are most likely to commit crime in later life. Preventive efforts in this area would pay dividends. Programmes which involve home visiting for high-risk families and helping teenage children have produced dramatic improvements. But the opportunities for determined initiatives of this type seem to fall between the departmental cracks. No one has the energy or conviction to take them up.

Recent differences between judges and ministers over sentencing policy are symptomatic of a dangerously widening gulf between the professionals and the politicians, and the third requirement is to bring these two groups together. The Criminal Justice Consultative Council, which has been instrumental in helping professionals work together, should be expanded to involve politicians, and it should be given a formal role in examining existing policy and planned legislation – or even proposing it.

Fourthly, we need a political commitment to researching and introducing new ways of dealing with convicted offenders. If, as should be the case, prison is to be reserved for serious offenders, there must be more acceptable non-custodial punishments. Widely regarded as a joke by the public, the current options are insufficiently unpleasant or visible to form an effective punishment or deterrent. Using community service as a form of punishment seriously devalues something that ought to be a voluntary matter, while tagging and curfews are too trivial for any but the most minor crimes. Genuinely hard labour – long hours of tough work on public projects – and corporal punishment may be distasteful to some, but they would meet society's need for punishment, providing deterrence without the disadvantages of prison.

Finally, the Prison Service can only provide the service the public expects if it is given the freedom and consistency of direction that so many observers have repeatedly called for. This can be done, though it may not appeal to any but the most innovative of governments. The Prison Service should enjoy statutory separation from the Home Office and the Home Secretary, in the same way as the police and probation services. It could be established by statute as a so-called non-departmental public body, with a formally appointed board which would have real teeth and the power to appoint and remove the Director General, rather than being merely advisory. Such a structure would achieve the autonomy intended by Lord Woolf, Sir Raymond Lygo and Kenneth Clarke. It would also ensure that the Director General did not hold or lose his job at the whim of a single minister. The distinction between policy and operations could be resolved definitively. Ministers already have available to them a vehicle of secondary legislation in the form of the Prison Rules, which govern aspects of what goes on in prison. These alone – or primary legislation – should be used for setting prisons policy. Parliament would be free to debate, and if necessary overturn, individual Prison Rules, thereby increasing democratic control over the Prison Service. Ministers would, of course, retain their control of spending by allocating funds and setting budgets, and they should have a more formal system of inspection, with a right to intervene if satisfactory standards were not being achieved. Such arrangements would serve to reduce some of the more extreme lurches in penal policy, for the long-term benefit of the public at large.

Further gains would be achieved by splitting the Prison Service up into four regional services and merging them with a restructured probation service. Regional services would be more manageable units, and they would not have the damagingly high national profile of the existing service. Merger with the probation service would bring together two closely related activities and eliminate some of the co-ordination problems that exist today, resulting in greater continuity in the treatment and supervision of offenders.

The Director General should be authorized to speak in public and to parliamentary select committees on the operational implications – positive and negative – of policies set by the government. This would happen automatically with a change in the constitutional status of the service. If population growth or budget cuts were threatening other key objectives of the Prison Service, such as rehabilitative work, the Director General would be expected to express such concerns publicly.

Crime in this country will not stand still. If we are content to fiddle about on the fringes of the problem, the prospects are bleak: we will drift unwittingly into a world in which increasing numbers of people are held in prison and more money is spent on the criminal justice system, but the rate of crime stubbornly refuses to drop signifcantly. It has happened in the United States, and it can happen here. Alternatively, we have the opportunity to adopt new and more radical approaches, learning from the experiences of other countries and developing solutions of our own.

The sacking of a Director General of the Prison Service is not significant in itself. I hope that the changes with which I have been associated in the Prison Service leave it much better able to play the role the public expects. But above all I hope that real lessons can be learned, and that the service will be given the autonomy, support and appreciation it deserves. I remain optimistic that this country can reduce the scourge of crime and remain a civilized place, provided it is led with vision, integrity and commitment. It is a challenge that calls for the most open of agendas, one to which we can all subscribe.

Index

Other than in the entry under his name,
Derek Lewis is referred to as DL.